A HISTORY
OF THE MISHNAIC LAW
OF WOMEN

PART THREE

STUDIES IN JUDAISM IN LATE ANTIQUITY

EDITED BY

JACOB NEUSNER

VOLUME THIRTY-THREE

A HISTORY
OF THE MISHNAIC LAW
OF WOMEN

PART THREE

A HISTORY OF THE MISHNAIC LAW OF WOMEN

BY

JACOB NEUSNER

University Professor
Professor of Religious Studies
The Ungerleider Distinguished Scholar of Judaic Studies
Brown University

PART THREE

NEDARIM, NAZIR

TRANSLATION AND EXPLANATION

Eugene, Oregon

Wipf and Stock Publishers
199 W 8th Ave, Suite 3
Eugene, OR 97401

A History of the Mishnaic Law of Women, Part 3
Nedarim, Nazir: Translation and Explanation
By Neusner, Jacob
Copyright©1980 by Neusner, Jacob
ISBN 13: 978-1-55635-357-4
ISBN 10: 1-55635-357-X
Publication date 3/20/2007
Previously published by E. J. Brill, 1980

To
The Protestant Theological Faculty of
Eberhard-Karls-Universität Tübingen
and to its Institutum Judaicum

with thanks for the hospitality and cordial friendship
shown to me on the occasion of my lectures delivered
in celebration of the 500th Anniversary Jubilee, 1477-1977.

October 7-15, 1977.

TABLE OF CONTENTS

Preface IX
Abbreviations and Bibliography XIII
Transliterations XX

NEDARIM

I.	Introduction to Nedarim	3
II.	Nedarim Chapter One	15
III.	Nedarim Chapter Two	21
IV.	Nedarim Chapter Three	29
V.	Nedarim Chapter Four	37
VI.	Nedarim Chapter Five	45
VII.	Nedarim Chapter Six	50
VIII.	Nedarim Chapter Seven	59
IX.	Nedarim Chapter Eight	66
X.	Nedarim Chapter Nine	72
XI.	Nedarim Chapter Ten	81
XII.	Nedarim Chapter Eleven	92

NAZIR

XIII.	Introduction to Nazir	105
XIV.	Nazir Chapter One	114
XV.	Nazir Chapter Two	121
XVI.	Nazir Chapter Three	132
XVII.	Nazir Chapter Four	140
XVIII.	Nazir Chapter Five	153
XIX.	Nazir Chapter Six	160
XX.	Nazir Chapter Seven	175
XXI.	Nazir Chapter Eight	181
XXII.	Nazir Chapter Nine	192

Index   198

PREFACE

This book joins Nedarim and Nazir. That is perfectly natural, since the two tractates address themselves to an identical, or nearly identical, agendum, and since they work out pretty much the same sorts of conceptual principles and problems in pretty much the same way. As we shall see, moreover, the two tractates speak to one another. The translation is meant to show the form-analytical traits and problems of the two tractates. The explanation gives a clear and straight-forward account of the exegetical results of form-analysis. It therefore spells out the original, primary meaning, intended by the framers of the several pericopae and of the tractate as a whole. Tosefta is explained very briefly and often in a perfunctory way, principally in relationship to Mishnah. I no longer treat Tosefta as an independent object of exegesis and now permit that compilation to play only a limited role in what follows.

The translation and explanation serve a single, very particular purpose, and in no way address all, or even most, of those many exegetical problems which occupy the great classical literature of Mishnah-exegesis and study of the *halakhah* of Mishnah and Talmud. My notion is that I herein explain what it is that the people who made up these sentences meant at the time that they made them up. The exclusion, of course, is self-evident: all those many issues generated by later thinkers and addressed to these same sentences for their (implied) judgments and responses. The intellectual structure and history of Rabbinic Judaism are one of the formidable achievements of the human mind. Surely an account of what lies at the very foundations of that structure and at the commencement of that history serves its purpose (achieved in the concluding part of the whole) without having to attend to those many legitimate issues and interests which arose later on, after Mishnah came to closure. Many times I have contemplated presenting only the conclusions, without an account of the texts and the meanings I believe inhere in their original form and sense. Each time I have concluded that conclusions without texts serve no important scholarly purpose, even though at the outset, the work of discovery and presentation would be greatly facilitated for me, and the reception of the results made easier for the reader.

Just as each division of Mishnah takes for granted the existence of the others, so no work on Mishnah may pretend to accomplish the whole of the work of description, interpretation, and philosophico-legal reconstruction and to take up the pretense that other works of reference and of scholarship are unavailable. One minor consequence is that I do not even trouble to list parallel passages, e.g., where a given pericope of Mishnah or Tosefta is alluded to or cited; these are exhaustively listed, for Tosefta, in Lieberman, and, for Mishnah, in Romm's edition. One major consequence is that, when I offer my simple conception of what it is that a pericope wishes to tell us at the very commencement of its historical journey, I no longer trouble to report other conceptions and why I reject them.

Let me now specify what the work aims to achieve. The purpose of the present work is to investigate the history of the formation of Rabbinic Judaism, down to the redaction of Mishnah in ca. 200. Even though attainment of that purpose presently seems remote, depending as it does upon the completion of the historical analysis of all of Mishnah-Tosefta, we have to keep in mind why we do the work and what we hope to learn. The sole issue here is *historical*. All discussion, both in the four exegetical parts and in the synthetic one to follow, is shaped to address the historical question announced in the title of the work. Questions of the history of exegesis and of the formation, formulation, transmission, and redaction of the literature of Mishnah-Tosefta, to which a fair amount of intellectual energy is devoted in *Purities,* here are not raised, as they were not dealt with at length in *Holy Things*. The reason is that the answers to these questions do not materially advance the single inquiry at hand, an investigation of the history of religions and of ideas. Methods for the finding of answers to certain long-standing literary and exegetical questions have proved their validity and do not require further demonstration in the present work. For the present purpose, moreover, it suffices to follow the text and pointing of Albeck-Yalon. Variant readings, while always interesting, have never made much difference to the historical results attained heretofore, despite their importance in ascertaining details of the law itself.

To conclude: This work is not called a *commentary*, but "translation and explanation," which I hope will more adequately define and delimit my purpose. A commentary may serve any number of useful and important purposes. It may be "scientific," that is, as the word is presently used, archaeological or philological. It may raise a wide range of quite distinctive and valid exegetical purposes, e.g., harmonistic, *halakhic*, atomistic, text-critical, and the like. It may constitute a supercommentary, not to Mishnah at all, but to a particular trend of Mishnah-commentaries. My contribution is defined by my purpose, to repeat: to attain a *history* of the Mishnaic law of women.

The history cannot be laid forth without a systematic, careful, and complete presentation of the relevant sources. This is accomplished in the *translation*.

These sources have also to be interpreted and explained, since no reader can be expected to effect the rather complex task of exegesis only at the time of turning to what I might offer in Part V as the history of these (by me, unexplained) texts. That is why, in addition to a fresh translation (the first in English of Tosefta, the first form-analytical one for Mishnah), I offer what I call an *explanation*, as I said, a simple and straightforward account of what I believe each pericope meant to the person who made it up.

Turning directly to the historical parts of the project without first learning the texts upon which they are based will not serve any useful purpose.

This book and its companions thankfully are dedicated to those universities which, in various ways, have chosen in the past few years to grant recognition to my scholarly efforts.

J.N.

ABBREVIATIONS AND BIBLIOGRAPHY

AE	=	*Tosafot* R. ʿAqiba Egger. From Mishnah, ed. Romm.
Ah.	=	ʾAhilot
Albeck	=	Ḥanokh Albeck, *Shishah sidré mishnah. Seder Nashim* (Tel Aviv, 1954).
Ar.	=	ʿArakhin
Arthur	=	Marylin B. Arthur, "The Origins of the Western Attitude toward Women," *Arethusa* 6, 1973, pp. 7-58.
A.Z.	=	ʿAbodah Zarah
B.	=	Babylonian Talmud
B.B.	=	Babaʾ Batraʾ
B.M.	=	Babaʾ Meṣiʿaʾ
B.Q.	=	Babaʾ Qammaʾ
Baer	=	Richard A. Bear, Jr., *Philo's Use of the Categories Male and Female* (Leiden, 1970).
Bailey	=	Derrick Sherwin Bailey, *Sexual Relation in Christian Thought* (N.Y., 1959).
Beauvoir	=	Simone de Beauvoir, *The Second Sex*. Translated and edited by H. M. Parshley (N.Y., 1953).
Ber.	=	Berakhot
Berger	=	Isaiah Berger, ed., *Analytical Index to The Jewish Quarterly Review, 1889-1908 (N.Y., 1966)*.
Berlin, 1968	=	Charles Berlin, *Harvard University Library. Catalogue of Hebrew Books* (Cambridge, 1968), I-VI.
Berlin, 1972	=	*Supplement* (Cambridge, 1972), I-III.
Berlin, 1971	=	*Widener Library Shelflist, 39. Judaica* (Cambridge 1971).
Bert.	=	ʿObadiah of Bertinoro. From Mishnah, ed. Romm.
Bes.	=	Beṣah
Bik.	=	Bikkurim
Blackman	=	Philip Blackman, *Mishnayoth.* Vol. III. *Order Nashim. Pointed Hebrew Text, Introductions, Translation, Notes, Appendix, Supplement, Indexes* (London, 1954).
C	=	H. Loewe, *The Mishnah of the Palestinian Talmud (Hammishnah ʿal pi ketab-yad Cambridge)* (Jerusalem, 1967).
Cohen	=	A. Cohen, *Sotah. Translated into English with Notes, Glossary, and Indices* (London, 1936).
Cohen, *Law*	=	Boaz Cohen, *Law and Tradition in Judaism* (N.Y., 1959).
Cohen, *Roman Law*	=	Boaz Cohen, *Jewish and Roman Law. A Comparative Study* (N.Y., 1966) I-II. See Smith *re* Cohen.
Corbett	=	Percy Ellwood Corbett, *The Roman Law of Marriage* (Oxford, 1930).
Daiches & Slotki	=	Samuel Daiches and Israel W. Slotki, *Kethuboth. Translated into English with Notes, Glossary, and Indices.* Pages 1-198 by Samuel Daiches [= b. Ket. 2a-36b]. Pages 198 to the end by Israel W. Slotki [= b. Ket. 36b = 112b] (London, 1936).
Daly	=	Mary Daly, *Beyond God the Father* (Boston, 1973).
Dem	=	Demaʾi
Deut.	=	Deuteronomy

Donaldson	=	James Donaldson, *Woman. Her Position and Influence in Ancient Greece and Rome, and Among the Early Christians* (N.Y., 1907).
Douglas *Meanings*	=	Mary Douglas, *Implicit Meanings. Essays in Anthropology* (London & Boston, 1975).
Douglas, *Symbols*	=	Mary Douglas, *Natural Symbols. Explorations in Cosmology* (N.Y., 1973).
Ed.	=	ʿEduyyot
EG	=	*Hiddushe Eliyyahu Migreiditz.* From Mishnah, ed. Romm (Vilna, 1887).
Epstein	=	Louis M. Epstein, *Marriage Laws in the Bible and the Talmud* (Cambridge, 1942).
Epstein, *Nusaḥ*	=	Y. N. H. Epstein, *Mabo lenusaḥ hammishnah* (Tel Aviv, 1954).
Epstein, *Tan.*	=	Y. N. H. Epstein, *Meboʾot lesifrut hattanaʾim. Mishnah tosefta, ummidrashé halakhah.* Ed. E. Ṣ. Melammed (Tel Aviv, 1957).
Erub.	=	ʿErubin
Evans-Pritchard	=	E. E. Evans-Pritchard, *The Position of Women in Primitive Societies and Other Essays in Social Anthropology* (N.Y., 1965).
Forkman	=	Göran, Forkman, *The Limits of the Religious Community. Expulsion from the Religious Community within the Qumran Sect, within Rabbinic Judaism, and within Primitive Christianity* (Lund, 1972).
Freedman	=	H. Freedman, *Nedarim. Translated into English with Notes, Glossary, and Indices* (London, 1936).
Freedman, *Qid.*	=	H. Freedman, *Kiddushin. Translated into English with Notes, Glossary, and Indices* (London, 1936).
Friedman	=	Shamma Friedman, "A Critical Study of Yevamot X with a Methodological Introduction," in H. Z. Dimitrovsky, ed., *Texts and Studies. Analecta Judaica.* (N.Y., 1977), I, pp. 275-442. The most important critical reading of Babylonia Talmudic literary problems of our day.
Goodwater	=	Leanna Goodwater, *Women in Antiquity: An Annotated Bibliography* (Metuchen, 1975).
GRA	=	Elijah ben Solomon Zalman ("Elijah Gaon" or "Vilna Gaon"), 1720-1797.
Git.	=	Giṭṭin
HA	=	Emanuel Hai Riqi. *Hon ʾashir.* In QMH.
Hag.	=	Ḥagigah
Hal.	=	Ḥallah
Hayyot	=	Yiṣḥaq Ḥayyot, *Zeraʿ yiṣhaq.* Ed. H. Y. L. Deutsch (N.Y., 1960).
HD	=	*Hasdé David.* David Pardo, *Ḥasdé David.* I. *Tosefta Zeraʿim Moʿed, Nashim* (Livorno; Repr.: 1976).
Hecker	=	Eugene A. Hecker, *A Short History of Women's Rights. From the Days of Augustus to the Present Time. With Special Reference to England and the United States* (N.Y., 1910).
Holy Things	=	Jacob Neusner, *A History of the Mishnaic Law of Holy Things* (Leiden, 1979-1980) I-VI.
Hor.	=	Horayot
Horner	=	I. B. Horner, *Women under Primitive Buddhism. Lay-women and Almswomen* (Delhi, Patna, Varanasi, 1930. Repr. 1975).
Hul.	=	Ḥullin
Hutner	=	*The Babylonian Talmud. With Variant Readings Collected from Manuscripts, Fragments of the "Genizah" and Early Printed Editions. And Collated Quotations from the Talmud in Early Rabbinic Literature, etc.*

	Tractate Kethuboth. Editor: Moshe Hershler. Director: Joshua Hutner (Jerusalem, 1977). I-II.
ID	= Nathan Lebam. *Imré daʿat.* In QMH.
Isaksson	= Abel Isaksson, *Marriage and Ministry in the New Temple. A Study with Special Reference to Mt. 19:13-12 and I Cor. 11:3-16* (Lund, 1965).
Janeway	= Elizabeth Janeway, *Man's World, Woman's Place: A Study in Social Mythology* (N.Y., 1971).
Jastrow	= Marcus Jastrow, *A Dictionary of the Targumim, the Talmud, Babli, and Yerushalmi, and the Midrashic Literature* (1904. Repr., N.Y., 1950) I-II.
K	= Georg Beer, *Faksimile-Ausgabe des Mishnacodex Kaufmann A 50* (Repr.: Jerusalem, 1968).
Kahana	= K. Kahana, *The Theory of Marriage in Jewish Law* (Leiden, 1966). This is surely the worst book on this subject.
Katsh	= Abraham I. Katsh. *Ginzé Mishna. One Hundred and Fifty-Nine Fragments from the Cairo Geniza in the Saltykov-Shchedrin Library in Leningrad Appearing for the First Time with an Introduction, Notes and Variants* (Jerusalem, 1970).
Kel.	= Kelim
Ker.	= Keritot
Kil.	= Kila'im
Klien	= B. D. Klien, *Nazir. Translated into English with Notes, Glossary, and Indices* (London, 1936).
KM	= *Kesef Mishneh.* Joseph Karo. Commentary to Maimonides, *Mishneh Torah.* Published in Venice, 1574-5. Text used: Standard version of Maimonides, *Mishneh Torah.*
Kutscher	= Eduard Yechezkel Kutscher, *Hebrew and Aramaic Studies* (Jerusalem, 1977). Edited by Zeev Ben Hayyim, Aharon Dotan, Gad Sarfatti, with Moshe Bar Asher.
Lasch	= Christopher Lasch, *Haven in a Heartless World* (N.Y., 1977).
Lacey	= W. K. Lacey, *The Family in Classical Greece* (Ithaca, 1968).
Levine, *Netinim*	= Baruch A. Levine, "Later Sources on the Netinim," *Orient and Occident. Essays presented to Cyrus H. Gordon on the Occasion of his Sixty-fifth Birthday,* ed. Harry A. Hoffner, Jr. (Kevelaer & Neukirchen-Vluyn, 1973), pp. 101-107.
Levine, *Mulugu*	= Baruch A. Levine, "Mulūgu/Melug: The Origins of a Talmudic Legal Institution," *Journal of the American Oriental Society* 88, 2, 1968, pp. 271-285.
Lieberman	= Saul Lieberman, *The Tosefta. According to Codex Vienna, with variants from Codices Erfurt, Genizah MSS. and Editio Princeps (Venice, 1521). Together with References to Parallel Passages in Talmudic Literature. And a Brief Commentary. The Order of Nashim.* I. *Yebamoth, Kethubuth, Nedarim, Nazir* (N.Y., 1967). II. *Sotah, Gittin, Kiddushin* (N.Y., 1973).
Lieberman, *TK*	= Saul Lieberman, *Tosefta Ki-fshutah. A Comprehensive Commentary on the Tosefta.* Part VI. *Order Nashim.* I. *Yebamot-Ketubot* (N.Y., 1967). II. *Nedarim, Nezirut* (N.Y., 1967). III. *Sotah, Gittin, Qiddushin* N.Y., 1973). In Hebrew.
Levy, *Wörterbuch*	= Jacob Levy, *Wörterbuch über die Talmudim und Midraschim* (1924. Repr., Darmstadt, 1963) I-IV.
Loewe	= Raphael Loewe, *The Position of Women in Judaism* (London, 1966).
M	= *Babylonian Talmud Codex Munich* (95) (Repr., Jerusalem, 1971).

M.	=	Mishnah
Ma.	=	Maʿaserot.
Maimonides, *Assev.*	=	B. D. Klien, trans., *The Code of Maimonides. Book Six. The Book of Asseverations* (New Haven and London, 1962).
Maimonides, *Comm.*	=	Moses b. Maimon, *Mishnah. Seder Nashim*. Trans. by Yosef Kappaḥ (Jerusalem, 1967).
Maimonides, *Holiness*	=	Louis I, Rabinowitz and Philip Grossman, trans., *The Code of Maimonides. Book Five. The Book of Holiness* (New Haven and London, 1965).
Maimonides, *Women*	=	Isaac Klein, trans., *The Code of Maimonides. Book Four. The Book of Women* (New Haven and London, 1972).
Mak.	=	Makkot
Makh.	=	Makhshirin
Me.	=	Meʿilah
Meg.	=	Megillah
Melammed, *Midrash*	=	E. S. Melammed, *Hayyaḥas sheben midrashé halakah lammishnah velattosefta* (Jerusalem, 1967).
Melammed, *Talmud*	=	E. Ṣ. Melammed, *Pirqé mabo lesifrut hattalmud* (Jerusalem, 1973).
Men.	=	Menaḥot
Mielziner	=	M. Mielziner, *The Jewish Law of Marriage and Divorce in Ancient and Modern Times and its Relation to the Law of of the State* (N.Y., 1901).
Miq.	=	Miqvaʾot
ML	=	*Mishneh Lammelekh*. Commentary to Maimonides, *Mishneh Torah*. Judah Rosannes 1657-1727. For source see KM.
M.Q.	=	Moʿed Qaṭan
MS	=	*Meleʾkhet Shelomo*. Shelomo bar Joshua Adeni, 1567-1625. From Mishnah, ed. Romm.
N	=	*Mishnah ʿim perush HaRambam. Defus Rishoʾn Napoli [5]252* [1492], (Jerusalem, 1970).
Naz.	=	Nazir
Ned.	=	Nedarim
Neg.	=	Negaʿim
Nid.	=	Niddah
Num.	=	Numbers
Noah	=	Aminoaḥ Noaḥ, *The Redaction of the Tractate Qiddushin in the Babylonian Talmud*. In Hebrew (Tel Aviv, 1977).
NS	=	Ṣevi Gutmacher, *Naḥalat ṣevi*. In QMH.
Oh.	=	ʾOhalot
Or.	=	ʿOrlah
Otwell	=	John T. Otwell, *And Sarah Laughed. The Status of Women in the Old Testament* (Philadelphia, 1977). Compendium of 800 references to women.
P	=	*Shishah sidré mishnah. Ketab yad Parma DeRossi 138* (Repr.: Jerusalem, 1970).
Pa	=	*Mishnah ketab yad Paris. Paris 328-329* (Repr.: Jerusalem, 1973).
Par.	=	Parah
PB	=	*Mishnah Codex Parma "B" DeRossi 497. Seder Tehoroth.* Introduction by M. Bar Asher (Repr.: Jerusalem, 1971).
Pes.	=	Pesaḥim
Pharisees	=	J. Neusner, *The Rabbinic Traditions about the Pharisees before 70* (Leiden, 1971) I-III.
Pomeroy	=	Sarah B. Pomeroy, *Goddesses, Whores, Wives, and Slaves. Women in Classical Antiquity* (N.Y., 1975).

Proulx & Schökel	=	P. Proulx and L. Alonso Schökel, "Las Sandalias del Mesias Esposo," *Biblica 1978:* 59, 1-37.
Purities	=	J. Neusner, *A History of the Mishnaic Law of Purities* (Leiden, 1974-1977) I-XXII.
QA	=	*Qorban Aharon.* Aaron Ibn Ḥayyim (d. 1632), *Qorban Aharon, Perush LaSefer Sifra* (Dessau, 1749).
Qehati	=	Pinḥas Qehati, *Seder Nashim* (Jerusalem, 1976) I-II
QH	=	Moshe Zakhuta, *Qol haramaz.* In QMH.
QMH	=	*Qebuṣat meforshé hammishnah* (Jerusalem, 1962).
QS	=	Ḥayyim Sofer, *Qol Sofer.* In QMH.
Rabad	=	Supercommentary to Maimonides, *Code.*
Rabad, Sifra	=	R. Abraham ben David, Commentary to Sifra. From *Sifra,* ed. Weiss.
Rabin, *Documents*	=	Chaim Rabin, *The Zadokite Documents. I. The Admonition. II. The Laws* (Oxford, 1958). Second Edition.
Rabin, *Studies*	=	Chaim Rabin, *Qumran Studies* (Oxford, 1957).
Rabinowitz	=	Louis I. Rabinowitz, "Levirate Marriage and *Ḥaliẓah,*" *Encyclopaedia Judaica* 11:122-131.
Rappaport	=	Ṣevi Hirsch Hakkohen Rappaport, *Torat Kohanim,* with the commentaries ʿ*Ezrat Kohanim* and *Tosefet HaʿEzrah* (Jerusalem, 1972).
Rawson	=	Beryl Rawson, "Family Life among the Lower Classes at Rome in the First Two Centuries of the Empire," *Classical Philology* 61, 2, 1966, pp. 71-83.
Reiter	=	Rayna R. Reiter, ed., *Toward an Anthropology of Women* (N.Y. and London, 1975).
Reuther	=	Rosemary Radford Ruether, *Religion and Sexism. Images of Women in the Jewish and Christian Traditions* (N.Y., 1974). A truly splendid essay.
R.H.	=	Rosh Hashshanah
Richter	=	Donald C. Richter, "The Position of Women in Classical Athens," *The Classical Journal* 67, 1971, pp. 1-8.
Rosaldo and Lamphere	=	Michelle Zimbalist Rosaldo and Louise Lamphere, eds., *Women, Culture, and Society* (Stanford, 1974).
San.	=	Sanhedrin
Sanday	=	Peggy R. Sanday, "Toward a Theory of the Status of Women," *American Anthropologist* 75, 1973, pp. 1682-1700.
Sens	=	Yaʿaqob David Ilan, *Tosafot Shenṣ* (Bene Beraq, 1973).
Shab.	=	Shabbat
Shabu.	=	Shabuʿot
Sheb.	=	Shebiʿit
Sheq.	=	Sheqalim
SifraFink.	=	*Sifra or Torat Kohanim. According to Codex Assemani LXVI.* With a Hebrew Introduction by Louis Finkelstein (N.Y., 1956).
SifraHillel	=	*Sifra.* With the Commentary of *Hillel b. R. Eliaqim.* Ed. by Shachne Koleditzky (Jerusalem, 1961).
Sifra ed. Weiss	=	*Sifra,* ed. Isaac Hirsch Weiss (repr.: N.Y., 1947).
SifHillel	=	*Sifré ... ʿim Perush ... Rabbenu Hillel bar Eliaqim.* Ed. Shachne Koleditzky (Jerusalem, 1958).
SifHorovitz	=	*Siphre d'Be Rab. Fasciculus primus: Siphre ad Numeros adjecto Siphre Zutta.* Ed. H. S. Horovitz (Leipzig, 1917).
SifIshShalom	=	*Sifre debe Rab. ʿIm Tosafot Meir ʿAyin.* Ed. Meir IshShalom (Friedman). (Vienna, 1864, repr.: N.Y., 1948).

SifLieberman	=	*Siphre Zutta (The Midrash of Lydda).* II. *The Talmud of Caesarea* (N.Y., 1968).
SifNeṣiv	=	*Sifré ... ʿEmeq HaNeṣiv.* Naftali Ṣevi Yehudah Berlin (Jerusalem, 1960).
SifPardo	=	*Sefer Sifre debe Rab.* David Pardo (Salonika, 1799). Repr.: Jerusalem, 1970).
SifVolk	=	*Sifre ... ʿim hagahot ... HaGRA veʿim perush Keter Kehunah.* Ṣevi Hirsch Hakkohen Volk. Ed. Yaʿaqob Hakkohen Volk (Jerusalem, 1954).
SifYasq	=	*Sifre Zutta leSeder Bamidbar ... ʾAmbuhaʾ deSifré.* Yaʿaqob Zeʾeb Yaskobitz (Lodz, 1929, repr.: Bene Beraq, 1967) I-II.
Simon	=	Maurice Simon, *Gittin. Translated into English with Notes, Glossary, and Indices* (London, 1936).
Slotki	=	Israel W. Slotki, *Yebamoth. Translated into English with Notes, Glossary, and Indices* (London, 1936).
Smith *re* Cohen	=	Morton Smith, review, Boaz Cohen, *Jewish and Roman Law, Journal of Biblical Literature* 1967, 86:238-241.
Sot.	=	Soṭah
Sotah-*Computer*	=	David E. Y. Sarna, Lawrence H. Schiffman, David Wm. Siktberg, and Michael J. Strassfeld, *A Computer-Aided Edition of the Tosefta Sotah. According to Codex Vienna. With variants from Codex Erfurt and Editio Princeps (Venice, 1521)* (Waltham, 1970).
Suk.	=	Sukkah
Swidler	=	Leonard Swidler, *Women in Judaism. The Status of Women in Formative Judaism* (Metuchen, 1976). Uncritical, ignorant, and polemical. Nothing more than an unanalyzed collection of sayings, embellished with hostile sermons. Poorly written, poorly conceived, poorly executed.
T.	=	Tosefta
T	=	*Sidré Mishnah. Neziqin, Qodoshim, Tohorot. Ketab yad Yerushalayim, 1336. Ketab Yad beniqud lefi massoret Teman.* (Repr.: Jerusalem, 1970). Introduction by S. Morag.
Ta.	=	Taʿanit
Tavard	=	George H. Tavard, *Woman in Christian Tradition* (Notre Dame, 1973).
Tem.	=	Temurah
Ter.	=	Terumot
Toh.	=	Ṭohorot
TR	=	Saul Lieberman, *Tosefet Rishonim.* II. *Seder Nashim, Neziqin, Qodoshim* (Jerusalem, 1938).
T.Y.	=	Ṭebul Yom
TYB	=	Tifeʾret Yisraʾel Boʿaz. See TYY.
TYT	=	*Tosafot Yom Tob.* Yom Tob Lipman Heller, 1579-1654. From reprint of Mishnah, ed. Romm.
TYY	=	*Tifeʾret Yisraʾel, Yakhin.* Israel ben Gedaliah Lipschütz, 1782-1860. (With supercommentary of Baruch Isaac Lipschütz = TYB.) From reprint of Mishnah, ed. Romm.
Unknown	=	*Mishnah. Sedarim Zeraim, Moed, Nashim. Unknown Edition. Printed in Pisaro or Constantinople.* (Jerusalem, 1970).
Uqs.	=	ʿUqṣin
V	=	*Talmud Babli. Nidpas ʿal yedé Daniel Bomberg bishenat 5282* [= 1552]. *Venezia.* (Venice, 1522). Repr.: Jerusalem, 1971).
V*	=	*Talmud Babli ...* [as above]. Zebaḥim.

Vat 130	=	*Manuscripts of the Babylonian Talmud. From the Collection of the Vatican Library.* (Jerusalem, 1972). Series A. Vol. III. *Vat. Ebr. 130: Ketubot, Gittin.*
Vat 110	=	As above: *Sotah, Nedarim, Nazir.*
Vat 112	=	*Manuscripts of the Babylonian Talmud. From the Collection of the Vatican Library* (Jerusalem, 1974). Series B. Vol. IV. *Ketubot.*
Vat 111	=	As above: Vol. VI *Yebamot, Qiddushin.*
Vermes, *English*	=	Geza Vermes, *The Dead Sea Scrolls in English* (Harmondsworth, 1975).
Vermes, *Perspective*	=	Geza Vermes, *The Dead Sea Scrolls. Qumran in Perspective* (London, 1977).
Wilson, *Patterns*	=	Bryan R. Wilson, ed., *Patterns of Sectarianism. Organisation and Ideology in Social and Religious Movements* (London, 1967).
Wilson, *Sects*	=	Bryan Wilson, *Religious Sects. A Sociological Study* (N.Y. & Toronto, 1970).
Wolff	=	Hans Julius Wolff, "Marriage Law and Family Organization in Ancient Athens. A Study on the Interrelation of Public and Private Law in the Greek City," *Traditio* 1944, 2:43-95.
Wright, F. A.	=	F. A. Wright, *Feminism in Greek Literature. From Homer to Aristotle* (London, 1923).
Wright, Helena	=	Helena Wright, *Sex and Society* (Seattle, 1968).
Y.	=	Yerushalmi. Palestinian Talmud.
Y.T.	=	Yom Ṭob
Yad.	=	Yadayim
Yadin	=	Yigael Yadin, *Bar Kokhba. The Rediscovery of the Legendary Hero of the Second Jewish Revolt against Rome* (N.Y., 1971).
Yaron	=	Reuven Yaron, *Introduction to the Law of the Aramaic Papyri* (Oxford, 1961).
Yeivin	=	Israel Yeivin, *A Collection of Mishnaic Geniza Fragments with Babylonian Vocalization. With Description of the Manuscripts and Indices* (Jerusalem, 1974).
Yeb.	=	Yebamot
Z	=	M. S. Zuckermandel, *Tosephta. Based on Erfurt and Vienna Codices* (Repr.: Jerusalem, 1963).
Zab.	=	Zabim
Zeb.	=	Zebaḥim
Zinserling	=	Verena Zinserling, *Women in Greece and Rome* (N.Y., 1973). Translated from the German by L.A. Jones.
ZY	=	*Zeraʿ yiṣḥaq.* By Yiṣḥaq Ḥayyot (Brooklyn, 1960).

TRANSLITERATIONS

א	=	ʾ	מ ם	=	M
ב	=	B	נ ן	=	N
ג	=	G	ס	=	S
ד	=	D	ע	=	ʿ
ה	=	H	פ ף	=	P
ו	=	W	צ ץ	=	Ṣ
ז	=	Z	ק	=	Q
ח	=	Ḥ	ר	=	R
ט	=	Ṭ	שׁ	=	Š
י	=	Y	שׂ	=	S
כ ך	=	K	ת	=	T
ל	=	L			

NEDARIM

CHAPTER ONE

INTRODUCTION TO NEDARIM

The present tractate, on vows, is among the more accessible of our division—and, indeed, of all of Mishnah—because many of its problems have to do with the interpretation of language and its implications, a task which, whether in Middle Hebrew or in English, imposes the same logical requirements of linguistic analysis. The tractate also poses few profound problems of explanation, because its basic, recurrent conceptions are clear and easily grasped (indeed, not a few are obvious and trite), and because there are few technicalities requiring patient mastery. While, as always, we shall encounter a small number of exegetical problems not to be solved within the limits of what Mishnah chooses to tell us, in the main Nedarim is among the genuinely pleasant and engaging intellectual exercises of Mishnah.

The tractate treats vows, how they are adopted, interpreted, and absolved, and, in this last rubric, the power of a husband to annul vows taken by his wife. It is that conception, introduced only at the end of the tractate and, as we shall see, essentially secondary to its principal thematic outline, which accounts for the inclusion of the tractate in the division of women. Had it ended with Chapter Nine, along with Nazir, it could have fit as comfortably alongside Shabuʿot as here. But Shabuʿot is devoted to matters of litigation and the use of oaths in resolving social and economic conflicts, while Nedarim and Nazir speak of matters of purely personal status, things an individual may or may not do in consequence of something he or she has said. It is for that reason, as much as for the substance of the concluding two chapters, that Nedarim, drawing Nazir in its wake as well, is given its present location. For if our division treats of the status of women and their relationship to men, its subterranean theme, expressed through its treatment of women, is the status of any individual in relationship to other individuals: private life of family, home, and village.

Nedarim, Nazir, and Sotah contain such information as Mishnah wishes to provide on the conduct of a marriage from the moment it has taken effect until death or divorce sever it. While, we recall, Ketubot contains some wise advice about what a wife owes her husband and *vice versa*, the sum and substance of Mishnah's sustained and rigorous investigation bear no such general character. For Mishnah wants to know, in respect to marriage, many particular things about matters of *relationship*. Its principal inquiry on any of its several topics relevant to marriage is into shifts and changes in the relationship of wife to husband. This of course is consistent with the points pertinent to the status of a woman *vis a vis* a man, at which Mishnah begins and ends: the creation of a marriage through Heavenly action (Yebamot) or human intervention (Qiddushin, Ketubot), and the cessation of a marriage through Heavenly action or through a writ of divorce (Gittin). In-between, we shall ask about the interplay between responsibilities to Heaven, on the one side, and the relationship of wife to husband, on the other. That is the gray area in which the woman owes fealty to Heaven and to husband alike. At Nazir she undertakes the disciplines described at Numbers Chapter Six; at Sotah she is investigated as required at Numbers Chapter Five, for her faithfulness at the instigation of a jealous husband (hence we must translate *sotah*, "*accused* wife," and not "*unfaithful* wife," a position on which Tosefta will concur). And here, at the outset, the much broader and more general topic is introduced, vows to Heaven which affect relationships on earth. That is, after all, what is at issue in Qiddushin and Gittin as well—only in the reverse: declarations made on earth and confirmed in Heaven as to the consecration, and cessation of consecration, of a woman to a particular man. So the middle of the account of woman, her relationship to herself and to others when she is a daughter or a wife, takes up declarations made to Heaven which shape a woman's status and relationships on earth.

What Mishnah here investigates, therefore, is the power of a person to affect his or her concrete and material relationships with other people through invoking the name of Heaven. This is done by stating, "May what I eat of your food be prohibited to me as a sacrifice is prohibited to me" (all expressed in the single word, *Qorban* [sacrifice]). Having said that, the person may not eat the food of the other. The reason is that the other person's food has been declared by the individual who took the vow to be in the status of a sacrifice. We know that what makes an ordinary beast into a holy beast, subject to the laws of sacrilege and set aside for the altar, is a verbal designation as a sacrifice. Here too what makes ordinary food into food in the status of Holy Things so far as a given individual is concerned is the designation of that ordinary food as Holy Things by the individual. The difference, of course, is that designating an animal as a beast for sacrifice is a public act. It affects the society at large, for no one may make use of said animal. Declaring that a dish of oatmeal is in the status of a *qorban*, by contrast, has no affect upon the cereal, except for the person who made the declaration. It would be fair to observe, therefore, that the fifth division, Qodoshm—e.g., Zebahim, Temurah, ʿArakhin—tells us about public and social sanctification, while the third division, Nashim—e.g., Qiddushin, Nedarim, Nazir—speaks of private and individual sanctification.

Now in contrast to its reverence for cultic sanctification, Mishnah looks down upon the subject-matter of this tractate (and, to a less articulate extent, the following one). Right at the outset, the redactor gives a powerful signal of his opinion of the whole: suitable folk (*keshārīm*) do not take vows to begin with, only evil people (*reshāʿīm*) do so. If one says, therefore, that something is subject to "the vows of the suitable folk," he has said nothing at all. Such people make no vows. There are, throughout, a certain distaste for vowing and a disdain for people who make vows. The latter are approached as irresponsible children. Given various openings toward the unbinding of their vows, they are, at the same time, forced to take seriously what they have said. The former are treated as a testing of Heaven and a trial of Heavenly patience and grace. So the sanctification of which tractates Yebamot and Qiddushin speak and the sanctity imposed by a vow, for a given individual, upon a mess of porridge, are quite distinct from one another. Mishnah takes expletive vows into its system. It does not admire them. But, in the nature of things, it must concede vows' power of sanctification, as it knows the power of language to effect consecration in more suitable circumstances. Mishnah therefore takes account of the sanctifying effect.

But it is a disreputable use of the holy. For so far as Mishnah is concerned, vows are a means of coercing people on earth by invoking the name and power of Heaven. Vows will be taken primarily under emotional duress and express impatience and frustration. They are not predictable and never follow upon a period of sober reflection. They are important in two relationships in particular: between one close friend and another, or between husband and wife. So vows come into play at the critical, therefore dangerous, points in the person's life. They disrupt the crucial *relationships* which define that life: marriage, friendship. They explode, jarring what should be predictable, indeed, what must be stable if life is to go on. So far as marriage is concerned, vows invoke the sacred to rip open the fabric of sacred relationships.

The weaker side to the party is commonly represented as taking a vow, very often the wife against her husband, or a harried guest against insistent host—who gives, dominates! Vows are the mode of aggression exercised by the less powerful party to the relationship. The weak invoke Heaven. The strong do not have to. For instance, as we shall see, a vow will be spit out by a guest who is importuned to join in a meal he does not want to eat. A wife will exclaim that she will derive no benefit whatsoever from her husband. A whole series of cases emerges from a vow taken by a person not to derive benefit from his friend, with the consequence that the friend, who wants to provide some sort of support for the person who has taken the vow, does so through a third party. The dependence is not any different, but is less obtrusive. *Who gives dominates:* the vow is an instrument to escape earthly domination in the name of Heaven. What it does, as we see, is to call down Heaven's sanctity upon the benefit—material or not—the donor wishes to give over. It is no wonder that, in analyzing vows, we once more call upon the conceptions of the gift to Heaven which forms the center of Holy Things.

If the prevailing atmosphere of our tractate is one of contempt for its subject-matter, nonetheless, as I said at the outset, the masters of the tractate have given us one of their best creations. In its perfectly logical unfolding of the topic from beginning through middle to end, it is a model of redactional good sense. In its clarity of conception and cogency of exposition, it is as close to perfection as any tractate we have seen. It even links itself to its neighboring divisions, fore and aft, through its neatly worked out concluding chapters, which, anywhere else in the tractate, will have produced a disruption in the unfolding of the theme, on the one hand, and in no way have accomplished their larger purpose, on the other. We start with a definition of language which effects a vow. We proceed to consider the affects of a vow upon what a person may or may not do (and, especially, may or may not *eat*). We conclude with close attention to how one may gain absolution from a vow, releasing its binding character on diverse grounds or pretexts. That is the whole story: beginning, middle, end, a structure so simple and logical that, if it were not also self-evident and absolutely obvious in the layout of the tractate, we should have been embarassed to claim to discern ("read in") on our own. Nothing impedes the logical flow of thematic exposition, and, with attention to the larger context of the division of Women, the redactor will remind us where we are and why: autonomous theme reshaped and moulded to fit a particular context, yet in no way violated or forced to yield its given nature, its integrity to its own topic. Vows in marriage remain *a propos* to the context so forcefully defined from the very beginning, and the end is integral and natural, far, far more than a tacked-on appendix.

Before we proceed to consider the layout of the tractate, we have to attend to the way in which Scripture, for its part, proposes to treat the theme at hand. It is only when we see an alternative account of what it is important to say *about* vows that we shall have clear perspective on the choice made and effected by our tractate's redactor. The relevant verses are Numbers 30:1-16, as follows:

> Moses said to the heads of the tribes of the people of Israel, "This is what the Lord has commanded. When a man vows a vow to the Lord, or swears an oath to bind himself by a pledge, he shall not break his word; he shall do according to all that proceeds out of his mouth.
> Or when a woman vows a vow to the Lord, and binds herself by a pledge, while within her father's house, in her youth, and her father hears of her vow and of her pledge by which has bound herself, and says nothing to her; then all her vows shall stand, and every pledge by which she has bound herself shall stand. But if her father expresses disapproval to her on the day that he hears of it, no vow of hers, no pledge by which she has bound herself, shall stand; and the Lord will forgive her, because her father opposed her. And if she is married to a husband while under her vows or any thoughtless utterance of her lips by which she has bound herself, and her husband hears of it, and says nothing to her on the day that he hears; then her vows shall stand, and her pledges by which she has bound herself shall stand. But if, on the day that her husband comes to hear of it, he expresses disapproval, then he shall make void her vow which was on her and the thoughtless utterance of her lips, by which she bound herself; and the Lord will forgive her. But any vow of a widow or of a divorced woman, anything by which she has bound herself, shall stand against her.
> And if she vowed in her husband's house, or bound herself by a pledge with an oath, and her husband heard of it, and said nothing to her, and did not oppose her; then all her vows shall stand, and every pledge by which she bound herself shall stand. But if her husband makes them null and void on the day that he hears them, then whatsoever proceeds out of her lips concerning her vows, or concerning her pledge of herself, shall not stand; her husband has made them void, and the Lord will forgive her. Any vow and any binding oath to afflict herself, her husband may establish, or her husband may make void. But if her husband says nothing to her from day to day, then he establishes all her vows, or all her pledges, that are upon her; he has established them, because he said nothing to her on the day that he heard of them. But if he makes them null and void after he has heard of them, then he shall bear her iniquity.
> These are the statutes which the Lord commanded Moses, as between a man and his wife, and between a father and his daughter, while in her youth, within her father's house.

From Scripture's perspective, we need hardly wonder why Nedarim is located where it is, since the important aspect of the topic—the father's or husband's right to abrogate or confirm the vows of a daughter or a wife—absolutely requires placing a tractate on vows in the context of women's law. Indeed, what we now appreciate is an amazing shift in the treatment of the topic. For Mishnah, while conceding that there is a special aspect of vows relevant to women, reconsiders the law in a neutral, non-sexual framework: vows taken by man or woman, and what we must know about them.

When we contemplate the tripartite construction of our tractate, we shall see how far it has redefined the agendum relevant to the theme of vows. What is nearly the whole story for the account of the topic in Numbers in Nedarim is a subordinate and secondary matter. As we shall now see, our tractate wants to know about the language which makes a vow effective, about the effects of vows, and about the absolution of vows and their effects, only at this last point taking into account the special case of the daughter or the wife, which forms the whole of Scripture's treatment of the topic.

The opening unit addresses three secondary questions, in the assumption that we all know the answers to the primary ones. That is, the tractate does not take up the obvious fact that if one says the normal language of vowing, e.g., "*Qorban* be what I taste of your food," then he or she is bound by that vow. First, it wants to know about *other* than normal language, for example, euphemisms. It touches upon the relationship between a vow and an oath. Second, there is language which produces no binding effect whatsoever, e.g., vows which are to begin with not taken seriously. Finally, there is language which produces only partial effect or is of limited consequence. This last unit forms a transition to the second principal division of the tractate.

I. *The Language of Vows.* 1:1-3:11

    A. *Euphemisms.* 1:1-2:5

1:1 All substitutes for language used to express vows are equivalent to vows, so too with bans, oaths, and Nazirite-vows. He who says, "I am forbidden by vow from you," "separated from you," etc., is bound by such a vow.

1:2 The foregoing illustrated.

1:3 He who says, "Not-unconsecrated-produce shall I not eat with you," is bound.

1:4 He who says, "An offering," "A whole-offering be what I eat with you" is bound [prohibited from eating with the other party].

2:1 And these vows are not binding at all: "May what I eat of yours be unconsecrated food," "Be like pig-meat," "Like an idol," etc. If one says, "*Qonam* if I sleep," or, "Speak," etc.—to this applies the law, "He shall not break his word." If he said, "By an oath I shall not sleep," it is binding.

2:2 He who says, "*Qorban* I shall not eat with you," is not bound. "By an oath I shall not eat with you," he is bound. Differences between vow and oath.

2:3 Continuation: There can be a vow within a vow, but no oath within an oath.

2:4 Vows which are not spelled out are subject to a more stringent rule and those which are spelled out are subject to a more lenient rule. Triplet.

2:5 If one used ambiguous language, the vow is of ambiguous status.

B. *Language of No Effect.* 3:1-4 + 5

3:1-3 Four types of vows did sages declare not binding: vows of incitement, vows of exaggeration, vows made in error, and vows made or broken under constraint.

3:4 They vow to murderers, robbers, or tax-collectors that produce is heave-offering even though it is not, or that it belongs to the state even though it does not + a triplet of Houses' disputes, clarifying this rule.

3:5 He who says, "Lo, these plants are *qorban* if they are not cut down," they are subject to redemption. "Lo, these plants are *qorban* until they are cut down," they are not subject to redemption.

C. *Language of Limited Effect.* 3:6-11

3:6-10 He who vows not to gain benefit from those who go down to the sea is permitted to enjoy benefit from those who dwell on dry land. He who vowed not to enjoy benefit from those who dwell on dry land is prohibited to enjoy benefit from those who go down to the sea, for those who go down to the sea are part of the generality of those who live on dry land—five matched exempla.

3:11 Triplet: If a man said, "*Qonam* be benefit which I enjoy from the children of Noah," he is permitted to enjoy benefit from Israelites and prohibited from nations of the world. "...if I have benefit from the seed of Abraham," he is prohibited to enjoy benefit from Israelites and permitted from the nations of the world.

The layout of the second unit is easy to discern, because Mishnah announces its two principal parts at the head of the unit. M. 4:1 tells us the difference between a vow not to derive (1) benefit from someone else and not to derive (2) food from him. The long and important components of the unit then tell us about a vow not to derive benefit in general and a vow not to make use of some sort of food in particular. A brief conclusion to this second element goes on the other particular things, e.g., clothing or furniture. But the main point of B is repeated at C, that is, the difference between a vow not to make use of a genus in general, and a species of a genus in particular. The former encompasses the latter, but the latter does not encompass the former. The final conception is how we interpret language used to limit the duration of a vow, e.g., "until Passover." This conception is worked out in painstaking detail but offers no complications or subtle refinements.

II. *The Binding Effects of Vows.* 4:1-8:6

    A. *Vows Not to Derive Benefit.* 4:1-5:6

4:1   There is no difference between him who is forbidden by vow from enjoying any benefit from his fellow and him who is forbidden by vow from deriving food from him except for setting foot in his house and using utensils in which food is not prepared.

4:2-3   He who is prohibited by vow from deriving benefit from his friend—the friend nonetheless pays his *sheqel*, pays back what he owes him, returns to him something he lost, etc.

4:4   He who is prohibited by vow from enjoying benefit from him—the friend goes in to visit him when he is sick, remaining standing, but not sitting down. And he heals the man, but not what belongs to him.

4:5   He who is forbidden by vow from enjoying benefit from his fellow, if this was before the Seventh Year, may not go down into his field or eat the produce that hangs over. In the Seventh Year while he may not go down into his field, he may eat the produce that hangs over from the man's property.

4:6   He who is forbidden by vow from deriving benefit from his fellow should not lend him anything nor borrow anything from him (triplet).

4:7-8   He who is forbidden by vow from deriving benefit from his fellow and has nothing to eat—the fellow goes to a storekeeper and says, "Mr. So-and-so is forbidden by vow from deriving benefit from me, and I don't know what I can do about it." And the storekeeper gives the other food and collects from the man. Triplet.

5:1-2   Partners who prohibited themselves by vow not to derive benefit from one another are prohibited from entering the common courtyard. Triplet.

5:3   He who is prohibited by vow from deriving benefit from his fellow, and the fellow has a bath-house or an olivepress which are hired out to other people—if the fellow has rights therein, the bathhouse or olivepress is prohibited. If he has no rights, the other is permitted.

5:4-5   If one said to his fellow, "Lo, I am *ḥerem* unto you," the one against whom the vow is made is prohibited from using what belongs to the one who made the vow. If he said, "Lo, you are *ḥerem* unto me," the one who takes the vow is prohibited from using what belongs to the other. If he said, "Lo, I am unto you and you are unto me *ḥerem*," both of them are prohibited.

5:6   He who is forbidden by vow from deriving benefit from his fellow and who has nothing to eat—the fellow gives food to someone else as a gift, and the one prohibited by vow then is permitted to make use of it.

B. Vows Not to Eat Certain Food. 6:1-7:2

6:1-3   He who takes a vow not to eat what is cooked is permitted to eat what is roasted or seethed. Five-part construction: He who takes a vow not to eat what is cooked in a pot is prohibited only from what is boiled therein. If he said, "*Qonam* be anything which goes down into a pot," he is prohibited from eating anything which is cooked in a pot.

6:4   Triplet: He who says, "*Qonam* if I taste fish or fishes," is prohibited to eat them in any form whatsoever.

6:5   He who vows not to have milk is permitted to eat curds.

6:6   He who vows not to eat meat is permitted to eat broth and meat sediment.

6:7-9   He who vows not to drink wine is permitted to eat a cooked dish which has a taste of wine. He who vows not to eat dates is permitted to have date-honey. Six-part construction. He who vows not to have wine is permitted to have apple-wine.

6:10   He who vows not to eat cabbage is forbidden to eat asparagus (a species of the cabbage-genus)—four-part construction.

7:1   He who vows not to eat vegetables is permitted to eat gourds.

7:2   He who vows not to eat grain is forbidden to eat dried Egyptian beans, so Meir.

C. Vows Not to Use Certain Objects. 7:3-5

7:3   He who vows not to wear clothing is permitted to wear sacking, curtains, or hangings.

7:4-5   He who vows not to enter a house is permitted to enter the upper room, so Meir. Sages: The upper room falls into the category of the house. He who vows not to use a bed is permitted to use a couch, so Meir. Sages: A couch is covered by the category of the bed.

D. The Temporal Limitation in Vows. 7:6-8:6

7:6-7   He who says "*Qonam* be these pieces of fruit for me," is prohibited from eating whatever he may exchange for those pieces of fruit and from whatever grows from them. If he says, "*Qonam* if I eat *these* pieces of fruit," he is permitted to eat whatever grows from them.

7:8-9   He who says, "*Qonam* be what you are making if I eat it until Passover," if she prepared these things before Passover, he may eat them after Passover. If he said, "*Qonam* be what you are making until Passover if I eat it," if she prepared things before Passover, he is prohibited from eating them before or after Passover.

8:1-3   Five part construction: He who says, "*Qonam* if I taste wine today," is prohibited until nightfall. Triplet along the same lines.

8:4-6   Five part construction, then two triplets: If he said, "Until the summer harvest," his vow applies until people bring in produce in baskets. If he said, "Until summer is over," it applies until the knives used in the harvest are put away, etc.

The concluding unit brings no surprises. It begins with very general considerations, then, as I said earlier, moves to what it particularly wishes to investigate. At the outset we consider grounds on the basis of which a sage will declare a vow to be null as at the outset, that is, never binding. We then turn to a brief account of a father's and husband's power jointly to annul the vows of a betrothed girl. The most important parts of the unit, C and D, deal with the husband's power to annul the vows of a wife. This is in two parts, though it may be reasonably argued that they are one. The first is a triplet involving Eliezer's views. The second is a more extensive set of special rules on the husband's power to annul the wife's vows: What sort of vows may he annul, and over what sort does he have no power? Are there vows which are null to begin with? How does the husband annul vows? These and similar questions are dealt with at some length. The unit ends with the consideration of vows made by women not subject to the authority of either a father or a husband. The concluding pericope links our tractate to its predecessor, Ketubot, a fitting redactional flourish, because it indicates in one small detail how much care has been lavished in the organization and presentation of our tractate.

III. *The Absolution of Vows.* 8:6-11:12

    A. *Grounds for the Absolution of Vows.* 8:6-9:10

He who says to his fellow, "*Qonam* be benefit I derive from you if you do not come and collect for your child a *kor* of wheat and two jugs of wine"—lo, this one can annul his vow without consultation with a sage, by saying to him, "Did you not speak only to do me honor? But this—not taking your wheat—is what I deem to be honorable."

9:1-2   Eliezer: They unloose a vow for a person by reference to the honor of his father or mother. They unloose a vow by reference to what happens unexpectedly.

9:3-4   Meir: There are things which appear to be equivalent to what happens unexpectedly but are not in fact treated as such. Meir: They unloose a vow by reference to what is written in the Torah.

9:5   They unloose a vow by reason of the wife's marriage-contract.

9:6-8   They unloose vows by reference to festival days and Sabbaths. ʿAqiba: A vow that is partly unloosed is deemed wholly unloosed.

9:9   They unloose a vow by reference to one's own honor and the honor of his children.

9:10   If one said, "*Qonam* if I marry that ugly Miss So-and-so," and she turns out to be beautiful—he is not bound by the oath.

    B. *The Annulment of the Vows of a Daughter.* 10:1-4

10:1-3   The father and husband of a betrothed girl must jointly annul her vows. If the one did and the other did not, it is not annulled.

10:4	A disciple of sages will annul the daughter's vows before she leaves his house, and the husband will annul them before she enters his domain.

C. *The Annulment of the Vows of a Wife.* 10:5-10:8

10:5-7	Triplet: An adult woman who waited twelve months and a widow who waited thirty days [and was not married], Eliezer says, Since the husband now is liable to support her, he has the power to annul her vows. Sages: He annuls her vows only after she enters his domain. A deceased childless brother's widow awaiting levirate marriage, whether with one or more levirs: Eliezer says, He annuls her vows. Joshua: If there is only one levir, he annuls the vow. If more, not. ʿAqiba: Neither one levir nor many may annul the vows. He who says to his wife, "All vows which you will vow from this time until I return from such-and-such a place are confirmed has said nothing. If he says, "Lo, they are annulled," Eliezer says, They are annulled. Sages: They are not annulled.
10:8	The annulment of vows may be done all day long, to sunset.

D. *The Husband's Power to Annul the Wife's Vows: Special Rules.* 11:1-8

11:1-2	These are vows which the husband annuls: matters inflicting self-punishment. Yosé: Only if they affect relationships between husband and wife may the husband annul such vows.
11:3	If she said, "*Qonam* if I derive benefit from anybody," he has not got the power to annul that vow.
11:4	If she said, "*Qonam* if I work for father," he does not have to annul that vow, which is null to begin with. ʿAqiba and Yoḥanan b. Nuri: Let him annul it—for diverse reasons.
11:5	Triplet: If his wife took a vow and he thought his daughter had done so, or *vice versa*—he has the power to go back and annul the vow. Abrogation done in error is null.
11:6	If she said, "*Qonam* be these figs and grapes," and he confirmed the vow concerning figs, the whole is confirmed. If he annulled the vow concerning figs, it is not annulled until he annuls the vow concerning grapes too.
11:7	If he said, "I was aware that there are vows, but I was not aware that there is the possibility of annulling them," he may later on annul the vow.
11:8	He who was prohibited by vow from giving any benefit to his son-in-law—how he may help his daughter.

E. *Vows of a Woman Not Subject to Abrogation.* 11:9-10

11:9	If a woman took a vow to take effect at the end of a given period and was married during that period, the husband has not got the power to annul the vow. If she took a vow in the domain of the husband to take effect after she left that domain, he does have the power to annul the vow for her.

11:10　　Nine sorts of girls make vows without the possibility of abrogation—there being no father with power to do so.

11:11　　If she said, "*Qonam* be any benefit I have of father... if I do work for you," the husband annuls that vow (in line with M. 11:1-2).

F.　*Redactional Conclusion.*　11:12

11:12　　Aforetimes they ruled: Three sorts of women go forth and collect their marriage-contract: She who says, "I am unclean for you," or "Heaven knows what is between you and me," or, "I am removed [by vow] from having sexual relations with all Jews." They reverted to rule that she cannot make such a statement.

The cogency evident in the logical unfolding and organization of the principal themes of the tractate and in the sophisticated formulary ambition of successive triplets, quintuplets, and the like, now will become clear in the actual conceptions themselves: the pericopae and their ideas.

CHAPTER TWO

NEDARIM CHAPTER ONE

This brief chapter defines the language by which one imposes a vow upon himself. Its main point is that substitutes for a word are as effective as the word, so that if one does not explicitly say, "Let it be to me as *qorban*," that is, equivalent to an offering, the normal usage, but rather says, "*Qonam*," he is subject to the vow through his euphemism. But it must be noted that if a person refers to some objects without the comparative ("*like* a sacrifice,") but instead "Altar," he may be interpreted to intend an oath, that is, "*By* the altar, such-and-so will I not do," in which case there is no vow at all. T. will want us to remember the difference between the language of a vow and the language of an oath. M. 1:1-2 announce that all substitute-language for a vow or equivalent is deemed effective. M. 1:2 spells out the sorts of substitute-language one may invent. M. 1:1B-I further explain other sorts of circumlocutions, besides substitute-language or euphemisms, which are effective.

M. 1:3-4 go on to a related but distinct question. What if one uses such language as, "Not-unconsecrated produce shall I not eat with you?" Then we understand that the man has vowed that he will eat *only* consecrated produce with the other, and this is prohibited. Likewise if he compares the food the other serves to something holy, then he cannot eat it. M. 1:4 goes on along these same lines. The concluding point is that a man may even declare his mouth, hand, or foot to be *qonam* if he talks, works, or walks with the other, and that vow is valid, so that he cannot do the things he has referred to. But the main point has to do with eating food at the other's house.

1:1-2

A. All substitutes for [language used to express] (1) vows are equivalent to vows,
    and for (2) bans (*ḥerem*) are equivalent to bans,
    and for (3) oaths are equivalent to oaths,
    and for (4) Nazirite-vows are equivalent to Nazirite-vows.

B. He who says to his fellow, (1) "I am forbidden by vow from you," (2) "I am separated from you," (3) "I am distanced from you,"

C. "if I eat your [food]," [or] "if I taste your [food],"

D. is bound [by such a vow].

E. [He who says,] "I am excommunicated from you"—

F. R. ʿAqiba in this case did incline to impose a stringent ruling.

G. [He who says], "As the vows of the evil folk...," has made a binding vow in the case of a Nazir, or in the case of [bringing] an offering, or in the case of an oath.

H. [He who says,] "As the vows of the suitable folk" has said nothing whatsoever.

I. "As their [suitable folks'] free-will offerings" ...he has made a binding vow in the case of a Nazir or in the case of [bringing] an offering.

M. 1:1

A. He who says to his fellow, "*Qonam,*" "*Qonaḥ,*" "*Qonas*"—lo, these are substitutes for Qorban [a vow to bring a sacrifice, and are valid].

B. [He who says to his fellow,] "*Ḥereq,*" "*Ḥerekh,*" "*Ḥeref,*" lo, these are substitutes for a *ḥerem* [ban].

C. [He who says to his fellow,] "*Naziq,*" "*Naziaḥ,*" "*Paziaḥ,*"—lo, these are substitutes for Nazirite-vows.

D. [He who says,] "*Shebutah,*" "*Shequqah,*"

E. [or if he] vowed [with the word], "*Mota,*"

F. lo, these are substitutes for *shebuʿah* [oath].

M. 1:2

The opening generalization, M. 1:1A, is carried forward at M. 1:2A-F. Indeed, the latter is a fairly systematic expansion of the former: M. 1:1A1 = M. 1:2A, M. 1:1A2 = M. 1:2B, M. 1:1A3 = M. 1:2D-F, M. 1:1A4 = M. 1:2C. M. 1:1B-D, E-F, are not, strictly speaking, substitutes for the language used of vows. G-I are a further, independent pericope, which deals with a distinct issue.

The point of M. 1:1A, M. 1:2 is that if one uses a substitute formulation for a vow, ban (*ḥerem*), oath, or Nazirite-vow, the language is as binding as if he had used the usual language. These substitutes are then illustrated. M. 1:1B-C's language is used to make a vow not to eat with the other party. C may be seen to continue any of the three formulations of B, "I am forbidden by vow from [eating] your [food] if I taste [your food]," and so on. E-F supplement B's list, since the language of excommunication is not much different from separation or distance, B2, 3. G contrasts with H, since, it is assumed, proper folk do not take vows of this sort. Its case is envisioned as follows. If one sees a Nazir passing by and says, "Lo, I am in accord with the vows of evil folk," he imposes upon himself the Nazirite-vow. If he said, "...in accord with the vows of suitable folk," he has said nothing. Righteous people do not take vows. But, I, sometimes suitable folk made a freewill offering as Nazirs or otherwise. But they do not make vows.

A. [He who says, "By] the right hand,"—lo, this is an oath.
B. "[By] the left hand,"—lo, this is an oath.
C. "By the Name," lo, this is an oath.
D. "For the Name," lo, this is a *qorban*.
E. "Like the freewill-offering of the evil folk,"—he has said nothing,
F. for the evil people do not bring freewill-offerings.
G. "Like the freewill-offering of the suitable folk"—
H. R. Judah says, "This is a valid vow in the case of a Nazirite-vow [M. 1:1G-I].
I. "For the pious men of old used to make freewill-offerings of Nazirite-vows.
J. "For there is not sufficient place [on the altar] for the bringing of offering in expiation for inadvertent sins in their behalf.
K. "So they would offer Nazirite-vows as freewill-offerings,
L. "so that they might bring an offering."
M. Rabban Simeon b. Gamaliel says, "[He who says,] 'Like the freewill offering of suitable folk' has not made a valid vow in the case of a Nazir.
N. "For the pious men of old did not make freewill-offerings of Nazirite-vows.
O. "For [in any case] if one wanted to bring a whole-offering, he might bring it. [If he wanted to bring] peace-offerings, he might bring them. [If he wanted to bring] a thank-offering and the four kinds of bread which go with it, he might bring [them].
P. "They did not make freewill-offerings of Nazirite-vows because they require atonement, since it says, *And he shall make atonement for him, because he sinned against the soul* (Num. 6:11)."

T. 1:1 L p. 100, ls. 1-9

A-D add complementary materials to M. D is a euphemism for a sacrifice, that is, "something for the Lord," hence an offering. The remainder of the pericope indicates that M. 1:1G-I express the view of Judah as against Simeon b. Gamaliel.

A. He who says, "I do not vow,"—lo, this one is permitted [not bound by a vow].
B. [He who says], "I already should have vowed,"—lo, this one is prohibited.
C. "It is [not] *qorban* if I taste it"—he is permitted.
D. "It is not *qorban*, and I shall not taste it"—he is prohibited.
E. Rabban Simeon b. Gamaliel says, "He who says, '[By] Mohi [Moses = by Him who sent Moses],' and 'As Mohi says,' lo, these are substitutes for an oath" [cf. M. 1:2E].
F. And so did Rabban Simeon b. Gamaliel say, "Two who were taking vows, one against the other—
G. "One of them said to his fellow, 'This loaf is *qorban* if I taste it,'
H. "his fellow said to him, 'It is not qorban if you taste it,'
I. "'Lo, I shall be a Nazir if I eat this bread,'

J. "his fellow said to him, 'I am not a Nazir if I eat it'—
K. "whichever one's words are null is prohibited."

T. 1:2 (continued) pp. 100-101, ls. 9-14

T. 1:2A-D further clarify the language of vows, a useful supplement to M. 1:1-2. The case of A has a man being coaxed to eat. He said, "I do not vow," and he did not eat. No vow is in place. If, B, he says, "I did not taste it even if I had not vowed, now I should have vowed," he is prohibited from eating. C is no different from A, and at D we interpret the language to mean, "If I do *not* taste it, it is not *qorban*." If he does taste it, then it is *qorban*. Simeon b. Gamaliel, E, gives us further substitute-language for oaths, now by the law of Moses and the one who spoke to Moses. The point of F-K is that the one whose intention has not been carried out is prohibited. Thus, G's man intends to say that he will *not* taste the food. If he does taste it, he is prohibited. The next says, "It is not *qorban* if you do taste it." So he wanted to be the first to taste it. If the wishes of the second are not carried out, that is, if the first man did not taste the food, the second party is prohibited.

1:3-4

A. He who says, "Not-unconsecrated-produce shall I not eat with you," "Not-valid-[food]," and, "Not-pure," "[Not] clean [for the altar]," or "Unclean," or "Remnant," or "Refuse"—
B. is bound.
C. [If he said, "May it be to me] like the lamb [of the daily whole-offering]," "Like the [temple-] sheds," "Like the wood," "Like the fire," "Like the altar," "Like the sanctuary," "Like Jerusalem"—
D. [if] he vowed by the name of one of any of the utensils used for the altar,
E. even though he has not used the word *qorban*—
F. lo, this one has vowed [in as binding a way as if he had vowed] by *qorban*.
G. R. Judah says, "He who says, 'Jerusalem,' has said nothing."

M. 1:3

A. He who says, "An offering," "A whole-offering," "A meal-offering," "A sin-offering," "A thank-offering," "Peace-offering,"—
B. "be what I eat with you,"
C. he is bound [prohibited from eating with the other party].
D. R. Judah permits [declares him not bound].
E. [If he says, "May what I eat of yours be] the *qorban*," "Like the *qorban*," "[By] a *qorban* [do I vow]"—
F. "be what I eat with you,"

G. he is bound.
H. [If he says,] "For a *qorban* shall be what I eat with you,"
I. R. Meir declares him bound.
J. He who says to his fellow, "*Qonam* be my mouth which speaks with you," or "My hand which works with you," or "My foot which walks with you,"
K. is bound.

M. 1:4

The chapter's concluding set turns to language which compares the host's food to Temple-food. M. 1:3 is divided into two parts, A-B, and C-G, but both make essentially the same point. If the metaphor is to food which one cannot eat, the vow is binding. Thus if he said, "What I eat with you will be not-unconsecrated," he cannot accept the meal, since it is as if he said, "Like an offering [*Qorban*]." If it is declared analogous to sacrificial substances or to cultic objects, it is binding. E is a gloss, supplying the exegetical center of the pericope: one does not have to use the word *qorban*, in line with M. 1:1A, or even a substitute for *qorban*, but a mere metaphor, to impose the vow upon himself. M. 1:4A-C + D go back over the same ground. Then M. 1:4E-K deal with the language of *qorban/qonam*. Judah's view, M. 1:4, is that since the man has not used the language, "*like* an offering," "*like* a whole-offering," and so on, he has said nothing at A-C (B. Ned. 13b). The point of H-I is that the man's meaning is, "May what I might eat with you be *for* a sacrifice." J lists ways in which a man prohibits himself from talking, working, or walking with his fellow.

L. R. Judah says, "He who says, 'Jerusalem,' has said nothing [M. 1:3G] unless he so intends as to vow by [what is done in] Jerusalem."
M. Sages concur with R. Judah in the case of him who says, "*Qorban*," "A whole-offering," "A meal-offering," "A sin-offering," "A thank-offering," "Peace-offerings," "if I eat with you"
N. for he has intended only to vow [by the life of] a sacrifice [*qorban*] itself.

T. 1:2 (concluded) L p. 101, ls. 15-17

T. now links M. 1:3 to M. 1:4. Sages concur with Judah's dissent at M. 1:4, for the reason given. The vow is by the life of the sacrificial animal.

A. [He who says,] "Jerusalem," "For Jerusalem," "In Jerusalem,"
"*Hekhal*," "For the *Hekhal*," "In the *Hekhal*,"
"Altar," "For the altar," "In the altar,"
"Lamb," "For the lamb," "In the lamb,"
"Sheds," "For the sheds," "In the sheds,"
"Wood, "For the wood," In the wood,"
"Fires," "For the fires," "On the fires,"

"Dishes [of frankincense]," "For the dishes," "On the dishes,"—
B. any one of these—"if I eat with you"
C. is bound.
D. [He who says,] "That I shall not eat with you [any of these]" is not bound.
E. [He who says,] "Unconsecrated food," "For unconsecrated food," "With unconsecrated food,"
F. whether he said, "That I shall eat with you," or whether he said, "That I shall not eat with you,"
G. is not bound.
H. [He who says,] "Not-unconsecrated-food if I shall eat with you," is bound.
I. [He who says,] "Unconsecrated food that I shall eat with you," "That I shall not eat with you," is not bound.
J. [If he said,] "If I shall not eat with you," he is not bound.
K. "Not-a-whole-offering shall I not eat with you"—
L. R. Jacob declares him bound.
M. And sages declare him not bound.
N. He who says, "Lo, it is unto me," even if he did not mention the word "*qorban*," lo this is a vow.
O. "It is *qorban* like my mother's flesh," "Like my sister's flesh," "Like a foreskin," "Like mixed seeds in a vineyard,"
P. he is not bound.
Q. For he has not declared anything to be sanctified.

T. 1:3 L pp. 101-102, ls. 17-25

A-C concur with M. 1:3C-F. The man says that what he will eat with the other will be "like Jerusalem" and so on. He is prohibited. But if he said, D, "Jerusalem," "*Hekhal*," "altar shall I not eat with you," this is an oath, and we interpret the language to mean, "*By* Jerusalem," "*By* the *Hekhal*," and so on. There is no prohibition now. At E-G the man has not prohibited anything. He simply has said that what he eats with the other will be unconsecrated, so there surely is no reason for him not to eat with the other. Even if the man said, "Not-unconsecrated food shall I not eat with you," we do not then interpret his language to mean, "Only consecrated food shall I eat with you." We consequently declare him to be permitted to eat with the other. At H he specifies that he will deem what he eats with the other as *not-unconsecrated*, rather than "as consecrated." He obviously is prohibited. I-J go back over the same ground. If the man says, K, "I shall not eat a not-whole-offering," we understand him to mean, "I shall only eat a whole-offering," and that is prohibited, so Jacob, L. Sages differ. The things mentioned at O are not subject to sanctification.

CHAPTER THREE

NEDARIM CHAPTER TWO

At M. 2:1-3 our chapter carries forward the definition of vows as distinct from oaths and the comparison of the two forms of language. If T. 1:5 were to state matters in behalf of M., there would be little difficulty in interpreting the opening unit of our chapter, M. 2:1-2 + 3, since T.'s version of the whole is remarkably lucid. It tells us that vows apply to matters which are subject to choice and to matters which are subject to commandment. But oaths apply only to matters of choice. One cannot take an oath not to carry out a commandment, for example. T. also says that oaths apply to something which is of material substance as well as to something which is not, while vows apply only to that which is of material substance. T. further organizes and places into a single scheme the several illustrative units of M. But it is M. with which we must contend.

M. 2:1A-E make the point that if a person vows concerning matters not subject to a vow for cultic purposes, the vow is null. Thus if he says, "May what I eat of yours be unconsecrated food," the vow is null. If, D-E, he says his wife is to him like his mother," that vow is treated as binding and has to be unbound on extrinsic grounds. M. 2:5 makes this same point again. Even though the vow strictly speaking is null, nonetheless sages propose to discourage people from taking such vows, by declaring them binding. Then, M. 2:1F-J, M. 2:2, we have a set of contrasts between oaths and vows, supplemented, moreover, at M. 2:3. The important points are given by T.'s exegesis of M., as indicated.

M. 2:4 deals with vows which are not fully spelled out and which require interpretation. In such cases we impose a strict interpretation. If someone made a vow that something is to him "like a devoted thing," if he specified, "a devoted thing belonging to the priests," it is not binding. But "a thing devoted to Heaven" produces a binding vow. If nothing has been specified, we impose the latter interpretation. There are three illustrations of this view. Meir and Judah then have a dispute related to it. The main point is Judah's, that language means one thing in Judah, another in Galilee. M. 2:5 carried forward the point that language may bear more than a single meaning, e.g., *ḥerem* means, "that which is devoted," and it also means a fish-net. If then someone claims he meant the latter, Meir holds that such a vow is null. If the person treats it as valid, however, then it is valid, and the person is punished. Sages, as at M. 2:1-2, treat the vow as null, so as to prevent people from dealing lightly with vows.

2:1-2

A. And these [vows] are not binding [at all]:
B. He who says,] "May what I eat of yours be unconsecrated food," "[Be] like pig-meat,"
"Like an idol," "Like hides pierced at the heart,"
"Like carrion," "Like *terefah*-meat,"
"Like abominations," "Like creeping things,"
"Like the dough-offering of Aaron," or "Like his heave-offering,"—
C. it is not binding.
D. He who says to his wife, "Lo, you are like mother to me,"—they open for him a door [for the unbinding of his oath] from some other source,
E. so that he may not behave lightly in such a matter.
I F. [He who says,] "*Qonam* if I sleep," or, "If I speak," or, "If I walk"—
G. he who says to his wife, "*Qonam* if I have sexual relations with you"—
H. lo, this is a case to which applies the law, *He shall not break his word* (Num. 30:2).
I. [If he said], "By an oath that I shall not sleep," "that I shall not speak," "that I shall not walk,"
J. it is binding.

M. 2:1

II A. [He who says], "*Qorban* I shall not eat with you!" "*Qorban* be what I eat with you!" "Not-*Qorban* be what I do not eat with you!"—
B. he is not bound.
C. "By an oath, I shall not eat with you!" "By an oath, if I shall eat with you," "Not by an oath I shall not eat with you,"
D. he is bound.
E. This rule is therefore more strict in the case of oaths than in the case of vows.
F. But [there is] a more strict rule which applies to vows than applies to oaths.
G. How so?
III H. [If] he said, "*Qonam* be the *Sukkah* which I am making!" "The *lulab* which I am taking!" "The *tefillin* which I am laying on"—
I. in the case of vows, it is binding.
J. In the case of oaths, it is not binding.
K. For an oath is not taken to transgress the commandments [of the Torah].

M. 2:2

The pericope at M. 2:1 is in three parts, A-C, a list of ten items, D-E + F-H, and I-J, which in fact link the foregoing materials to M. 2:1. If a man says, "Let such-and-such be an offering," it is changed and deemed sanctified. But if he said, "Let such-and-such be pig's meat," the thing is not changed and not deemed transformed. That is the point of A-C. Having spelled out the language which imposes a binding vow or oath, we now consider language which may or may not do so. The importantce of A-C is to indicate that inappropriate similes are meaningless. Why? Because a vow is valid only when it refers to something which is subject to a vow, e.g., language or similes appropriate for the cult. These are things (B) which are prohibited or which are not subject to a vow at all. Therefore if one says, "Let whatever I eat at your house be to me like prohibited food," he has said nothing. That is so whether the thing is prohibited, e.g., pig-meat, or prohibited only to non-priests and not vowed for the cult, e.g., the dough-offering given to the priest.

The next set of M. 2:1 contrasts D-E with F-H. F is somewhat jarring, because the important contrast is D and G. If a man says to his wife, "Lo, you are prohibited to me like my mother," sages find a means of unbinding the oath. If he uses the language specified at G, he has to keep his vow, H. I-J go over the ground of F, which therefore will have been intruded at the point at which redactional work linking M. 2:1 to M. 2:2 was undertaken. I-J make the same point about oaths as has been made about vows, treating the two as equivalent. An oath takes effect when so phrased, just as much as a *Qonam*-statement does.

The contrast drawn at M. 2:1F + H, I-J is repeated at M. 2:2A-B, C-D. Then E-F + G-K provide yet a third contrast, now with an elaborate introduction at E-F. It is on this basis that I treat M. 2:1 and M. 2:2 together, even though M. 2:1A-E are distinct from what follows. Once more the difference is the use of *qorban* as against *by an oath*, M. 2:2A-B *vs*, C-D. H-K then make matters explicit. *Qorban*-language is invalid and the man is not bound. It is understood to mean, "By the life of the sacrifice," and this language is null. The point of M. 2:2E-F is clear as stated. Then we have the excellent case of H-J, explained at K. The vow is valid concerning the object which is mentioned. But one cannot take an oath not to build a *sukkah*, since the oath will apply to the man himself, not merely to the object. The man cannot remove from himself the (prior) obligation to keep the commandments. T. 1:5 must now make some better sense of M. 2:2A-D by spelling out a difference between vows and oaths which will account for the distinction here made between them.

    A. He who vows by the Torah—lo, this is not binding.
    B. He who vows by what is written in the Torah—lo, this is binding.

C. [He who vows] by what is in the Torah and by what is written in it—it is binding.

D. What is a vow which imposes a prohibition [of that which is permitted] in the Torah?

F. He who says, "Lo, I take upon myself that I shall not eat meat, and that I shall not drink wine, as on the day on which I saw Jerusalem in ruins, or as on the day on which so-and-so was slain"—

G. it is binding.

T. 1:4 L p. 102, ls. 25-28

T. illustrates the point of M. 2:1A-C, the difference between vowing concerning something subject to a vow, and vowing concerning something not subject to a vow, that is, B *vs.* A. At A the man vows by the Torah, understood to mean, by the sanctity of the Torah. That is not something subject to a vow. But at B he vows by what is written therein, that is including references to the offerings which are inscribed and commanded in Scripture. That is the difference between the two sorts of vows, exactly as in M. D-G then invoke the language of Num. 30:3, "Two impose a prohibition by vow." One is able to prohibit what ordinarily is permitted, and such a vow is binding, as at M. 2:1F-H.

A. A more strict rule applies to vows than to oaths, and to oaths than to vows.

B. For vows apply to matters which are subject to choice as well as to those which are subject to commandment,

C. which is not the case with oaths [M. 2:2H-K].

D. A more strict rule applies to oaths.

E. For oaths apply to something which is of substance and to something which is not of substance,

F. which is not the case of vows.

G. In the case of vows, how so?

H. *[If] one said, "Qonam is the Sukkah which I am making," "the lulab which I am taking," "the tefillin which I am putting on"*—

I. *it is binding in the case of vows and not binding in the case of oaths* [M. 2:2H-J].

J. How so?

K. *If he said, "Qonam if sleep, if speak, if walk"* [M. 2:1F],

L. it is binding in the case of oaths, and not binding in the case of vows [M. 2:1I-J].

M. "*Qonam* is my mouth if it speaks with you, my hands if they work with you, my feet if they walk with you"—

N. it is binding in the case of vows and binding in the case of oaths [M. 1:4J-K].

T. 1:5 L pp. 102-103, ls. 28-38

T.'s excellent pericope makes sense of M.'s several units, as I said, presenting a far more lucid statement than does M. The point of A-C is clear by reference to M. 2:2H-K. A person may declare the *Sukkah* to be *qonam*, so that he cannot make use of the *Sukkah*. But he cannot take an oath binding himself not to dwell in a *Sukkah*. So vows apply to things which are a matter of choice and a matter of a commandment, but oaths cannot be made contrary to what is commanded in the Torah. G-I thus illustrate A-C, just as J-L illustrate D-F. One may take an oath concerning something which is not material, e.g., an action or a statement, K. But he cannot take a vow concerning such a matter, K-L. M-N invoke M. 1:4 and show why the language of M is valid. If one declares *qonam* (that is, the language of a vow) to be his mouth if it speaks with the other, then he has vowed concerning something of substance, his mouth, as well as a deed done with his mouth, the speaking. The point is that this is binding in the case of vows; there is no issue as to oaths. The reason is that, as E says, vows apply to something which is of substance. It is hard to imagine a more effective exposition of M. than is provided by T.

2:3

A. There is a vow within a vow, but there is no oath within an oath.
B. How so?
C. [If] he said, "Lo, I am a Nazir if I eat," "Lo, I am a Nazir if I eat,"
D. [and if] he ate,
E. he is liable for each such statement [and observes two spells of Naziriteship].
F. [If he said], "By an oath I shall not eat," "By an oath I shall not eat,"
G. and he ate,
H. he is liable for one count only.

M. 2:3

We have yet one more point of contrast between vows and oaths, A, spelled out at the contrast of C-E, F-H. M. carries its own exegesis, A, and therefore requires no comment.

2:4

A. Vows which are not spelled out are subject to a more stringent rule, and [vows] which are spelled out are subject to a more lenient rule.
B. How so?
I C. [If] he said, "Lo, it is to me like salted meat," "Like wine used for idolatrous worship,"
D. if his vow referred to things belonging to Heaven, it is binding.
E. If it is of things belonging to idolatry that he vowed, it is not binding.

F. But if he vowed without specification, it is binding [as at D].
II G. [If he said,] "Lo, it is to me like a devoted thing,"
H. if he said, "Like a thing devoted to Heaven," it is binding.
I. If [he said,] "Like a thing devoted to priests," it is not binding.
J. And if he said it without further specification, it is binding [as at H].
III K. [If he said,] "Lo, it is unto me like tithe,"
L. if he vowed that it was like tithe of cattle, it is binding.
M. If it was like tithe of the threshing floor, it is not binding.
N. And if he said it without further specification, it is binding [as at L].
O. "[If he said], 'Lo, it is to me like heave-offering,'
P. "if he vowed that it was like heave-offering of the chamber [of the Temple], it is binding.
Q. "And if it was like that of the threshing-floor, it is not binding.
S. "And if it was without further specification, it is binding," the words of R. Meir.
T. R. Judah says, "A statement referring without specification to heave-offering made in Judah is binding. But in Galilee, it is not binding.
U. "For the men of Galilee are not familiar with heave-offering belonging to the chamber.
V. "Statements that something is devoted, without further specification, in Judah are not binding, and in Galilee they are binding.
W. "For the Galileans are not familiar with things devoted to the priests."

M. 2:4

The formal traits are fairly obvious: three illustrations of A, as indicated. What appears to be a fourth, beginning at O, in fact has its own frame of reference, the dispute between Meir, O-S, and Judah, with its gloss at U, and the further set of V-W. Judah's point of interest is not to dispute the basic notion of A-N, but Meir's application thereof at O-S. The point is that we treat as binding ("more stringent rule") vows which do not carry with them their own exegesis. Thus if there is a possibility of interpreting a vow as valid or as invalid, and the vow carries no specification, it is treated as valid. This is spelled out at C-F, which depend upon (or concur with) M. 2:1A-C. Something which is *ḥerem* ("devoted") to Heaven cannot be used for any purpose whatsoever. What is *ḥerem* to the priests is deemed to be the property of the priests, available for any secular purpose whatsoever (M. Ar. 8:6). Tithe of cattle is subject to a vow; it is deemed to be sanctified and treated as an offering (Lev. 27:32). Tithe separated at the threshing floor is first tithe, which goes to the Levites. Once the heave-offering of the first tithe is removed, the first tithe falls into the status of unconsecrated food (M. Hag. 2:5).

The case of Meir, O-S, refers to heave-offering of the Temple-chamber, that is, *sheqels* which are vowed for use in the purchase of sacrifices. Heave-offering separated at the threshing-floor is prohibited (once more, along the lines of M. 2:1A-C) and the rest follows. Judah's point, clear as given, depends on the fact that Galileans are not likely to refer to something they do not see very often. When a vow made in Galilee refers without further specification to heave-offering, we do not assume it refers to heave-offering of the chamber. Galileans also are not used to devotions to the priesthood but only to Heaven. This is essentially separate from the foregoing, yielding an artificial dispute.

    A. *Vows which are not spelled out are subject to a more stringent rule* [M. Ned. 2:4A]:
    B. "Why did you take an oath?"
    C. [If] he said, "I do not know. But I saw my buddies taking oaths that way,"
    D. it is binding.
    E. "[If] one vowed [to be a Nazirite] and violated his vow,
    F. "they do not accept an inquiry from him [about releasing the vow]
    G. "until he will act as if he is bound by the vow for at least as many days as he acted as if he was not bound by it," the words of R. Meir.
    H. Said R. Yosé, "Under what circumstances?
    I. "When it is a vow lasting for a long time.
    J. "But if it was a vow which was to last for a short time, it is sufficient for him to observe it for thirty days."
    K. R. Judah says, "A statement referring to heave-offering not bearing further specification made in Judah is binding" [M. 2:4T].
    L. R. Eleazar b. R. Ṣadoq says, "Statements that something is devoted, without further specification, are not binding in Judah and are binding in Galilee" [M. 2:4V].

                                            T. 1:6 L p. 103, ls. 35-40

While A cites M. as indicated, B-D provide an illustration of a separate situation from M.'s. That is the case also with E-J, which deal with a vow to be a Nazirite and how we cope with an only partially-fulfilled spell of Naziriteship. K-L then go over M.'s ground.

2:5

I   A. [If] one vowed by "*ḥerem*," but then he said, "I vowed only concerning that which is a *ḥerem* [a net] of the sea,"
II   B. [or if he vowed] by "*qorban*" but then he said, "I vowed only concerning *qorban* [offerings] to kings,"
III C. [if he said,] "Lo, ʿaṣmi [my bone] is *qorban*," and explained, "I vowed only concerning the ʿeṣem which I placed before me by which to vow,"
IV D. [if he said,] "*Qonam* is that benefit which my wife derives from me,"
    E. and he said, "I vowed only concerning my first wife, whom I have already divorced"—

F. "in all these cases they do not accept inquiry concerning them. But if they accept inquiry, they punish and treat them strictly," the words of R. Meir.

G. And sages say, "They find an opening for them from in some other place [by some pretext].

H. "And they instruct them that they not treat vows lightly."

M. 2:5

Since Chapter Three will treat the problem of granting absolution for vows and suitable grounds thereof, the present unit broaches the coming topic, while concluding the foregoing one. A-E present four parallel cases. The man has taken a vow using a word which bears two meanings, e.g., *ḥerem* as devoted thing or as fish-net, *eṣem* as self or as bone, C, and so on. Meir's view is that these vows are null, and there is no need to grant absolution for them. But if the person who took such a vow approaches a sage for the release of the vow, the sage punishes the person, imposing a strict ruling. Sages deem the vows valid, on which account absolution *is* required on the foundations of some pretext other than a trait intrinsic to the vow itself. The vow therefore is not released on the ground that the words were not meant to impose a vow, e.g., as at D-E. Their view is what links our unit's problem to M. 2:4, that is, M. 2:4/O-W.

CHAPTER FOUR

NEDARIM CHAPTER THREE

The chapter is in two parts, M. 3:1-3 + 4,5, and M. 3:6-10 + 11. The interest of the former is in vows deemed not binding. These are impaired at the outset and therefore never valid, so they impose no requirement to seek sages' absolution. They are of four kinds: vows of incitement, e.g., to purchase an object at a given price; vows of exaggeration; vows made on the basis of erroneous information; and vows made (and broken) under constraint. Each of these vows is illustrated at M. 3:1-3. M. 3:4 takes up the theme of vows made under constraint, introducing a triplet of Houses' disputes clarifying some minor questions, and ending with illustration of the one of the Houses' disputes.

M. 3:5 is an anomaly, bearing no obvious relation to what precedes or what follows. But it is devoted to interpreting the language of a vow and so forms an introduction to M. 3:6-11's main interest, which is in interpreting the language of vows, and it probably has been given its position on that account. M. 3:6-10 present five cases in which we carefully interpret the language used in a vow to determine the range of applicability of that vow. M. 3:11 then gives three more instances of the same procedure. These extensive materials are lucid and pose no major exegetical problems.

3:1-3

A. Four [types of] vows did sages declare not binding:

(1) Vows of incitement, (2) vows of exaggeration, (3) vows made in error, and (4) vows [broken] under constraint.

(1) B. *Vows of incitement:* How so?

C. [If] one was selling something and said, "*Qonam* if I chop the price down for you to under a *sela*," and the other says, "*Qonam* if I pay you more than a *sheqel*,"

D. [then] both of them agree at three *denars*.

E. R. Eliezer b. Jacob says, "Also: He who wants to force his fellow by a vow to eat with him says, 'Any vow which I am going to vow is null,'—so long as he is mindful at the moment of his vow."

M. 3:1

(2) A. *Vows of exaggeration:*

B. [If] he said, "*Qonam* if I did not see [walking] on this road as many as went out of Egypt,"

C. "...if I did not see a snake as big as the beam of an olive-press."
(3) D. *Vows made in error:*
E. "...if I ate," or "...if I drank," and he remembered that he ate or drank;
F. "...if I eat," or "...if I drink" and he forgot and ate and drank.
G. [If] he said, "*Qonam* be any benefit my wife gets from me, for she stole my purse," "for she beat up my son,"
and he found out that she had not beaten up his son,
or he found out that she had not stolen it.
H. [If] he saw people eating figs [belonging to him] and said, "Lo, they are *qorban* to you!" and they turned out to be his father and brothers, and there were others with them—
I. the House of Shammai say, "They are permitted, and those with them are prohibited."
J. And the House of Hillel say, "These and those [men] are permitted [to eat the figs]."

M. 3:2

(4) A. *Vows [broken] under constraint:*
B. [If] one's fellow imposed a vow on him to eat with him, but he got sick, or his son got sick, or a river [overflowed and] stopped him—lo, these are vows [broken] under constraint.

M. 3:3

The illustrative materials, M. 3:1B-E, 3:2A-C, D-F + G, M. 3:3, do not follow a single pattern. M. 3:1B-C hardly require D. M. 3:2A-C and D-F match the former and show that G is a sizable, needless interpolation. M. 3:2H-J, moreover, introduce a quite subtle problem. M. 3:3 follows the formal pattern of M. 3:2A-C, D-F. So in all the formal articulation of M. 3:1A is not the work of a single hand, and, at M. 3:2G, H-J, the work is rather poorly done.

The point throughout is that, in cases such as these, one need not consult a sage, since the vows were not valid to begin with. The first, M. 3:1B-E, is made simply in the pressure of a business transaction. The seller wants a *sela*, four *denars*, and the buyer offers a *sheqel*, two. The rest follows. Both in fact intended to agree on a price of three but exaggerated the matter. Eliezer b. Jacob, E, glosses this case by making the matter explicit. One has the right in advance to annul his vow, in the stated case. The vows of exaggeration, M. 3:2A-C, follow suit. Those made in error, D-F, are null because they were made depending on false facts, E, F, and G.

The interpolated Houses' dispute, M. 3:2H-J, has a man see people eating his figs. If he had known that his father and brothers were among those eating his figs, he would not have made such a vow. Clearly, so far as the vow affected his brother or father, it is null, as a vow made in error. But what about the other people? These after all are subjected to a vow not made in error. On that account the Shammaites impose the vow in its valid segment. The Hillelites deem a vow which is partially unloosened to be wholly unbound.

M. 3:3, as we noticed, speaks of vows which a man cannot keep because of conditions beyond his control. But they are invalid at the outset, in the theory that, if the man had known that he would be unable to keep his vow, he would not have made it. Accordingly, this vow at the outset is as invalid as all the others. M. 3:4 gives us better examples of vows made under constraint than these.

    A.   *R. Eliezer b. Jacob says, "He who wants to force his fellow by a vow to eat with him* [M. 3:1E],
    B.   "and this one vowed that he would not eat with him,
    C.   "even though both take oaths against one another,
    D.   "lo, these are deemed vows of incitement."
    E.   [If one said], "*Qonam* if I was not counted for a Passover whose fat-tail weighed ten *litrim*,"
    F.   "if I did not drink wine worth a golden *denar* for a *log*,"
    G.   "*if I did not see a snake as big as the beam of an olivepress*" [M. 3:2C]—
    H.   just as vows of exaggeration are not binding, so oaths of exaggeration are not binding.

T. 2:1 L p. 104, ls. 1-5

T. improves the language of M. 3:1E and links vows of incitement to those of exaggeration.

3:4

    A.   They take a vow to murderers, robbers, or tax-collectors
    B.   that [produce] is heave-offering, even though it is not heave-offering;
    C.   that [property] belongs to the state, even though it does not belong to the state.
I   D.   The House of Shammai say, "In any form of words they vow except in the form of an oath."
    E.   And the House of Hillel say, "Even in the form of an oath."
II   F.   The House of Shammai say, "One should not [volunteer to] take a vow at the outset."
    G.   And the House of Hillel say, "Also: One [voluntarily] takes a vow at the outset."
III   H.   The House of Shammai say, "[One takes a vow] only in the matter concerning which the vow is imposed."
    I.   And the House of Hillel say, "Also: concerning that in which the vow is not imposed."

J. How so?

K. [If] they said to him, "Say: '*Qonam* be any benefit my wife has with me!' " and he said, "*Qonam* be any benefit my wife and children have with me!"—

L. The House of Shammai say, "His wife is permitted, and his children prohibited."

M. And the House of Hillel say, "These and those are permitted."

M. 3:4

The introductory illustrations, B, C, surely are redundant. One would have been enough to make A's point. Then we have the triplet of Houses' disputes, spelling out the circumstances and conditions of A. The Shammaites exclude an oath, insist that the vow be subject to constraint (M. 3:1A4), and apply only to what the one is forced to mention. The Hillelites in all instances take a broader view. The illustration of M. 3:4H-I at J-M is clear as stated. The Shammaites prohibit the children from deriving benefit from their father, since he need not have mentioned them in his vow.

A. They attribute [produce subject to seizure] by assessors and tax-collectors to heave-offering, or to gentile ownership, or to the ownership of the government.

B. But they do not attribute ownership to another Israelite.

T. 2:2 L p. 104, ls. 5-6

The gloss of M. 3:4A-C excludes the possibility of getting someone else in trouble.

3:5

A. [He who says], "Lo, these plants are *qorban*, if they are not cut down,"

B. "This cloak is *qorban* if it is not burned"—

C. they are subject to redemption.

D. "Lo, these plants are *qorban* until they are cut down,"

E. "This cloak is *qorban* until it is burned"—

F. they are not subject to redemption

M. 3:5

The difference between A-C and D-F, in this exquisitely balanced pericope, is that at A-C, the plants or cloak are sanctified when the man says they are *qorban*. They therefore may be redeemed. At D-F, the plants or cloak cannot be redeemed so long as they are *not* cut down or burned, that is, so long as they have not yet been consecrated.

The facts of the case involve a man who declares his field to be sanctified for the upkeep of the Temple, if it is not cut down, e.g., by a tax-collector. He obviously has the possibility of redeeming the crop which thereby has been sanctified when it was not cut down. The point is that we do not maintain that the produce has not been sanctified on grounds that it is a vow made in error. That is, there is no valid claim that the man assumed the produce *would* be cut down and, when it turns out not to be cut down, it therefore is not subject to the original statement. On the contrary, it is subject to what he has said. But it also is available for redemption. In the second case, the man most certainly has sanctified the produce, on the one hand, but so long as the produce is not cut down (or the cloak burned), there is no possibility of redeeming it. Why not? Because as soon as he does redeem the produce, it goes back to the status of sanctification, unless it is cut down, so too with the cloak (Albeck, pp. 155, 361).

> A. [He who says], "*Lo, these plants are qorban until they are cut down,*" "*This cloak is qorban until it is burned,*" [M. 3:5D]—.
> B. "This cow is *qorban*, until it is slaughtered,"
> C. once they have been cut down, burned, or slaughtered, they have gone forth to the status of unconsecrated objects.
>
> T. 2:3 L p. 104, ls. 7-8

T. clarifies the question left open at M. 3:5D-F. Maimonides (*Trespass* 4:11) gives a still clearer picture of the case:

> If one said, "These plants shall be an offering if they are not cut down today," or "this cloak shall be an offering if it is not burned today," and the day passed without the trees being cut down or the cloak being burned, they were consecrated and could be redeemed like all other consecrated things, after which they might be enjoyed. But if one said, "These plants shall be an offering until they are cut down," they could not be redeemed. For whenever they would be redeemed, they would become consecrated again until cut down, and as soon as they were cut down, they did not require redemption but might be enjoyed forthwith...

3:6-10

I A. He who vows [not to gain benefit] from those who go down to the sea is permitted [to enjoy benefit] from those who dwell on dry land.
  B. [He who vowed not to enjoy benefit] from those who dwell on dry land is prohibited [to enjoy benefit] from those who go down to the sea,
  C. for those who go down to the sea are part of the generality of those who live on dry land.
  D. [Those who go down to the sea includes] not the like of those who go from Acre to Jaffa but the one who sails out of sight of land.

M. 3:6

II A. He who vows [not to enjoy benefit] from those who see the sun is prohibited even [to enjoy benefit] even from the blind.

B. For he intended [to separate himself] only from the one whom the sun sees.

M. 3:7

III A. He who vows [not to enjoy benefit] from black-haired men is prohibited [to enjoy benefit] from bald people and from white-haired people.

B. But he is permitted [to enjoy benefit] from women and children,

C. for only men are called black-haired.

M. 3:8

IV A. He who vows [not to enjoy benefit] from creatures that are [already] born is permitted [to enjoy benefit] from those creatures who may be born [thereafter].

B. [If he vowed not to enjoy benefit] from those who may be born [thereafter], he is prohibited [to enjoy benefit] from those who are born.

C. R. Meir permits [him to enjoy benefit] also from those who are born.

D. And sages say, "This one intended [to separate himself] only from anyone [whose nature it is to be] brought forth [living creatures]."

M. 3:9

V A. He who vows [not to enjoy benefit] from those who rest on the Sabbath is prohibited [to enjoy benefit] both from Israelites and from Samaritans.

B. [If he vowed not to enjoy benefit] from garlic-eaters, he is forbidden [to derive benefit] from Israelites and Samaritans.

C. [If he vowed not to enjoy benefit] from those who ascend to Jerusalem, he is forbidden [to enjoy benefit] from Israelites but permitted [to enjoy benefit] from Samaritans.

M. 3:10

The pericope, which makes an obvious point, is formally less disciplined than it appears on the surface, because of the extensive glosses, e.g., M. 3:6C, D, M. 3:7B, M. 3:8C, M. 3:9C-D. M. 3:10 is really outside of the formal and conceptual framework of the rest. Still, the one who framed the whole had a clear idea of what he wanted to say, which is that we interpret the language used in a vow in accord with some sort of orderly and objective principle. It seems to me that the authority of M. 2:4-5 will not have been uncomfortable with this set. The curious dispute at M. 3:9 leaves sages in the position of having the man prohibited from enjoying benefit of anything which brings forth living creatures, thus excluding all but fish and birds, which bring forth eggs. M. 3:11 now goes over the same ground, with a different formulary pattern.

3:11

I A. [If a man said,] "*Qonam* if I have benefit from the children of Noah," he is permitted [to enjoy benefit] from Israelites and prohibited [to enjoy benefit] from the nations of the world.

B. "...if I have benefit from the seed of Abraham," he is prohibited [to enjoy benefit] from Israelites, and permitted [to enjoy benefit] from the nations of the world.

II C. [If he said, "*Qonam*] if I have benefit from Israelites," he buys for more and sells for less.

D. "...if Israelites enjoy benefit from me," he buys for less and sells for more—

E. (if anyone will pay attention to him!)

F. "...if I derive benefit from them and they from me"—he derives benefit from strangers.

III G. [If he said,] "*Qonam* if I derive benefit from the uncircumcised," he is permitted [to derive benefit] from uncircumcised Israelites, but prohibited [from deriving benefit] from circumcised gentiles.

H. "*Qonam* if I derive benefit from the circumcised"—he is prohibited [to derive benefit] from uncircumcised Israelites and permitted [to derive benefit] from circumcised gentiles.

I. Fot the word "uncircumcised" is used only as a name for gentiles, as it is written, *For all the nations are uncircumcised, and the whole house of Israel is uncircumcised at heart* (Jer. 9:26).

J. And it says, "*This uncircumcised Philistine* (1 Sam. 17:36).

K. And it says, *Lest the daughters of the Philistines rejoice, lest the daughters of the uncircumcised triumph* (11 Sam. 1:20).

L. R. Eleazar b. ʿAzariah says, "The foreskin is disgusting, for evil men are shamed by reference to it, as it is written, *For all the nations are uncircumcized.*"

M. R. Ishmael says, "Great is circumcision, for thirteen covenants are made thereby."

N. R. Yosé says, "Great is circumcision, since it overrides the prohibitions of the Sabbath, which is subject to strict rules."

O. R. Joshua b. Qorḥa says, "Great is circumcision, for it was not suspended even for a moment for the sake of Moses, the righteous."

P. R. Neḥemiah says, "Great is circumcision, for it overrides the prohibition [against removing the marks of] *negaʿim.*"

Q. Rabbi says, "Great is circumcision, for, despite all the commandments which Abraham our father carried out, he was called complete and whole only when he had circumcized himself as it is said, *Walk before me and be perfect* (Gen. 17:1).

R. "Another matter: Great is circumcision, for if it were not for that, the Holy One, blessed be he, would not have created his world, since it says, *Thus says the Lord: But for my covenant day and night, I should not have set forth the ordinances of heaven and earth* (Jer. 33:25)."

M. 3:11

There are two obvious divisions, M. 3:11A-H + I, and J-R. The former is a triplet, along the lines of M. 3:6-10. E and F gloss C and D. G-H then require the sizable explanation of I, and the rest is a set of encomia.

    A. He who vows not to derive benefit from Israelites is prohibited from deriving benefit from proselytes.
    B. [He who vows not to derive benefit] from proselytes is permitted to derive benefit from Israelites.
    C. He who vows not to derive benefit from Israelites is prohibited from deriving benefit from priests or Levites.
    D. [He who vows not to derive benefit] from priests and Levites is permitted to derive benefit from Israelites.
    E. He who vows not to derive benefit from priests is permitted to derive benefit from Levites.
    F. He who vows not to derive benefit from Levites is permitted to derive benefit from priests.
    G. He who vows not to derive benefit from garlic-eaters—
    H. R. Judah prohibits [him from deriving benefit] also from Samaritans [M. 3:10B].
    I. He who vows that Israelites will not derive benefit from him *buys for less and sells for more* [M. 3:11D].
    J. R. Yosé says, "They do not pay attention to him" [M. 3:11E].
    K. It does not say, *For you are going to take a wife from the Philistines* (Judges 14:3) who are idolators, who have sexual relations with women prohibited to them, who are murderers, but *who are uncircumcized.*
    L. And so we observe that the judgment of the nations of the world is sealed only on account of uncircumcision, since it says, *And all of them who are uncircumcized fall by the sword* (Ez. 32:23-25).

T. 2:4 L p. 105, ls. 12-15

    A. *Rabbi says, "Great is circumcision, for, despite all the commandments which Abraham our father carried out, he was called complete and whole only when he had circumcized himself, as it is said, Walk before me and be perfect"* (Gen. 17:1) [M. 3:11Q].

T. 2:5 L p. 105, ls. 16-17

    A. Another matter: Great is circumcision, for it is deemed equivalent to all the other commandment in the Torah put together,
    B. since it says, *Lo, the blood of the covenant which the Lord made* (Ex. 24:8).

T. 2:6 L p. 105, ls. 17-19

    A. Another matter: Great is circumcision, for if it were not for that, the heaven and the earth could not endure, since it says, *Thus says the Lord: But for my covenant day and night, I should not have set forth the ordinances of heaven and earth* (Jer. 33:25).

T. 2:7 (continued) L p. 105, ls. 19-20

A-B, C, D, E, and F, make obvious points about how some divisions are encompassed in others, e.g., priests also are Israelites, but Israelites are not priests, C, D. H refers us back to M. 3:10B, not given in Judah's name. The rest of the units are clear as given.

CHAPTER FIVE

NEDARIM CHAPTER FOUR

We turn to the theme of the relationship between a person who vows not to receive benefit from another party and that other party. The chapter is remarkably coherent both in formal and in conceptual characteristics. As to the former, we find the recurring formulary, *He who is forbidden by vow from enjoying benefit from his fellow* at M. 4:1A, 4:2A, 4:4A, 4:5A, 4:6A, and M. 4:7A—six units. But several are clearly composites, so the formulary pattern is imposed at the ultimate stratum of redaction.

The oath may have the form of prohibiting all benefit or only food. M. 4:1A-B define the difference between these two kinds of oath. If one is prohibited from deriving benefit from the other in general, he cannot use the property of the other. If he is prohibited from deriving food in particular, he cannot use the other's food or anything used in the preparation of food. M. 4:2-3 then take up the matter of prohibiting oneself from deriving benefit from another party and define the sorts of benefits one may derive and those one may not derive. The person against whom the vow has been taken may do favors for the man's wife and children, for example, or may restore to the man something he has lost. M. 4:2-3 deal with property, cultic, and religious relationships. M. 4:4 carries this theme forward, now with reference to certain personal contacts, e.g., visiting the one who took the vow when he falls sick, sharing the same bath-tub, bed, table, dish, and task of labor. M. 4:5 introduces a rather special problem, use of the fellow's property not in the Seventh Year and in the Seventh Year. M. 4:6 completes the matter by prohibiting the fellow against whom the vow is taken from a situation in which the latter does a favor for the former, since the former in due course will be expected to do a favor for the latter, which of course is to be avoided. Finally, at M. 4:7-8, we define ways in which the one against whom the vow is taken *may* help out the one who took the vow, without forcing the latter to violate his vow. What he does is to set up a condition by which others will help the one who took the vow, and in due course, the one against whom the vow is taken will compensate them. But this he does without making explicit promises. M. 4:7-8 present a triplet of examples on this conception. Chapter Five will continue the exploration of this rather interesting theme.

4:1

A. There is no difference between him who is forbidden by vow from enjoying any benefit from his fellow and him who is forbidden by vow from deriving food from him,

B. except for setting foot in his [the fellow's] house and [using his] utensils in which food is not prepared.

C. He who is forbidden by vow from deriving food from his fellow—[the fellow] should not lend him a sifter, a sieve, a millstone, or an oven. But he may lend him a shirt, a ring, a cloak, earrings, or anything in which food is not prepared.

D. But in a place in which such things as these are rented out [for money or food], it is forbidden to do so.

M. 4:1

A-B provide a formal introduction to the entire chapter, the principal units of which begin, *He who is forbidden by vow from enjoying benefit from his fellow*. At the outset we distinguish the one prohibited by vow from enjoying benefit in general from the one prohibited by vow from deriving food in particular. It is the former status which is of special interest, not the latter, which is dropped after this pericope. The conception is clear as given at A-B. The point about not using utensils for food, B, then is expanded at C, itself further clarified by D. If the clothing may be rented out, not merely lent, then the friend may not lend them out, because he thereby forgives the cost of rental, with which the one who took the vow may purchase food.

4:2-3

A. He who is prohibited by vow from deriving benefit from his friend—

B. he [the friend] nonetheless (1) pays out his *sheqel* [half-*sheqel* tax to the Temple],

C. (2) pays back his debt,

D. and (3) returns to him something which he [the one who took the vow] has lost.

E. But in a place in which for this action a reward is paid out, the benefit [of the reward] should fall to the sanctuary.

M. 4:2

A. (1) And he takes up his heave-offering or his tithes with his permission.

B. (2) And he offers in his behalf bird-offerings for (1) *Zab*-men or (2) *Zab*-women, (3) bird-offering for women who have just given birth, (4) sin-offerings, and (5) guilt-offerings.

C. (3) And he teaches him *midrash*, laws and stories.

D. But he does not teach him Scripture.

E. But he teaches his sons and daughters Scripture.

F. (4) And he takes care of his wife and children, even though he [who vowed] is liable for their care.

G. (5) But he should not take care of his domesticated animal, whether unclean or clean.

H. R. Eliezer says, "He takes care of the unclean one, and he does not take care of the clean one."

I. They said to him, "What is the difference between the unclean one and the clean one?"

J. He said to them, "As to the clean one: its soul belongs to Heaven, and its body belongs to him. But as to the unclean one, its soul and its body belong to Heaven [it is prohibited to him]."

K. They said to him, "Also the unclean one: its soul belongs to Heaven, but its body belongs to him.

L. "For if he wants, lo, he can sell it to gentiles or feed it to dogs."

M. 4:3

M. 4:2 follows the formal traits of M. 4:1, with its qualification at E modeled after M. 4:1D. But since M. 4:3 depends upon M. 4:2A, I treat the two together. The former defines property relationships, the latter, mainly cultic and religious ones. The formal character of M. 4:2 requires no comment. The point is that the friend pays the *sheqel*, settles the debts, and returns a lost object to the one who has taken the vow. In all these instances, the benefit to the one subject to the vow is indirect, not direct, as at M. 4:7-8. Returning the lost object is simply restoring what the one subjected to the vow actually owns. If, E, the man from whom the one made the vow cannot derive benefit declines to accept the reward, the man subject to the vow has to pay it out, lest he benefit from the action of the other. He gives it over to the sanctuary.

I see five items in M. 4:3A-G, but of course the entries are not carefully balanced against one another. It is equally possible to view M. 4:3 as divided into these units, independent of one another: A-B, C-E, F, and G-K, the latter a dispute, G-H, followed by a debate, I-L, in which the opposition (G) gets the last word and wins the point. The fellow may fulfill the man's sacred obligation, A, or serve as officiating priest for his offerings, B, along the lines of M. 4:2B, C. Payment is not received for the teaching of M. 4:3C, but it is for M. 4:3D. E links that item to M. 4:3F. G's point is that when the animal gets fat, the added value will be enjoyed by the one who has taken the vow. That is why, in Eliezer's view, the friend may take care of the unclean one, since, as he says, J, the soul and body of the unclean one belong to Heaven: the man may not eat the animal if he wants to. Sages' reply is a good one and settles the matter. Any increase in the weight of the animal benefits the man who took the vow, and this is without regard to whether the animal is clean or unclean, since, if it is unclean, the man who took the vow may sell the animal and gain an advantage in any event.

4:4

A. He who is prohibited by vow from enjoying benefit from him—he [the fellow] goes in to visit him when he is sick,

B. remaining standing but not sitting down.

C. And he heals him himself, but not what belongs to him.

D. He washes with him in a large bath tub, but not in a small one.

E. He sleeps with him in the same bed.

F. R. Judah says, "In the sunny season [does he share a bed], but not in the rainy reason, because at that time he gives the other the benefit [of the warmth of his body]."

G. And he sits with him on the same couch,

H. and eats with him at the same table, but not from the same bowl.

I. But he eats with him from the same bowl which is passed around.

J. He may not eat with him from the same feeding-bowl that is set before workers.

K. "And he may not work with him in the same furrow," the words of R. Meir.

L. And sages say, "He works with him but at a distance."

M. 4:4

The established formulary at M. 4:4A now introduces a set of rules on personal services and points of social contact, A-C, D, H-J, K-L, evidently four distinct themes. The themes are laid out rather smoothly, so that the bed introduces the table, then the bowl on the table, then the workers eating from the same bowl, then workers laboring together in the same furrow—a rather fine piece of linkage, in logical and proper order, of distinct considerations and themes. When the fellow, who is not supposed to give benefit to the one who has taken the vow, visits, he remains standing, so that he will not stay for a long time and give pleasure to the sick one (B. Ned. 38b, Simeon). It is an obligation to provide healing to the man. But he does not have to provide healing for his cattle (C) (B. Ned. 41b). D introduces using in common the same bath-tub, bed, and couch. Where joint use is no advantage, it is permitted, that is, not a small tub, in which, by his presence, the fellow raises the water-level; and not a common bed when the warmth of the bodies is a benefit, F. G forms the transition to the consideration of eating. They may eat together. But if they share a bowl, the fellow may leave the one who has taken the vow a larger or better portion, so they may not do so. I qualifies H. J makes the same point as H. The dispute of K-L concerns whether or not the fellow may help in work and so provide assistance.

B. *There is no difference between him who is forbidden by vow from enjoying any benefit from his fellow without specification, and him who is forbidden by vow from deriving food from him, except for setting food in his house and using utensils with which food is not prepared* [M. 4:1A-B].

C. He who is forbidden by vow from deriving benefit from his fellow and who died—

D. he [the fellow] brings a coffin and shrouds for him, wailing pipes and wailing women,

E. for the dead get no benefit [from these things].

F. He gives testimony in his behalf in property cases and in criminal cases.

G. [If] he fell ill, he [the fellow] goes into visit him [M. 4:4A].

H. But if the [one who took the vow] had someone ill in his house, the fellow does not go in to visit him. But he inquires after his welfare.

I. [If] he [the fellow] was a priest, he tosses the blood of his sin-offering in his behalf, and the blood of his guilt-offering [M. 4:3B],

J. for the sake of peace.

K. He washes with him in the same bath tub and *sleeps with him in the same bed* [M. 4:4D-E].

L. R. Judah says, "He sleeps with him in a small bed in the sunny season and in a large bed in the rainy season [M. 4:4F].

M. "He washes with him in a large bath tub and sweats with him in a small steam-bath" [M. 4:4D].

T. 2:7 (concluded) L pp. 105-106, ls. 20-27

T. works its way through the materials of M. 4:1-4. It adds a new item at C-E and F. In the former case the fellow benefits not the deceased but his family, along the lines of M. 4:3F, and in the latter he does his duty, as at M. 4:2. The reworking of M. 4:4 is clear as indicated. Judah's saying at M. 4:4F is given with greater precision.

4:5

A. He who is forbidden by vow from enjoying benefit from his fellow,

B. [if this was] before the Seventh Year, he may not go down into his field and he may not eat produce that hangs over [from the property of the other].

C. But [if this was] in the Seventh Year, while he may not go down into his field, he may eat the produce that hangs over [from the property of the other].

D. [If] he vowed that he would not derive food from him,

E. [if this was] before the Seventh Year, he goes down into his field but does not eat the produce.

F. And [if this was] in the Seventh Year, he goes down [into the field] and eats the produce.

M. 4:5

The formal perfection of this pericope requires no comment. It is essentially a replay of M. 4:1. The item is distinct from the foregoing and makes the point that produce in the Seventh Year is ownerless, but the field remains in the possession of the owner. Hence the contrast between B and C. If, then, the man cannot derive food, D, he is permitted to set foot in the field (M. 4:1A-B), but not to eat the produce, before the Seventh Year, and (obviously) to eat the produce in the Seventh Year. In point of fact, we have our first illustration of M. 4:1's distinction between prohibiting oneself by vow from deriving benefit in general, and eating food in particular.

A. *He who is forbidden by vow from enjoying benefit from his fellow—*
B. *before the Seventh Year may not go down into his field and may not eat* what is planted there [M. 4:5A-B].
C. In the Seventh Year he may go down into his field and eat what is planted there.

T. 2:8 L p. 106, ls. 27-29

T.'s theory, C, is that the field, as well as its contents, is ownerless (compare B. Ned. 42b). T. has NTY‛WT for M.'s NWṬWṬ.

4:6

A. He who is forbidden by a vow from deriving benefit from his fellow—
I B. should not lend him [his fellow] anything, nor should [the one who took the vow] borrow anything from him.
II C. He should not lend him money nor should he borrow money from him.
III D. He should not sell him anything, nor should he buy anything from him.
E. [If] he said to him, "Lend me your cow,"
F. [and] he said to him, "It is not available,"
G. and he said to him, "*Qonam* be my field if I ever again plough my field with it [the cow],"—
H. if he [himself] usually ploughed, while he is prohibited, everyone else is permitted [to plough his field with that cow].
I. If he did not usually plough his own field, then he and everyone else in the world are prohibited [from ploughing the field with that cow].

M. 4:6

There are two distinct units, M. 4:5A-D, and E-I. They hardly relate to one another. The interest turns at A-D to what the one who takes the vow may do in regard to the one against whom the vow is taken. The former cannot lend or borrow anything, lend or borrow money (B, C) or do any business (D). If the one who takes the vow does a favor for the one against whom the vow is taken, then the former may, in due course, accept a favor from the latter, which is not allowed by the terms of the vow.

E-G set up a case, settled at H-I. We have to interpret the man's language. If the man usually ploughed himself, not using his workers for that purpose, then he cannot use that cow. He was refering only to himself. But others may do so. If he usually did not do the ploughing himself, then in his mind was the notion that no one was going to plough his field with that cow. I simply cannot account for the location of this item here.

4:7-8

I A. He who is forbidden by vow from deriving benefit from his fellow and has nothing to eat—

B. he [the fellow] goes to a storekeeper and says, "Mr. So-and-so is forbidden by vow from deriving benefit from me, and I don't know what I can do about it."

C. And he [the storekeeper] gives food to him [who took the vow] and then goes and collects from this one [against whom the vow was taken].

II D. [If] he [against whom the vow was taken] had to build his house [that of the one prohibited by vow from deriving benefit],

or to set up his fence,

or to cut the grain in his field,

he [the fellow] goes to the workers and says to them, "Mr. So-and-so is forbidden by vow from deriving benefit from me, and I don't know what I can do about it."

E. [Then] they [the workers] do the work with him [who took the vow] and come and collect their salary from this one [against whom the vow was taken].

M. 4:7

III A. [If] they were going on a journey and he [who had forbidden himself by a vow from deriving benefit from his fellow] had nothing to eat,

B. he [against whom the vow was taken] gives something to another as a gift, and the other [who took the vow] is permitted to make use of it.

C. If there is no one else with them, he [against whom the vow was taken] leaves it on a rock or on a fence and says, "Lo, these things are ownerless property for anyone who wants them."

D. Then the other [who is prohibited by vow from deriving benefit from his fellow] takes what he wants and eats it.

E. And R. Yosé prohibits [such a procedure].

M. 4:8

The triplet makes its points clearly. M. 4:7A-C and D-E are carefully matched. M. 4:8 completes the picture, but does not adhere so closely to the established formal pattern. Yosé's objection is that he sees the procedure as a gift, pure and simple.

    A. "[He who says,] 'This loaf of bread is sanctified,'
    B. "and either he or his fellow ate it,
    C. "lo, this one has committed an act of sacrilege.
    D. "Therefore it is subject to redemption.
    E. "If he said, 'Lo, it is [incumbent] on me,' and he ate it,
    F. "he has trangressed by committing sacrilege to the extent of his thanks for enjoying the loaf of bread.
    G. "[If] someone else ate it, lo, that one has not committed sacrilege.
    H. "Therefore it is not subject to redemption," the words of R. Meir.
    I. R. Simeon says, "Neither this one nor that one has committed sacrilege."
    J. *Then the other one takes it and eats it* [M. 4:8D].
    K. *R. Yosé prohibits* because his vow has come before his act of declaring the food to be ownerless property [M. 4:8E].

    T. 2:9 (continued) L pp. 106 ls. 29-33

A-D pose no problems. If someone sanctifies a loaf of bread, and then he or someone else eats it, he has done sacrilege. The loaf, of course, may be redeemed for money, and the coins then are consecrated in its stead. What if the man uses the language, "This is unto *me*" meaning, "Sacred *only* unto me"? Then the loaf is consecrated so far as he is concerned, F. But someone else who ate it has not committed sacrilege, since the loaf was consecrated only for the person who formulated matters in that way. The sacrilege is then defined at F. Meir's view is that the loaf is not subject to redemption, because it is sacred only in the limited sense just now defined. Simeon says it is not consecrated at all, I. I do not know why this case is relevant here.

J cites M., and Yosé's reason is spelled out. The vow was in force before the man declared the food to be ownerless property. So long as the other party has not acquired possession, the property declared ownerless does not leave the domain of the one who declares it to be ownerless. It follows that, if the one who is prohibited by vow takes possession of the property, it is as if he received it as a gift.

CHAPTER SIX

NEDARIM CHAPTER FIVE

This brief chapter continues the inquiry into the consequence of prohibiting oneself by vow from enjoying benefit from someone else. If two people do so to one another and share a courtyard, neither may use the shared property. Eliezer b. Jacob maintains that each uses the courtyard in the theory that the whole was stipulated to be his when the two entered into partnership. This same view is repeated in a triplet, M. 5:1-2. M. 5:3 makes the further, obvious point that if the person prohibited by vow from giving benefit to the one who took the vow owns a bath-house or olive-press which he rents out, and if when he rents out his property, he retains a right to it, then the one who took the vow cannot make use of the property. If the owner retains no right to it when it is subject to rental, then the one who took the vow may make use of it. M. 5:4-5 again have two people unable to use one another's property. We return to the issue of the common court. There is property owned in joint tenancy by all the people who live in a town. This property may not be used by either party. There also is property not deemed owned by any individual but regarded as wholly public. Both may make use of that property. M. 5:6 is a singleton which repeats the point of M. 4:8 and adds to it a wildly inappropriate precedent. This is the mark of the end of a major unit of inquiry.

5:1-2

I   A. Partners who prohibited themselves by vow from deriving benefit from one another are prohibited from entering the common courtyard.

B. R. Eliezer b. Jacob says, "This one enters the part which is his, and that one enters the part which is his."

C. And both of them are prohibited from setting up a millstone and oven there, or from raising chickens.

II   D. [If] one of them was prohibited by vow from deriving benefit from his fellow, he should not enter into the common courtyard.

E. R. Eliezer b. Jacob says, "He can say to him, 'Into the part which is mine I enter, but I do not enter into the part which is yours.' "

F. And they force the one who has taken the vow to sell his share [to the other].

M. 5:1

III   A. [If] a third party ["someone from the market"] was prohibited by vow from deriving benefit from one of them, he should not enter into the common courtyard.

B. R. Eliezer b. Jacob says, "He can say to him, 'Into the part which belongs to your fellow I enter, but I do not enter into your part.' "

M. 5:2

The purest example of the form is at M. 5:2A-B, which shows that M. 5:1C and M. 5:1F are secondary interpolations. The conception of the anonymous authority in the triplet, M. 5:1A, D, and M. 5:2A, is that every part of the shared property is held in *joint* tenancy. Eliezer holds that each has a *sole* right everywhere in the courtyard, in the theory that, at the moment he is in a given location, it is stipulated that that location is wholly his. All parties concur at C. Each has the right to prevent the other from taking over in permanent use any part of the courtyard, and if he does not exercise that right, then he turns out to give a benefit to the other party, which is prohibited. If one party is subject to a vow not to derive benefit from the other, then that party must sell the other party his share of the courtyard, a view which Eliezer, E, need not accept, but which must be adopted by the authority of D.

L. Just as both of them [the two men who have prohibited themselves by a vow from deriving benefit from one another] are prohibited from dwelling in the common courtyard [M. 5:1A], so they are prohibited from living in the same alleyway.

M. Just as both of them are prohibited from raising chickens, so both of them are prohibited from raising small cattle [M. 5:1C].

N. If one of them was accustomed to prohibiting others by vow from deriving benefit from his share, they force the one who is accustomed to do so to sell his share [M. 5:1F].

T. 2:9 (continued) L pp. 106-107, ls. 33-36

T.'s gloss of M. 5:1 is clear as stated.

5:3

A. He who is prohibited by vow from deriving benefit from his fellow, and he [the fellow] has a bath-house or an olive-press in town which are hired out [to other people]—

B. if he [the fellow] has rights therein it [the bath-house of olive-press] is prohibited [to the other].

C. [If] he has no rights therein, he [the other] is permitted.

D. He who says to his fellow, "*Qonam* if I enter *your* house," or "...if I buy your field,"

E. [if the other party] died or sold them to a third party, he [the one who took the vow, now] is permitted [to enter the house or the field].

F. [If he said], "*Qonam* if I enter *this* house" or "...if I purchase this field"—

G. [if the other party] died or sold it to a third party, it is [nonetheless] forbidden.

M. 5:3

We have two fairly obvious propositions, A-C, D-G. They are not quite in alignment with one another. The former speaks of a man who owns a bath-house or an olive-press. He rents it out to others. Now if, when he does so, he does not rent out the entire usufruct of the property but keeps a right to himself to make use of it, then the one prohibited by vow from deriving benefit from him cannot make use of that property, because it still in some measure remains in the domain of the one from whom he who has taken the vow cannot derive benefit. Otherwise he may.

The second statement is along equally obvious lines. If the person speaks of a house in the other's domain, then, when the house no longer lies in the other's domain, the one who took the vow may make use of it. But if he spoke of that particular house, without regard to its ownership by the other, he may never again enter that house. None of this is very surprising.

5:4-5

I A. [If one said to his fellow,] "Lo, I am *herem* unto you,"
   B. the one against whom the vow is made is prohibited [from using what belongs to the other, who made the vow].
II C. [If he said,] "Lo, you are *herem* unto me,"
   D. the one who takes the vow is prohibited [from benefitting from the other].
III E. [If he said,] "Lo, I am unto you and you are unto me [*herem*]," both of them are prohibited.
   F. But both of them are permitted [to make use of property belonging to] the immigrants from Babylonia [that is, inalienable property, which is deemed ownerless].
   G. And they are forbidden [to make use of property] belonging to that town [which each citizen owns jointly with all others].

M. 5:4

A. What is something which belongs to the immigrants from Babylonia [F]?
B. For example, the Temple mount and courtyards, and the well which is in the middle of the way.
C. And what are things which belong to that town [G]?
D. For example, the town square, the bath-house, the synagogue, the ark, and the scrolls.
E. And he who writes over his share to the *nasi* [of the court allows the fellow, prohibited by vow, the derive benefit from those things which are deemed to be held jointly by the town's citizens].

F. R. Judah says, "All the same is the one who writes over his share to the *nasi* and the one who writes over his share to an ordinary person.

G. "What is the difference between him who writes over his share to the *nasi* and the one who writes over his share to an ordinary person?

H. "For: the one who writes over his share to the *nasi* does not have to grant him title. [But the one who writes over his share to an ordinary person does have to grant him title]."

I. And sages say, "All the same are this one and that one. They have to grant title.

J. "They referred to the *nasi* only because they spoke of prevailing conditions."

K. R. Judah says, "The Galileans do not have to write [their share over to the *nasi*]. For their forefathers already have written over their share in their behalf."

M. 5:5

The gloss of M. 5:4F-G, M. 5:5, is somewhat disproportionate to the thing glossed. The point of the triplet, M. 5:4A-E, is so obvious that it can only be deemed an introduction to F, G. It therefore appears that the "gloss" has generated the basic pericope. The difference at F, G, is familiar from M. 5:1's sages' viewpoint. If property is owned by none, then both may use it. If it is owned by all, then neither may use it. M. 5:5E is framed in a peculiar way, since it lacks an apodosis, though in context what is required is readily supplied. The dispute, F-H *vs.* I-J, represents a tertiary exegesis. That is, it is meant to explain M. 5:5E, which itself is part of the interpretation of M. 5:4F-G. Judah wants to know the meaning of the formulation of E and takes it to be inclusive. The one who has taken the vow may write over his share in the common property of the town either to the *nasi* of the town or to anyone else. Then he posits a difference between doing so to the one and to the other, on the stated grounds of G-H. This is clever but, sages maintain, pointless. K then is a further addition to the whole, independent of the foregoing.

O. A public square through which the public way passes, lo, this belongs to the immigrants from Babylonia.

P. But if the public way does not pass through, lo, it belongs to the men of that town.

T. 2:9 (concluded) p. 107, ls. 36-37

A. He who is prohibited by vow from deriving benefit from his town or from the people of his town,

B. and someone came from the outside and lived there for thirty days—

C. he is permitted to derive benefit from him.

D. [But if he was prohibited by vow from deriving benefit] from those who dwell in his town, and someone came from the outside and lived there for thirty days, he is prohibited [from deriving benefit from him].

F. He who is prohibited by vow from deriving benefit from his fellow [in a vow made] in his presence—

G. they accept inquiry from him only in his presence.

H. [But if he vowed not to derive benefit from his fellow] not in his presence,

I. they accept inquiry from him either in his presence or not in his presence.

T. 2:10 L p. 107, ls. 38-41

The difference between A-C and D is that in the latter case, the outsider's residence places him under the man's vow, a supplement to M. 5:4-5. If the fellow knew about the vow, F, he must be present at the absolution, G. If not, H, it is not necessary.

5:6

A. He who is forbidden by vow from deriving benefit from his fellow and who has nothing to eat—

B. he [the fellow] gives it [food] to someone else as a gift, and this one [prohibited by vow] is permitted [to make use of] it.

C. MʿŚH B: There was someone in Bet Ḥoron whose father was prohibited by vow from deriving benefit from him.

And he [the man in Bet Ḥoron] was marrying off his son, and he said to his fellow, "The courtyard and the banquet are given over to you as a gift. But they are before you only so that father may come and eat with us at the banquet."

The other party said, "Now if they really are mine, then lo, they are consecrated to heaven!"

He said to him, "I didn't give you what's mine so you would consecrate it to Heaven!"

He said to him, "You did not give me what's yours except so that you and your father could eat and drink and make friends again, and so the sin [for violating the oath] could rest on his [my] head!"

Now the case came before sages. They ruled, "Any act of donation which is not so [given] that, if one sanctified it to Heaven, it is sanctified, is no act of donation."

M. 5:6

A-B go over the ground of M. 4:8A-B. The case is relevant in general but hardly to the particular rule of B, which is not illustrated by C (!).

CHAPTER SEVEN

NEDARIM CHAPTER SIX

We now come to a new unit of inquiry, the interpretation of the language used in a vow. Our chapter is a good deal more interesting than it appears to be on the surface. For while superficially it seems to present one rather obvious conception after another, underneath it raises profound issues of categorization and taxonomy. If, for example, we refer to a genus, do we thereby include the diverse species thereof? If we refer to the species, do we also comprehend the genus? And again, if I prohibit myself by a vow from using wine, may I consume something with the flavor of wine? If we say that I may do so, then what about prohibiting myself from using a particular glass of wine? Then I should refrain from using that wine, so long as it is discernible, e.g., if it imparts a flavor to something else. Furthermore, what appears to be a dreary set of catalogues turns out to exhibit a measure of formal sophistication, in the inclusion, on one sequence of ideas, of a coming formal pattern, as at M. 6:7-9. In all, therefore, we must not be taken in by what seems to be repetitious and arid, purely formal materials to assume that no important problems or issues are under discussion, for the opposite is the case.

The main point of this chapter and the following two is that one who vows not to eat one thing is permitted to eat something akin. If, however, he so phrased his vow as to cover a whole genus of food, then, of course, he may not make use of any food of that type. He may refer to a particular thing or to a generality, with the expected, different consequences. Our chapter is in two main parts, M. 6:1-3 + 4, 5, and M. 6:6,7-9 + 10.

The first set deals at the outset with processing, then with the issue of the genus and the species. If one vows not to eat food which is cooked, he may eat food which is roasted or seethed. If he refers to a process applicable to a given sort of food, then if he says, "I vow not to eat *something* pickled," he is prohibited from eating picked vegetables. But if he says, "I vow not to eat *anything* pickled" (that is, omitting the definite article), he, of course, cannot eat anything pickled, vegetable or not. M. 6:5 goes on to treat milk and curd. One who vows not to eat milk may eat curd. If he vows not to eat curd, he may eat milk.

M. 6:6 introduces the second group, starting with concern for the flavor of the forbidden substance. If the substance in general is prohibited, we pay no attention to the flavor. But if a particular quantity of that substance is prohibited, we treat it as we do forbidden meat and prohibit anything bearing the flavor. M. 6:7 repeats that viewpoint—which is sages' *vis à vis* Judah—and then proceeds to introduce the following construction, M. 6:8-9. M. 6:9 restates the materials of M. 6:8 as sages of M. 6:8 *vis à vis* Judah b. Betera will want them. Judah b. Betera holds that if one vows not to eat something, and a derivative of that thing bears its name, one also cannot use the derivative. This would apply, for example, to a vow not to eat dates. They produce date-honey. If one vows not to eat dates, he may not eat date-honey, so Judah b. Betera. Sages reject this view. Their conception is stated both at M. 6:8 and again in a major construction at M. 6:9. M. 6:10 is distinct, going over the issue of the genus and the species.

6:1-3

A. He who takes a vow not to eat what is cooked is permitted [to eat what is] roasted or seethed.

B. [If] he said, "*Qonam* if I taste cooked food," he is prohibited from eating what is loosely cooked in a pot, but permitted to eat which is solidly cooked in a pot.

C. And he is permitted to eat a lightly boiled egg or gourds prepared in hot ashes.

M. 6:1

I A. He who takes a vow not to eat what is cooked in a pot is prohibited only from what is boiled [therein].

B. [If] he said, "*Qonam* if I taste anything which goes down into a pot," he is prohibited from eating anything which is cooked in a pot.

M. 6:2

II A. [He who takes a vow not to eat] what is pickled is prohibited only from eating pickled vegetables.

B. [If he said, "*Qonam*] if I taste anything pickled," he is prohibited from anything eating anything which is pickled.

III C. [If he took a vow not to eat what is] seethed, he is forbidden only from eating seethed meat.

D. [If he said, "*Qonam*] if I taste anything seethed," he is prohibited from eating anything which is seethed.

IV E. "[He who takes a vow not to eat] what is roasted is prohibited only from eating roasted meat," the words of R. Judah.

F. [If he said, "*Qonam*] if I taste anything roasted," he is prohibited from eating anything which is roasted.

V G. [He who takes a vow not to eat] what is salted is prohibited only from eating salted fish.

H. [If he said, "*Qonam*] if I eat anything salted," then he is prohibited from eating anything at all which is salted.

M. 6:3

The formal traits of the unit are clear. M. 6:2-3 constitute a highly disciplined, five-part construction. The inclusion of Judah at M. 6:3E is curious, but it does not break the pattern. The principal conception is stated at M. 6:1A-B, bearing a gloss at C, then restated interminably in many examples. If one phrases matters in one way, the prohibition is of one sort, and if he does so in another, he prohibits much more. If he says he will not eat what is cooked, he thereby permits himself that which is excluded: what is roasted or seethed. If he phrases matters to prohibit cooked food, then he excludes food which is properly cooked. This conception is rephrased in a much tighter way at M. 6:2-3. If he is specific—"cooked in a pot"—then the food cooked in the usual way is prohibited. If he vows not to eat anything which has been *in* a pot, the prohibition is much more general. The statements at M. 6:3 are still clearer.

6:4

I A. [He who says, "*Qonam*] if I taste fish or fishes," is prohibited [to eat] them, whether large or small, salted or unsalted, raw or cooked.
    B. But he is permitted to eat pickled chopped fish and brine.
II C. He who vows not to eat small fish is prohibited from eating pickled chopped fish. But he is permitted to eat brine and fish-brine.
III D. He who vowed [not to eat] pickled chopped fish is prohibited from eating brine and fish-brine.

M. 6:4

We have a tripartite construction, A-B, C, and C, specifying the implication of the several references, fish and pickled fish, brine and fish-brine.

6:5

A. He who vows not to have milk is permitted to eat curds.
B. And R. Yosé prohibits [eating curds].
C. [If he vowed not to eat] curds, he is permitted to have milk.
D. Abba Saul says, "He who vows not to eat cheese is prohibited to eat it whether it is salted or unsalted."

M. 6:5

The formal pattern begins with A + C, then bears B's view. D is a secondary accretion. The point is clear as given.

6:6

A. He who takes a vow not to eat meat is permitted to eat broth and meat-sediment.
B. And R. Judah prohibits [him from eating broth and meat-sediment].

C. Said R. Judah, M'SH W: "R. Tarfon prohibited me from eating eggs which were roasted with it [meat].

D. They said to him, "And that is the point! Under what circumstances? When he will say, 'This meat is prohibited to me.'

E. "For he who vows not to eat something which is mixed with something else, if there is sufficient [of the prohibited substance] to impart a flavor, is prohibited [from eating the mixture].''

M. 6:6

The dispute, A-B, is given a kind of debate by the addition of D-E. Sages' point is that the specific piece of meat is prohibited, and so is anything bearing its flavor. But "meat in general" is not meant to exclude the taste of meat. T. has Judah explicitly reject this argument.

A. He who vows not to eat what is cooked is prohibited from eating what roasted and what is seethed and what is boiled [M. 6:1B].

B. And he is prohibited from eating soft bisquits, because sick people eat their bread with them.

C. He who vows [not to eat] what goes down into a pot is prohibited from eating what goes down into a pan [M. 6:2].

D. [He who vows not to eat] what goes down into a pan is permitted to eat what goes down into a pot.

T. 3:1 L p. 107, ls. 1-3

A. [He who vows not to eat what] is prepared in a pot is permitted to eat what is prepared in a pan.

B. [He who vows not to eat what] is prepared in a pan is permitted to eat what is prepared in a pot.

C. [He who vows not to eat what] goes down into an oven is prohibited from eating only bread alone.

D. [He who vows not to eat what] is prepared in an oven is prohibited from eating anything which is prepared in an oven.

E. He who vows [not to eat] what is curdled is permitted to eat cheese.

F. He who vows not to eat cheese is prohibited from eating what is curdled [M. 6:5].

G. He who vows not to eat the meat sediment is permitted to eat the broth. He who vows not to eat the broth is permitted to eat the sediment.

H. R. Judah says, "If he said, '*Qonam* if I eat meat,' he is prohibited to eat it, its broth, and its meat-sediment" [M. 6:6].

T. 3:2 L pp. 107-108, ls. 308

A. He who takes a vow not to eat meat is prohibited from eating every kind of meat [M. 6:6].

B. He is prohibited from eating the head, the feet, and the windpipe, and [he is prohibited from eating] fowl.

C. But he is permitted to eat the flesh of fish and locusts.

D. Rabban Simeon b. Gamaliel says, "He who vows not to eat meat is

54

prohibited from eating all kinds of meat. But he is permitted to eat the head, the feet, and the windpipe, fowl, fish, and locusts."

E. And so did Rabban Simeon b. Gamaliel say, "The innards are not the meat, and people who eat them are not men."

F. R. Simeon b. Eleazer says, "If he said, '*Qonam* if I eat fish,' he is prohibited from eating big fish but permitted to eat little ones.

G. "[If he said, '*Qonam* if] I eat little fish,' he is prohibited from eating little ones but permitted to eat big ones.

H. "[If he said, '*Qonam*] if I eat fish,' he is prohibited from eating big fish and prohibited from eating little fish," [M. 6:4A].

T. 3:5 L p. 109, ls. 21-29

T. complements M., explaining what M. 6:1B does not spell out. What is interesting is the matched stichs, T. 3:1C-D, T. 3:2A-B. What is cooked in a pot can be cooked in a pan, e.g., in a smaller quantity. But there are things cooked in a pan which cannot be cooked in a pot at all. The rest is clear as given. Judah's point is that the broth and sediment contain the flavor of the meat. T. 3:5A goes over the issues of M. 6:6 and makes its own points, then T. 3:5F-H refine M. 6:4.

6:7-9

A. He who vows not to drink wine is permitted to eat a cooked dish which has the taste of wine.

B. [If] he said, "*Qonam* if I taste this wine," and it fell into a cooked dish, if there is sufficient [wine] to impart a flavor, lo, this is prohibited.

C. He who takes a vow not to eat grapes is permitted to drink wine.

D. [He who takes a vow not to eat] olives is permitted to have olive-oil.

E. [If] he said, "*Qonam*! if I eat these olives or grapes," he is prohibited to eat them and what exudes from them.

M. 6:7

A. He who takes a vow not to eat dates is permitted to have date-honey.

B. [He who takes a vow not to eat] winter-grapes is permitted to have the vinegar made from winter-grapes.

C. R. Judah b. Betera says, "Anything which is called after the name of that which is made from it, and one takes a vow not to have it—he is prohibited also from eating that which comes from it."

D. But sages permit.

M. 6:8

I A. He who takes a vow not to have wine is permitted to have apple-wine.
II B. [He who takes a vow not to have] oil is permitted to have sesame oil.
III C. He who takes a vow not to have honey is permitted to have date-honey.
IV D. He who takes a vow not to have vinegar is permitted to have the vinegar of winter-grapes.

V   E.   He who takes a vow not to have leeks is permitted to have shallots.
VI F.   He who takes a vow not to have vegetables is permitted to have wild vegetables,
     G. since they have a special name.

M. 6:9

I treat M. 6:7-9 together because M. 6:9 goes over the ground of M. 6:7, 8, stating matters in an excellent formal construction. M. 6:7 repeats the main point of M. 6:6's sages. That is, if one vows not to drink wine, he may eat something which has a wine-flavor. But if he vows not to have a particular glass of wine, then he cannot eat anything bearing a sufficient quantity of that particular wine to impart a flavor—that is, precisely the conception of M. 6:6. M. 6:7C, D, E, make that point at E, but a separate point at C, D, and so form a transition between M. 6:6-7B and M. 6:8, 9, 10. The first point, C, D, is that if one vows not to eat grapes, he may make use of grapes when they are in the form of wine, so too with oil. If, however, he specifies the particular grapes or olives, then he cannot make use of anything which derives from those particular grapes or olives, just as at M. 6:6, 7A-B. M. 6:8, B, appear to make the same point as M. 6:7C, D. But Judah b. Betera offers an interesting observation, which shows that M. 6:8A, B, do not go over the ground of M. 6:7C, D at all. If something produces a derivative and bears the name of the derivative, then if one vows not to have that thing, he also cannot have its derivative. Dates, for instance, are called honey, which they produce. If one vows not to have dates, he cannot have honey. So C-D restate the view of A, B, from sages' perspective, and place Judah in opposition. Then, as we see, M. 6:9 restates sages' view, which produces a repetition of M. 6:8A, B at M. 6:9C, D, respectively.

A. *[He who takes a vow not to eat] oil is permitted to eat sesame-oil* [M. 6:9B].

B. But in a place in which they make use of sesame-oil as a staple, he is prohibited even from using sesame-oil.

C. *R. Judah b. Betera says, "Anything which is called after the name of that which is made from it, and one takes a vow not to have it—he is prohibited also from eating that which comes from it"* [M. 6:8C].

D. R. Simeon b. Eleazar says, "If something is usually eaten and what exudes from it is usually eaten, and one has vowed not to eat it, he is prohibited also from eating what exudes from it.

E. "If he takes a vow not to eat what exudes from it, he is prohibited from eating it as well.

F. "What is usually eaten, but that which exudes from it is not usually eaten, and one has taken a vow not to eat it—he is permitted to eat what exudes from it.

G. "[If he took a vow not to eat] what exudes from it, he is permitted to eat it.

H. "What is not usually eaten and what exudes from it is usually eaten and one has taken a vow not to eat it—this one has intended his vow to cover only what exudes from it."

T. 3:3 L p. 108, ls. 9-16

T. 3:3A-B make the point that if the man can have meant sesame-oil, he is prohibited from using that. Simeon b. Eleazar has a different criterion from Judah b. Betera, and it is stated with great clarity. He distinguishes in terms of edibility. If one vows not to eat an edible substance which produces an edible substance, the latter is prohibited along with the former, and *vice versa*, D-E. F-H then are clear as stated. Since everything mentioned in M. is edible, Simeon's conception, while relevant, does not illuminate anything we have at M. 6:7-9.

A. He who takes a vow not to wear anything made of wool is permitted to wear something made of flax.

[If he took a vow not to wear something made] of flax, he is permitted [to wear something made] of wool.

B. R. Simeon b. Eleazar says, "As to that which is usually used for clothing, and that which comes from it is usually used for clothing, and one has taken a vow not to make use of it—he is prohibited also from making use of what comes from it.

C. "[If he took a vow] not to use what comes from it, he is prohibited from making use of it.

D. "As to something usually used for clothing, but what comes from it is not usually used for clothing, and one has taken a vow not to use it—he is permitted to make use of what comes from it.

E. "[If he took a vow not to use] what comes from it, he is permitted to make use of it.

F. "As to something which is not usually used for clothing but what comes from it is usually used for wearing, and one has taken a vow not to make use of it,

G. "this one has intended only to refrain from using what comes from it."

T. 3:4 L pp. 108-109, ls. 16-21

T. 3:4 is located at M. 6:7-9 because Simeon's saying at T. 3:3 relates to Judah b. Betera's, M. 6:8/T. 3:3. But in fact it takes up the theme of M. 7:3 (below, p. 61). B refers to sheep-skin, which also yields wool, D, to goat-skin, which is used, and goat-hair, which is not.

6:10

I A. [He who takes a vow not to eat] cabbage is forbidden from asparagus [deemed a species of the cabbage-genus].

B. [He who takes a vow not to eat] asparagus is permitted to have cabbage.
II C. [He who takes a vow not to have] grits is forbidden to have grits-pottage.
D. And R. Yosé permits it.
E. [He who takes a vow not to eat] grits-pottage is permitted to have grits.
III F. [He who takes a vow not to eat] grits-pottage is forbidden to eat garlic.
G. And R. Yosé permits it.
H. [He who takes a vow not to eat] garlic is permitted to eat grits-pottage.
IV I. [He who takes a vow not to eat] lentils is forbidden from eating lentil-cakes.
J. And R. Yosé permits.
K. [He who takes a vow not to eat] lentil-cakes is permitted to eat lentils.
L. [He who says, "*Qonam*] if I taste [a grain of] wheat or wheat [ground up in any form]" is forbidden from eating it, whether it is ground up or in the form of bread.
M. [If he said, "*Qonam* if I eat] a grit [or] grits in any form," he is forbidden from eating them whether raw or cooked.
N. R. Judah says, "[If he said,] '*Qonam* if I eat either a grit or a [grain of] wheat,' he is permitted to chew them raw."

M. 6:10

The pericope is in two parts, A-K and L-N. The formal traits of the former set of four matched entries do not require the dispute introduced at D, G, and J, but are defined by the pattern, *forbidden/permitted*, as at A-B, C + E, F + H, and I + K. The anonymous authority behind the four units maintains that if one refers to the genus, he prohibits the species thereof. But if he refers to the species, he does not prohibit the genus. For example, grits-pottage includes garlic, F, but garlic does not exhaustively define grits-pottage, H. Yosé rejects this view, holding that, for the present purpose, the genus does not encompass the species. At L, M, we have a vow using the singular and plural of the item, e.g., grit-grits. This is deemed to cover all forms of the item. Judah has a quibble to add, which is that if one refers to *eating*, then one may not eat such a thing, but with it one may do something which does not fall into the category of normal eating, e.g., merely chewing.

A. He who in the Seventh Year takes a vow not to eat vegetables is prohibited from eating wild vegetables.
B. [If he vowed not to eat] gourds, he is prohibited only from eating Greek gourds alone.
C. *[If he vowed not to eat] cabbage, he is prohibited from eating asparagus. [If he vowed not to eat] asparagus, he is permitted to eat cabbage* [M. 6:10A-B].

D. If he vowed not to eat leeks, in a place in which they call shallots leeks, he is prohibited to eat shallots.

E. [If he vowed not to eat] shallots, he is permitted to eat leeks [M. 6:9E].

F. [If he vowed not to eat] onions, he is prohibited from eating scallions.

G. And R. Yosé permits it.

H. [If he vowed not to eat] scallions, he is permitted to eat onions.

I. *[If he vowed not to eat] lentils, he is prohibited from eating lentil-cakes.*

J. *And R. Yosé permits* [M. 6:10I-J].

K. [If he vowed not to eat] grits-porrage, he is permitted to eat garlic [= Yosé, M. 6:10F-G].

T. 3:6 L pp. 109-110, ls. 30-36

We interpret the vow against vegetables differently if it is taken in the Seventh Year. Then, when people do not cultivate gardens, the man is assumed to refer to wild vegetables as well as cultivated ones. The rest of T. 3:6 expands M. 6:10 by rephrasing matters or supplying further entries in accord with Yosé's view.

A. R. Judah says, "[If he said,] '*Qonam* be a grit if I taste it.' he is permitted to eat them raw but prohibited from eating them cooked.

B. "[If he said, '*Qonam* be] grits if I taste them,' he is prohibited from eating them raw but permitted to eat them cooked.

C. "[If he said, 'Qonam be] a grain of wheat if I taste it,' he is permitted to chew it but prohibited from baking it.

D. ["If he said, '*Qonam*] be grains of wheat if I taste them,' he is prohibited from chewing them and prohibited from baking them."

T. 3:7 L p. 110, ls. 36-38

T. rephrases M. 6:10L-N. A single grit would refer to cooked grits, therefore raw ones are permitted, A, and B restates the matter.

CHAPTER EIGHT

NEDARIM CHAPTER SEVEN

The same basic theme continues, the clarification of the meaning and limits of language used in vows. M. 7:1-5 carry forward familiar concerns, while M. 7:6-9 take up fresh issues. At M. 7:1 we ask whether gourds are included in the general category of vegetables, and, at M. 7:2, whether dried Egyptian beans go into the category of grain, because they are ground for flour. M. 7:3 moves on to the definition of clothing, which excludes sacking, curtains, or hangings, then a prohibition of wool, which does not encompass wool-shearings, in the theory that by 'wool' the person meant 'clothing made of wool.' M. 7:4-5 conclude in a very impressive formal exercise which makes the point that if one vows not to enter a house, he may go into the upper room, so far as Meir is concerned. Sages deem the upper room to fall into the category of the house. All parties concur that a vow not to enter the upper room has no affect upon the right to enter the house proper.

M. 7:6-7 and M. 7:8-9 make important but obvious points of clarification of linguistic constructions. If a person vows not to *derive benefit* from pieces of fruit, then not only the fruit, but whatever is yielded by the fruit is prohibited. If he vows not to *eat* pieces of fruit, then that is what he may not do. But he may derive benefit from what is yielded by the fruit. Thus he may derive benefit from juice yielded by the fruit. This point is made a second time, now with reference to the wife's work, and the repetition is important solely in linking the whole to what follows, M. 7:8-9. So M. 7:6-9 should be deemed a carefully formed intermediate unit. Now we distinguish between a vow not to derive benefit up to Passover from what the wife is making, and a vow not to derive benefit from what the wife is making up to Passover. In the latter instance the man may never derive benefit from what the wife makes up to Passover. M. 7:9, finally, has the man prohibit the wife not to go to the father's house before the festival of Sukkot, saying that she may not derive benefit on his account before Passover if she does so. But that means that if she goes *after* Passover, there is no penalty to be invoked, since the benefit she now should not enjoy was prohibited only until Passover. In this case the man's vow is null. But he should not make that sort of vow; the wife, for her part, should not go until Sukkot. D-F make the further, equally obvious point that if the husband prohibits the wife from enjoying benefit up to Sukkot if she goes to her father's house before Passover, and she does so, she cannot derive benefit from him until Sukkot. I take it this self-evident fact is stated only to complete the construction.

7:1

A. He who vows not to eat vegetables is permitted to eat gourds.
B. And R. ʿAqiba prohibits [him from eating gourds].
C. They said to R. ʿAqiba, "And does not a man say to his messenger, 'Buy me vegetables,' to which the other replies [upon his return home] 'I found only gourds'?"
D. He said to them, "And that is just how things are! But would he say to him, 'I found only pulse?'
E. "But gourds are in the general category of vegetables, while pulse is not in the general category of vegetables."
F. And [if he vowed not to eat vegetables] he is prohibited from eating Egyptian beans when they are fresh, but he is permitted to eat them when they are dried.

M. 7:1

A is continued at F, with the dispute, B, bearing a sizable exposition of ʿAqiba's position. Gourds are not in the category of vegetables. Fresh Egyptian beans are, but dried ones are ground into flour. The issue of gourds devolves upon whether or not, in common speech, people regard them as vegetables. Sages' saying sets up ʿAqiba's reply and cannot be taken seriously as an autonomous argument. D-E are clear as given.

7:2

A. "He who vows not to eat grain is forbidden to eat dried Egyptian beans," the words of R. Meir.
B. And sages say, "He is prohibited only from eating the five varieties [wheat, barley, spelt, goat-grass, and oats]."
C. R. Meir says, "He who vows not to eat [field] produce is forbidden only to eat the five varieties.
D. "But he who vows not to eat grain is prohibited from eating all kinds of grain."
E. But he is permitted to eat fruit of trees and vegetables.

M. 7:2

M. 7:1F treats dried Egyptian beans as a kind of grain, not as a vegetable. Meir, A, C-D, clearly concurs. Sages deem *grain* to include only the five varieties listed. D goes over the ground of A, of course, and now would encompass even pulse. E further explains the meaning of grain.

7:3

A. He who vows not to wear clothing is permitted to wear sacking, curtains, or hangings.

B. [If] he said, "*Qonam* if wool touches me," he is permitted to wear wool-shearings.

C. [If he said, "*Qonam* if] flax touches me," he is permitted to wear stalks of flax.

D. R. Judah says, "All depends upon the one who makes the vow:

E. "[If] he was bearing a burden and was sweating and breathing heavily [and] said, '*Qonam* if wool and flax touch me,' he is permitted to wear them as clothing but prohibited to throw them over onto his back [as a bundle]."

· M. 7:3

Judah, D-E, does not meet the position of A-C head-on. On the contrary, I should be inclined to see the two sets as complementary to one another. The point of A-C is clear as given. At B, C, we interpret the vow to refer to wool or flax used as clothing. Judah's saying does not differ from that conception that we interpret the language of the person contextually. If the person may be referring to clothing, we assume that he is. But if it is clear that he is vowing against repeating what he is doing, which is bearing a burden of wool or flax, then, of course, we shall so interpret what he has said.

A. He who vows not to eat the produce of a given year is prohibited from eating all the produce of that year.

B. But he is permitted to eat [meat of the] calves, lambs, sheep, and milk, and pigeons [produced that year].

C. If he said, "[*Qonam* if I taste what is] produced in [this] year," he is prohibited from eating all of them.

D. He who vows not to eat summer fruit is prohibited only from eating figs alone.

T. 4:1 L p. 110, ls. 1-3

A. Rabban Simeon b. Gamaliel says, "Grapes also fall into the category of summer-fruit."

T. 4:2 L pp. 110-111, ls. 3-4

A. He who vows not to eat *pe'ah* is prohibited from eating cucumbers, gourds, and chate-melons but permitted to eat fruit which grows on trees.

B. He who vows not to drink fruit-juice is prohibited from all kinds of sweet juice but permitted to drink wine.

C. He who vows not to eat spices is prohibited [eating] from raw spices but permitted cooked spices.

D. If he said, "Lo, they are prohibited to my mouth," "Lo, they are incumbent on me," he then is prohibited from eating them whether they are raw or cooked.

E. He who vows not to eat bread is prohibited only from eating bread which comes from the five varieties [of grain of the Land] [M. 7:2B].

F. He who vows not to eat grain is *prohibited from eating Egyptian beans when they are fresh but permitted to eat them when they are dried* [M. 7:1F].

G. And he is permitted to eat rice, split grain, groats of wheat, and barley-groats.

H. He who vows not to wear clothing is prohibited from putting on a belt or a *fascia*.

I. But he is permitted to put on a leather coat, a spread, shoes, pants, and a hat.

T. 4:3 L p. 111, ls. 4:11

A. Under what circumstances did *R. Judah say, "All depends upon the one who makes a vow"* [M. Ned. 7:3D]?

B. If he was bearing a burden of wool and was suffering on its account and said, "*Qonam* if wool touches me again," he is prohibited from carrying it but permitted to wear it.

C. If he was wearing wool and was suffering on its account and said, "*Qonam* be wool if it touches me," he is prohibited from wearing it but permitted to carry it in a bundle.

T. 4:4 L p. 111, ls. 11-13

T. complements M. as indicated. The language of "produce" is assumed to refer to fruit or vegetables, not to animals, unless, M. 4:1C, it is stated in a very general way. The dispute on summer fruit is clear as given, T. 4:1D, T. 4:2. *Pe'ah*, T. 4:3A, seems to refer to plants which have plaited leaves. T. 4:3C-D go over the ground of specific as against rather general phrasing of the vow. E brings us to M. 7:2B, F to M. 7:1F, and H-I, T. 4:4, to M. 7:3. The exposition of Judah's saying is better than M.'s, but matters were not obscure to begin with.

7:4-5

I A. "He who vows not to enter a house is permitted to enter the upper room," the words of R. Meir.

B. And sages say, "The upper room is covered by the category of the house [and he is prohibited from entering it]."

C. He who vows not to enter the upper room is permitted to enter the house.

M. 7:4

II A. "He who vows not to use a bed is permitted to use a couch," the words of R. Meir.

B. And sages say, "A couch is covered by the category of the bed [and he is prohibited from making use of a couch]."

C. He who vows not to make use of a couch is permitted to make use of a bed.

D. He who vows not to enter a city is permitted to enter into the border of the city but prohibited from entering into its confines.

E. But he who vows not to enter a house is prohibited from entering beyond the jamb of the door and inwards.

M. 7:5

M. 7:4 and M. 7:5A-C follow the same formal pattern. M. 7:5D and E are independent; *but* (ʾBL) at M. 7:5E links M. 7:5E to D. Meir's two disputes repeat the same point, which is made articulate by sages. Both parties, of course, will concur on C, since making mention of "the upper room" or "the couch" does not invoke the encompassing category of the house or the bed. The border of the city, D, is the two thousand cubits round about in all directions. These begin from the confines. The confines are seventy *amah* and four *tefaḥs* around the city in all directions. The midpoint of the door-jamb marks the beginning of the house proper. How this contrasts to D is not self-evident.

7:6-7

A. [He who says,] "*Qonam* be these pieces of fruit for me," "They are *qonam* for my mouth," "They are *Qonam* to my mouth,"—

B. he is prohibited [from eating] whatever he may exchange for those [pieces of fruit] and whatever grows from them as well.

C. [If he says, "*Qonam* if] I eat [these pieces of fruit]," ["*Qonam*] if I taste them,"

D. he is permitted to eat whatever he may exchange for those pieces of fruit and whatever grows from them.

E. [This is the case] of something the seed of which perishes.

F. But in the case of something the seed of which does not perish, even what grows from what grows from it is prohibited.

M. 7:6

A. He who says to his wife, "*Qonam* be [the results of] the work of your hands for me," "They are *qonam* for my mouth," "They are *qonam* to my mouth"—

B. he is prohibited to make use of things exchanged for them or things which grow from them as well.

C. [If he said, "*Qonam*] that I shall not eat," or "That I shall not taste,"

D. then he is permitted to eat or taste things exchanged for them and things which grow from them.

E. This is the rule for something the seed of which perishes.

F. But in the case of something the seed of which does not perish, even things which grow from the things which grow from them are prohibited.

M. 7:7

M. wishes to contrast a prohibition against something and whatever derives from it with a prohibition limited to the thing itself, A-B as against

C-D in both M. 7:6 and M. 7:7. E-F in both pericopae then gloss the foregoing. If he speaks of deriving benefit from the pieces of fruit in general, then the prohibition extends to whatever the fruit yields, either in exchange or in further growth. But if he says he will not *eat* or *taste* those pieces of fruit, that is what he cannot do with them. But he may derive benefit from them in any other way. In the case of something the seed of which does not perish, E-F, however, part of the original produce is in the later yield of the seed.

7:8-9

A. [He who says, "*Qonam*] be what you are making if I eat it until Passover," "Be what you are making if I wear it until Passover,"—
B. [if] she prepared [these things] before Passover, he is permitted to eat or to wear [what she has made] after Passover.
C. [If he said, "*Qonam* be to me] what you are making until Passover if I eat it," "What you are making until Passover if I wear it,"—
D. [if] she prepared these things before Passover, he is prohibited from eating or wearing [what she has made] after Passover.

M. 7:8

A. [He who says, "*Qonam*] be what you enjoy on my account before Passover if you go to your father's house before the Festival of Sukkot,"
B. [if] she went before Passover, she is prohibited from deriving benefit from him until Passover.
C. [If she went] after Passover, he is subject to the rule, *He shall not profane his word* (Num. 30:2).
D. [He who says, "*Qonam*] be what you enjoy on my account up to the Festival of Sukkot if you go to your father's house before Passover,"
E. and she went to her father's house before Passover,
F. she is prohibited from deriving benefit from him up to the Festival of Sukkot.
G. But she is permitted to go to her father's house after Passover.

M. 7:9

Continuing M. 7:7A but shifting the discourse, M. 7:8 sets up a contrast between A-B and C-D. In the former case the man vows not *to make use up to Passover* of what the wife makes. He may use these things after Passover. In the latter case, he vows not to make use *of what she makes up to Passover*. At no time may he derive benefit from what she makes before Passover. The reason is clear from the language he has used: What you make is *prohibited* to me *until* Passover, as against, what you make *until* Passover is *prohibited* to me. M. 7:9A has the man prohibit his wife from deriving benefit from him up to Passover if she goes home before Sukkot.

B makes the obvious point that, if she goes to the father's house before Passover, she cannot derive benefit from her husband until Passover. That is, after all, what the husband has said. If she went after Passover but before Sukkot, his vow is null, since he has not made an enforceable provision for this situation. But she surely should not go to the father's house before Sukkot. If the man now prohibits the wife from enjoying benefit from him up to Sukkot if she goes to the father's house before Passover and she does so, she cannot derive benefit from him up to Sukkot. But, G, the prohibition applied only to Passover, as D explicitly says—a needless clarification.

> A. [He who says,] "*Qonam* be this loaf of bread which I am tasting if I go to such-and-such a place tomorrow"—
> B. if he ate it, lo, he is subject to not going to that place.
> C. And if he went to that place, he is subject to the rule, *He shall not profane his word* (Num. 30:2).
>
> T. 4:5 L p. 111, ls. 13-15

> A. Even though there are vows which we have said are not binding, how do we know that one should not make such a vow with the plan of annulling it?
> B. Scripture says, *He shall not profane his word* (Num. 30:2).
> C. That is to say, he should not treat his words as profane [and unconsecrated].
> D. Another matter: *He should not profane his word*—
> E. Even a sage does not annul his vow for himself.
> F. [If he said to him, "Lend me your spade," [and the other said, "*Qonam* be this spade] if it is mine," "*Qonam* be these things to me if I have a spade [at all],"
> G. one may be sure that he has no spade at all.
>
> T. 4:6 L pp. 111-112, ls. 15-19

T. now treats the situation in which a man makes an essentially unenforceable vow, as at M. 7:9A-C. If the man eats the loaf, A, he now is not permitted to go to that place, B. And if he does so, he has violated his vow. But the bread is not available to be subject to the vow which he originally made. This sort of procedure, T. 4:6, is legal but improper and should be discouraged. T. 4:6F-G are independent. The point of F is that once the man says what he says, the spade is prohibited for his use and thus leaves his domain, which is why G follows.

CHAPTER NINE

NEDARIM CHAPTER EIGHT

The concluding discussion of how we interpret and apply the language used in vows is presented in this chapter, which contains three units, M. 8:1-3, M. 8:4-6, and M. 8:7. A good bit of formal care is exhibited in all three. The first set, a five-part construction followed by a triplet, deals with time-limits on a vow. If one says, "*Qonam* if I taste wine today," the day ends with nightfall. We then deal successively with week, month, year, and septennate. Next we have language referring to the arrival of Passover and its conclusion. M. 8:4-6 carries this same theme onward. If one vows that he will not do so-and-so until the summer harvest, the meaning is, until people bring in produce in baskets. If it is until the summer-harvest is over, the vow is effective until the harvest-knives are put away. We further ask about the rainy seasons, and, then, about the problem of the intercalated year. Finally, by way of transition to the concluding unit, we ask about the normal usage and intention of someone, e.g., who vows not to drink wine until Passover. He means, until the time that people usually drink wine on Passover, so the man may drink wine on Passover itself. M. 8:7 presents two doublets, each in perfect formal structure, about the loosing of vows, a fine transition to the concluding unit of the tractate. If one says that he will not benefit from the other unless the other takes a gift for his children, the fellow annuls the vow without consulting a sage (= M. 3:1). If, likewise, people were nagging a man to marry his sister's daughter and he said, "*Qonam* be what she enjoys which is mine for all times," the vow applies only to the circumstance of marriage, not to any other situation. The inclusion at M. 8:7B of annulling the vow without a sage's intervention at this point seems to be a secondary detail of internal exegesis, but in context of Chapter Nine it forms a significant transition, which, as we shall note, T. for its part makes explicit.

8:1-3

I   A. [He who says,] "*Qonam* if I taste wine today," is prohibited only to nightfall.
II B. [If he referred to] "this week," he is prohibited the entire week, and the Sabbath [which is coming is included] in that past week.
III C. [If he referred to] "this month," he is prohibited that entire month, but the day of the New Month [is assigned] to the coming month.

IV D. [If he referred to] "this year," he is prohibited that entire year, but the New Year ['s day] is assigned to the year which follows.

V E. [If he referred to] "this septennate," he is prohibited that entire septennate, and the Seventh Year is assigned to the last septennate [and is included in the vow].

F. And if he said, "One day," "One week," "One month," "One year," "One septennate," he is prohibited from that day until the same day [or month, year, or septennate following].

M. 8:1

I A. [If he said], "To Passover," he is prohibited until it comes.

II B. [If he said,] "Until it will be [Passover]," he is prohibited until it is over.

III C. [If he said,] "Until before Passover,"

D. R. Meir says, "He is prohibited until it comes."

E. R. Yosé says, "He is prohibited until is is over."

M. 8:2

A. [If he said,] "Until harvest," "Until vintage," "Until olive-gathering," he is forbidden only until it comes.

B. This is the general principle: As to any occasion whose time is fixed, if he said, "Until it comes," he is prohibited until it comes.

C. [If] he said, "Until it will be," he is prohibited until it is over.

D. But as to any occasion whose time is not fixed, whether he said, "Until it will be," and whether he said, "Until it comes," he is prohibited only until it comes.

M. 8:3

The set consists of two parts, M. 8:1A-E, glossed at F, and M. 8:2, M. 8:3A, the whole glossed by M. 8:3B-D. The point is clear throughout. If the man specifies a particular period of time during which he will not drink wine, that period of time requires definition, as indicated. If, F, he specified a day, week, or month, and so on, these periods are measured from that moment and for a period of twenty-four hours, seven days, and so on. The language of M. 8:2A and B is clear as given. M. 8:2C refers to (L)PNY Passover, producing the indicated dispute, D-E. M. 8:3A is not independent, for B-C explain M. 8:2, and then D explains A.

8:4-6

I A. [If he said,] "Until summer [harvest]," "Until it will be summer [harvest]," it applies until the people will begin to bring in produce in baskets.

II B. [If he said,] "Until summer [harvest] is over," it applies until the knives are put away.

III C. [If he said], "Until the harvest," it applies until the people begin to harvest the wheat-crop but not the barley-crop.

68 NEDARIM CHAPTER EIGHT 8:4-6

D. All is in accord with the place in which he takes his oath:
E. If it was in the mountain, [we follow conditions in] the mountain.
F. And if it was in the valley, [we follow conditions in] the valley.

M. 8:4

IV A. [If he said,] "Until the rains," "Until the rains will come," it applies until the second shower has fallen [in November].

B. Rabban Simeon b. Gamaliel says, "Until the time of the second shower comes."

V C. "[If he said,] 'Until the rains stop,' it applies until Nisan is wholly passed," the words of R. Meir.

D. R. Judah says, "Until Passover is passed."

I E. [If he said,] "*Qonam* be wine if I taste it this year," and the year received an intercalated month, he is prohibited during the year and the added month.

II F. [If he said,] "Until the beginning of Adar," it applies until the beginning of the First Adar [not the intercalated one].

III G. [If he said], "Until the end of Adar," it applies until the end of the First Adar.

I H. R Judah says, "[If he said,] '*Qonam* be wine if I taste it until Passover will be,' he is prohibited only up to the night of Passover.

I. "For this man intended to refer only until the time that people usually drink wine."

M. 8:5

II A. [If] he said, "*Qonam* be meat if I taste it until there will be the fast," he is prohibited only up to the night of the fast.

B. For this man intended to refer only to the time at which people usually eat meat.

III C. R. Yosé his son says, "[If he said,] '*Qonam* be garlic if I taste it until it will be the Sabbath,' he is prohibited only up to the night of the Sabbath.

D. "For this man intended to refer only to the time at which people usually eat garlic."

M. 8:6

I am inclined to think that at M. 8:4-5D we have a five-part construction, as indicated, with a major interpolation at M. 8:4D-F, and a further triplet at M. 8:5E-G. M. 8:5H-I belong with M. 8:6A-B, C-D. The main points of M. 8:4A-C, 8:5A-E + F-G, hardly require comment. The language used at various points receives definition. D-F form a useful gloss of M. 8:4A-C: in terms of conditions prevailing in the mountains. The disputes of M. 8:5A-B, C-D, are about matters of detail. The intention of the man is interpreted at M. 8:5H-I, just as Judah makes explicit. If he vowed not to drink wine until Passover, he meant, up to that point at Passover at which people drink wine, so too with eating meat before the Day of Atonement. Judah's son carries his father's reasoning forward with the third entry of the triplet, M. 8:6C-D. The concluding pericope, M. 8:7, will present a further essay on interpreting what people generally are thinking when they make various statements.

> A. He who makes a vow "until the summer" in [the mountains of] Galilee and went down into the valleys, even though the summer came in the valleys, is prohibited until the summer comes to Galilee [M. 8:4D-F].
> B. Said R. Yosé, "At first they ruled, 'He who is prohibited by vow from deriving benefit from his fellow without further specification until Passover is prohibited until the moment at which the Passover-lamb is slaughtered.
> C. "After the Temple was destroyed, the vow remained in effect for the entire day" [M. 8:5H-I].
> D. This is the general principle: As to any occasion whose time is fixed, he is prohibited until before it [M. 8:2C]:
> E. *R. Meir says, "He is prohibited until it comes."*
> F. *R. Yosé says, "He is prohibited until it is over"* [M. Ned. 8:2].
> G. [If he said,] "Until the rains end," he is prohibited until the first night of Passover [M. 8:5C-D].
> H. [If he said], "Until the Sukkot are torn down," he is prohibited until the last night of the Festival [of Sukkot].
> I. [If he said], "Until Adar," it means, the first [M. 8:5F-G].
> J. And if the year was intercalated with the addition of a second Adar, he is prohibited until the second Adar.
>
> T. 4:7 L p. 112, ls. 19-26

T. systematically glosses M., as indicated, adding its own materials. The conditions defining the vow are personal to the one who takes it. Yosé refers to the situation prevailing before the destruction of the Temple; the same point is made of the day of the waving of the ^comer. D-F go over the ground of M. 8:2, the meaning of PNYW. G-J then review M. 8:5.

B. Ned. 62b restates T. 4:7A in a somewhat clearer way: "He who vows in Galilee, 'Until the fruit-harvest, and then descends to the valleys, though the fruit-harvest has begun in the valley, he is forbidden until the fruit-harvest in [the mountains of] Galilee."

8:7

> A. He who says to his fellow, "*Qonam* be benefit I derive from you, if you do not come and collect for your child a *kor* of wheat and two jugs of wine,"—
> B. lo, this one [the fellow] can annul his vow without consultation with a sage,
> C. and say to him, "Did you not speak only to do me honor? But this [*not* taking your wheat and wine for my children] is what I deem to be honorable!"
> D. And so: He who says to his fellow, "*Qonam* be benefit you derive from

me, if you do not come and give my son a *kor* of wheat and two jugs of wine"—

E. R. Meir says, "He is prohibited until he will give [what the other has demanded]."

F. And sages say, "Also: This one can annul his vow without consultation with a sage,

G. "and one [who made the vow] says to him, 'Lo, it is as if I have received what I demanded.' "

H. [If] they were nagging him to marry the daughter of his sister and he said, "*Qonam* be what she enjoys which is mine for all times"—

I. and so he who divorces his wife and says, "*Qonam* be what my wife enjoys of mine for all time"—

J. lo, these are permitted to derive benefit from him.

K. For this man intended [his vow] only with reference to [actual] marriage with them.

L. [If] one was nagging his friend to eat with him [and the other] said, "*Qonam* be your house if I enter it," "if I drink a single drop of cold water of yours,"

M. he is permitted to enter his house and to drink cold water of his.

N. For this man intended [his vow] only with reference to eating and drinking [but not merely coming into the house or taking a glass of cold water].

M. 8:7

We have two doublets, A-C + D-G, and H-K + L-N. The care at formal patterning is obvious and impressive, marred by only a single interpolation, I. The point in all instances is that we interpret the intent of the one who takes the vow in such wise as to place limits upon the vow's effectiveness. The stress that this is done without consultation with a sage, moreover, proves to be a significant redactional device, linking Chapter Nine to the concluding elements of this long unit on the interpretation of the language of vows. A-C are self-evident. The point of the dispute at D-G is sages' view that the one who made the vow in this instance may annul its effects. T. will assign the point in dispute to the first case as much as the second. In the concluding doubtlet, the important exegesis is provided by M. itself, at K and N.

A. *He who says to his fellow, "Qonam if I derive any benefit whatsoever from you, if you do not come and collect for your child a kor of wheat and two jugs of wine,"* [M. 8:7A]—

B. and [between-times] an occasion of mourning befell him, or [he was prevented] by constraint, or [he had an occasion for a banquet], or there were rains—

C. he is permitted [the vow is not binding].

D. "But under all circumstances he is prohibited [from deeming the vow null] until he will find absolution for his vow through the ruling of a sage," the words of R. Meir.

E. And sages say, "*Also: This one can annul his vow without consultation with a sage.*

"*He may say to him, 'Did you not speak only to do me honor? But this [not taking your wheat and wine for my children] is what I deem to be honorable!'* " [M. Ned. 8:7B-C].

F. And so: *He who says to his fellow, "Qonam if you derive benefit from me, if you do not come and give my son a kor of wheat and two jugs of wine"* [M. Ned. 8:7D].

G. *[If] one was nagging his fellow to eat with him* during a banquet *[and] said, "Qonam be your house if I enter it"* [M. 8:7L],

H. during the banquet, he is prohibited from going in there.

I. After the banquet, he is permitted to go in there.

J. R. Judah says, "If one was nagging his fellow during the festival to eat with him and said to him, '*Qonam* be your house, if I enter it,'

"during the festival he is prohibited from entering it.

"After the festival he is permitted to enter it."

T. 4:8 L pp. 112-113, ls. 26-35

A. *[If] one was nagging his fellow to eat with him* during a banquet *and said to him, "Qonam be your house if I enter it,"* during the banquet, he is prohibited from going in there. After the banquet he is permitted to go in there.

B. *[If] he said, "Qonam be your house if I enter it," "If I drink a single drop of cold water of yours,"* [M. 8:7L],

C. *he is permitted to enter his house* [M. 8:7M]

D. and to wash with him in cold water.

E. But he is prohibited from eating or drinking with him.

T. 4:9 L p. 113, ls. 35-38

As is T.'s way, the restatement of M. 8:7A provides the occasion to read into M. 8:7 the considerations of M. 9:1ff., that is, circumstances which allow for the annulment of a vow. The dispute now is whether or not, under these particular circumstances—not envisaged at M. 8:7 but important in Chapter Nine—a sage must be consulted or not. In order to accomplish this feat of redactional exegesis, T. must then reorient sages' saying as well, E. Then F repeats M. 8:7D with the indication that here too the stated dispute applies. But, of course, what M. 8:7 has under dispute is a quite different point. T. 4:8G-J apply M.'s principle to T.'s somewhat more subtle case. We go so far in interpretating the vow as to limit the time at which the vow is effective. T. 4:9 repeats the same matter.

CHAPTER TEN

NEDARIM CHAPTER NINE

Six grounds for absolution of a vow—whether or not a sage in particular has to declare it null—are laid out in our chapter, at M. 9:1A, 9:2A, 9:4A, 9:5A, 9:6A, and 9:9A, each opening, *They unloose a vow by*...The theory in each case is that if a man confesses that, had he known such-and-such would be affected or would be the effect, he would not have vowed, the vow is null. Such a confession, if the pretext is acceptable, absolves him of the vow, e.g., if he turns out to be unable to carry out one of the commandments, if he vows with the result that he or his children suffer disgrace, and similar conceptions. While authorities of both Yavneh and Usha make their appearance, the whole surely is the work of the final formulation. Some of the proposed grounds are in the names of individuals, others in the names of the generality of sages, yet the formal structure of the chapter, neatly laid out as it is, is indifferent to that fact.

The first two conceptions, that we unloose a vow by reference to the honor of the person's father and mother, and that we unloose a vow by reference to something which takes place after the vow has been made, are assigned to Eliezer. Sages in both cases reject Eliezer's remarkably lenient view, with the correct conception that if such a pretext for absolution were to be validated, then there never would be valid vowing.

M. 9:3-4 give us two rulings of Meir. In the first he takes up the position of sages *vis à vis* Eliezer. He concurs that one cannot use as a pretext something which happens only after the vow has been made. At the moment of the vow, there were no false assumptions. But, he says, some things appear to have taken place later on but in fact are not so at all. If a man vows and states a reason for his vow, and the reason turns out to be null, then the vow may also be nullified, and this is even after the fact. He gives the pretext about vowing and turning out not to be able to carry out a Scriptural commandment.

The third unit is formed by M. 9:5-10, which rests upon M. 9:5A, 9:6A, and 9:9A, with each of these propositions richly illustrated. The first is that the state of a wife's marriage-contract may serve as pretext, with illustration through a precedent of ʿAqiba. The second, M. 9:6, has a suitable pretext in the incapacity of the man properly to observe Sabbaths or festivals. This yields an immense secondary conception. If a vow is released for a single day, e.g., a Sabbath, is it then permanently and wholly null? ʿAqiba is cited to the effect that if a vow is partially nullified, it is wholly released (= the House of Hillel at M. 3:4), and the whole of M. 9:7 and M. 9:8 form two immense illustrations of ʿAqiba's principle. M. 9:9 then allows as a pretext the shame of oneself or one's children. M. 9:10 reverts to the issue of M. 9:2-3, a change in circumstances which was not foreseen when the vow was taken.

9:1-2

A. R. Eliezer says, "They unloose a vow for a person by [reference to] the honor of his father or mother."
B. And sages prohibit.
C. Said R. Ṣadoq, "Before they unloose a vow for him by [reference to] the honor of his father or mother, let them unloose his vow by reference to the honor of the Omnipresent.
D. "If so, there will be no vows!"
E. But sages concede to R. Eliezer that, in a matter which is between him and his mother or father, they unloose his vow by [reference to] the honor of his father or mother.

M. 9:1

A. And further did R. Eliezer say, "They unloose a vow by reference to what happens unexpectedly [a new fact]."
B. And sages prohibit.
C. How so?
D. [If] he said, "*Qonam* be what I enjoy which derives from so-and-so," and the person was appointed a scribe,
E. or the person was marrying off his son in the near future,
F. and he [who took the vow] then said, "If I had known that he would be appointed a scribe,
"or that he would be marrying off his son in the near future,
"I should never have made such an oath!"—
G. [If he said,] "*Qonam* be this house if I enter it," and it was turned into a synagogue,
H. [If he said, "If I had known that it would be made into a synagogue, I should never have made such an oath"—
I. R. Eliezer permits [declares the vow to be unbound].
J. And sages prohibit [declare the vow to remain binding].

M. 9:2

The formal traits of M. 9:1 require that we set aside Ṣadoq's interpolation on sages' side, C-D; the pericope's basic elements, A-B, are clear. The concession at E is unimpressive, since Eliezer's basic point has nothing to do with so limited a frame as what sages allow. Eliezer would permit a man to say that if he had known that he would bring dishonor upon his parents, he would never have made such a vow. Such, Eliezer's view, would constitute grounds for absolution. In point of fact M. 9:9 will come close to exactly the same principle. M. 9:2A-B follow the form established at M. 9:1A-B. Then we have a rather elaborate set of illustrations, D-F, G-H, followed by the fixed formulary, I-J. The points are clear as given.

9:3-4

A. R. Meir says, "There are things which appear to be equivalent to what happens unexpectedly, but are not, in fact, treated as equivalent to what happens unexpectedly."

B. And sages do not concur with him.

C. How so?

D. [If] he said, "*Qonam* that I shall never marry so-and-so, for her father is evil,"

E. [and] they told him, "He died," or "He has repented,"—

F. [if he said], "*Qonam* be this house, that I shall not enter it, for there is a bad dog inside," or, "snake inside,"

G. [and] they told him, "The dog died," or, "The snake was killed,"—

H. lo, these appear to be equivalent to that which happens unexpectedly, yet are not treated as equivalent to that which happens unexpectedly.

I. And sages do not concur with him.

M. 9:3

A. And further did R. Meir say, "They unloose his [vow] by reference to what is written in the Torah, saying to him,

B. "'If you had known that you would transgress the commandment, *You shall not take vengeance*, or, *You shall not bear a grudge* [Lev. 19:18], or, *You shall not hate your brother in your heart* (Lev. 19:17), or, *You shall love your neighbor as yourself* (Lev. 19:18), or *That your brother may live with you* (Lev. 25:36), [would you have taken such a vow?] Now what happens if he becomes poor and you will be unable to help him out?'

C. "And he says, 'If I had known that matters were thus, I should never have taken such a vow'—

D. "lo, this [vow] is loosed."

M. 9:4

Meir's two units, M. 9:3 and M. 9:4 are conceptually distinct. At M. 9:3 he carries forward the discussion of M. 9:2, with the claim that, while, in line with sages' view, one does not grant absolution for a vow on the grounds of what happens unexpectedly, if one specifies a reason for his vow and his reason turns out to be nullified in the course of events, then the vow is absolved. This, Meir holds, is not equivalent to absolving the man of his vow on grounds of unexpected or unforeseen events. So he proposes an interesting gloss to sages' position *vis à vis* Eliezer at M. 9:2. His two cases, D-E, F-G, are clear as given. In both we treat the explanation of the vow, ("For her father is evil") as a condition of the vow. If then the condition is nullified, so is the vow. M. 3:2 will concur. Meir's further position, M. 9:4, invokes Scriptural commandments as grounds for nullifying the vow. Sages at M. 9:1E will concur with reference to honoring parents.

9:5

A. They unloose a man's vow by reason of the wife's marriage-contract.
B. M^cSH B: A certain man vowed not to derive benefit from his wife.
C. And her marriage-contract called for a payment of four hundred *denars*.
D. And he came before R. ʿAqiba, who required him to pay off her marriage-contract.
E. He said to him, "Rabbi, my father left [an estate worth] eight hundred *denars*, and my brother received four hundred, and I four hundred. Is it not enough for her if she collects two hundred and I keep two hundred?"
F. R. ʿAqiba said to him, "Even if you have to sell the hair of your head, you still have to pay off her marriage-contract."
G. He said to him, "Now if I had ever known that things were so, I should never have taken such a vow."
H. And R. ʿAqiba declared the vow to be not binding.

M. 9:5

M. 9:5A continues the basic formulary pattern, and the precedent, B-H, suitably illustrates the rule. The man enjoyed benefit from the marriage-contract and had to pay it back.

A. He who prohibits himself by a vow from deriving benefit from a house [and] an upper room.
B. and finds out that, before his vow, they had fallen to him by inheritance or had been given to him as a gift,
C. [and said], "If I had known that that was the case, I should never have taken such a vow," lo, this [vow] is not binding.
D. M^cSH B: A certain man prohibited his wife by vow from going up to Jerusalem.
E. And she went and treated his vow as not binding.
F. And he turned to R. Yosé.
G. He [Yosé] said to him, "Now if you had known that she would treat your words as null [when she was] not in your presence, would you have imposed such a vow on her?"
H. He said to him, "Never!"
I. And R. Yosé declared [the vow] not binding.
J. R. Ishmael b. R. Yosé says, "They say to him, 'If someone had appeased you, would you have taken such a vow?'

K. "If he says, 'No,'
L. "then, lo, this [vow] is not binding."
M. R. Judah b. Betera says, "They say to him, 'If you [then] had this [present] attitude, would you have taken such a vow?'
N. "If he says, 'No,'
O. "then, lo, this [vow] is not binding."

T. 5:1 (continued) L pp. 113-114, ls. 1-7

T. 5:1A-C, D-I, J-L, and M-O give us four examples of Meir's position at M. 9:4. These are vows which are annulled not because of something which happens unexpectedly, but because of an assumed fact or a condition (stated or not) which turns out to be invalid. The man did not assume that, before his vow, he had inherited the house; obviously, had he known that that was so, he would not have taken such a vow. It is not nullified; it is null to begin with.

9:6-8

A. They unloose [vows] by reference to festival days and Sabbaths.
B. At first they said, "On those particular days [the vows] are not binding, but for all other days they are binding."
C. But then R. ʿAqiba came along and taught that the vow part of which is unloosed is wholly unloosed.

M. 9:6

A. How so?
B. [If] he said, "*Qonam* be what I enjoy from any one of you"—
C. [if] his vow with reference to any one of them was declared not binding, the vow with reference to all of them was declared not binding.
D. [If he said, "*Qonam*] be what I enjoy from this one and from that one,"
E. [if] the vow pertaining to the first was declared not binding, all of them are no longer subject to the vow.
F. [If] the vow pertaining to the last one of them was declared not binding, the last one is permitted [to give benefit to the man] but the rest of them are prohibited.
G. [If the vow] was declared not binding for one in the middle, from him and onward, it is not binding, but from him and backward, it is binding.
H. [If he said,] "Let what I enjoy of this one's be *qorban*, and of that one's be *qorban*," they require an opening [absolution] for each and every one of them.

M. 9:7

A. [If he said,] "*Qonam* be wine, because it is bad for the belly,"
B. [and] they told him, "But isn't old wine good for the belly?"
C. he is permitted to drink old wine.
D. And not old wine alone is permitted.

E. But all wine [is permitted].
F. [If he said,] "*Qonam* be an onion if I taste it, for onions are bad for the heart,"
H. then Cyprus onions are permitted for him.
I. And not Cyprus onions alone are permitted,
J. but all onions [are permitted].
K. There was a case along these lines, and R. Meir declared him permitted to eat all onions.

M. 9:8

M. 9:6's point is that if someone vowed to fast for a given period of time and then admits that had he known it was prohibited to fast on the Sabbath or on a festival, he would not have vowed, he may be absolved from his vow. But A is hardly the point of what is a huge construction.

A serves as an introduction to M. 9:6B-C + M. 9:7, 8. By itself A hardly requires the following clarifications. B-C form a suitable secondary connection between A and C + M 9:7, 8. Then the whole of M. 9:7 and M. 9:8 illustrates ʿAqiba's position, in particular at M. 9:7A + B-C. Some complications of that illustration are laid forth at M. 9:7D-G + H. I see no reason to doubt M. 9:7 is a unitary composition. A still more suitable illustration is given by M. 9:8, with its extended "amplifications" at D-E, I-J, making clear the link to ʿAqiba's original principle. M. 9:8 also must be seen as a unitary composition, but, of course, one quite independent of M. 9:7. So we have in hand two distinct essays in the application of ʿAqiba's view that a vow loosed in part is wholly unbound.

The secondary development of the principle at M. 9:7D-H requires further attention. Why is it, in particular, that the contrast between E and F is drawn? Because at C the vow affecting the whole lot depends upon the first. It was in regard to the first vow that the language, *Qonam*, was invoked to begin with. And that same reasoning accounts for F and G. And whence that reasoning, if not H? For there we have the affective language severally invoked in the context of each and every person, in which case each and every one has to be subjected to absolution. A vow, distinct and individual, has affected each one. So in this instance unbinding one vow has no affect upon the others. Once more M. supplies its own exegesis.

P. R. Nathan says, "There is a sort of vow, part of which is not binding and part of which is binding [*vs.* M. 9:6C].
Q. "How so?
R. "[If] he took a vow not to eat fruit in a basket in which were *shuah*-figs, [and then] he said, 'Had I known that there were *shuah*-figs in it, I should have taken a vow only in regard to the rest of what is in the basket,' he is permitted to eat the *shuah*-figs in the basket but prohibited from eating any of the other fruit in the basket.

78   NEDARIM CHAPTER NINE 9:6-8

S. "[If] he took a vow not to eat onions, [and then] he said, 'Now if I had known that Cyprus onions are good for the heart, I should have taken a vow only not to eat other kinds of onions,' he is permitted to eat Cyprus figs but prohibited from eating all other kinds of figs" [M. 9:8F-H].

T. [Now this was the case] *until R. ʿAqiba came along and taught that an oath, part of which is unloosed is wholly unloosed* [M. 9:6C].

U. *How so?*

V. *[If] he says, "Qonam be what I enjoy from any one of you, and [if] his vow with respect to one of them is declared not binding, then the vow with reference to all of them is declared not binding* [M. Ned. 9:7A-C].

W. *[If he said], "Qonam be what I enjoy from this one and from that one and from the other one, and the vow pertaining to the one in the middle was declared not binding, then from him and onward, it is not binding, but from him and backward, it is binding* [M. Ned. 9:7G].

X. [If he said,] "*Qonam* be what I enjoy from so-and-so," and then he hesitated for a time sufficient to say something and went and said, "Also for so-and-so," he is prohibited in the case of the first, but permitted in the case of the second.

Y. How much is an interval sufficient to say something?

Z. Time enough for a master to ask after the welfare of his disciple.

ZZ. [If] he said, "*Qonam* be what I enjoy from Mr. So-and-so, and further, from Mr. Such-and-such,"

AA. [or if he said], "For Mr. So-and-so and Mr. Such-and-such, *Qonam* be benefit I derive," lo, these are deemed to be two separate and distinct vows.

BB. [If] the first is declared not binding, then the second is not binding.

CC. [If] the second is not binding, the first has not been declared not binding [and has to be unloosed on its own] [M. 9:7E, F].

T. 5:1 (concluded) L pp. 114-115, ls. 8-19

A. [If he said,] "Qonam be benefit I derive from Mr. So-and-so and from anyone from whom I may obtain absolution on his account"—

B. they go and obtain absolution in respect to the first and then go and gain absolution in respect to the second [statement].

T. 5:2 L p. 115, ls. 19-20

Nathan phrases M. 9:8 in such wise as to reject ʿAqiba's principle. There can be no doubt that his pericope is meant to differ head-on with ʿAqiba's position. T. proceeds in its own direction at X-Z. But T. thus introduces its reasoning on M. 9:7E, F. ZZ-CC revert to M. 9:7E, F. The point at ZZ is that the man has linked the second vow to the first with the language, and *further*. At AA, the same is the case. Even though we have distinct vows, AA, we still invoke M.'s conception at BB, CC.

T. 5:2's point is that the first vow has to be absolved first of all. So long as it is not unbound, he still is permitted to derive benefit from all sages, and no vow is brought for absolution before its prohibition is binding (Lieberman, p. 115, to ls. 20).

A. [If] he intended to take a vow by a whole-offering and took a vow by a Nazirite's vow,
B. by an offering, and took a vow by an oath,
C. it is not binding.
D. [If he intended to take a vow] by a whole-offering and took a vow by an offering,
E. by a *ḥerem* and took a vow by that which is sanctified [to the Temple],
F. it is binding.

T. 5:3 L p. 115, ls. 21-22

A. [If] he took a vow by a Nazirite-vow, an offering, and an oath, they unloose his vow by a single pretext covering all of them.
B. [If] he said, "I have taken a vow but I do not know by which of these two I have taken a vow," they unloose his vow through a single pretext covering all of them.

T. 5:4 L p. 115, ls. 22-24

The point is that at D, E, the *whole-offering* is of the same genus as *offering*. When we come to absolve him of the vow, we say, "If you had known that such-and-such was the case, would you have vowed by a Nazirite-vow or an oath or an offering," without seeking a pretext for each and every one of them (*TK* p. 473).

A. He who takes a vow not to derive benefit from a town (and) seeks absolution from a sage in that town
B. and does not scruple that he grants absolution in his own interest.
C. [If he takes a vow not to derive benefit from] an Israelite, he seeks absolution from a sage who is an Israelite,
D. and does not scruple that he grants absolution in his own interest.

T. 5:5 L p. 115, ls. 24-26

At A the man can seek absolution from a sage in some other town. So only after the fact is A-B's procedure acceptable. But at C-D, there is no choice and at the outset the man is permitted to seek absolution in this way, since he has taken a vow not to derive benefit from all sages (Lieberman, p. 115, to ls. 24, 25).

9:9

A. They unloose a vow for a man by reference to his own honor and by reference to the honor of his children.
B. They say to him, "Had you known that the next day they would say about you, 'That's the way of so-and-so, going around divorcing his wives.'
C. "and that about your daughters they'd be saying, 'They're daughters of a divorcee! What did their mother do to get herself divorced' [would you have taken a vow]?"

D. And [if] he then said, "Had I known that things would be that way, I should never have taken such a vow,"

E. lo, this [vow] is not binding.

M. 9:9

B + C illustrate both of A's pretexts, a fine work of expansion.

9:10

A. [If one said,] "*Qonam* if I marry that ugly Miss So-and-so," and lo, she is beautiful,

B. "...dark...," and lo, she is light,

C. "...short...," and lo, she is tall,

D. he is permitted [to marry] her,

E. not because she was ugly and turned beautiful, dark and turned light, short and turned tall, but because the vow [to begin with] was based on erroneous facts.

F. M'ŚH B: A certain man prohibited by vow that from the daughter of his sister he should derive benefit.

G. And they brought her into the house of R. Ishmael and made her beautiful.

H. Said to him R. Ishmael, "My son, did you ever take a vow about this lass?"

I. He said to him, "Never!"

J. And R. Ishmael declared his [vow] not binding.

K. That moment R. Ishmael wept and said, "Israelite girls really are beautiful, but poverty makes them ugly."

L. And when R. Ishmael died, Israelite girls took up a lamentation, saying, "Israelite girls, weep over R. Ishmael."

M. And that is what [Scripture] says for Saul, "*Israelite girls, weep for Saul [who clothed you in scarlet delicately, who put ornaments of gold upon your apparel]*" (11 Samuel 1:24).

M. 9:10

A-E are a supplement to M. 9:2, 3 illustrating the view of M. 9:2's sages and M. 9:3's Meir. This is a matter of misconstruction of facts. In line with M. 3:2, this vow does not even require absolution. But Ishmael rejects A/E and allows the marriage even when the original facts were correct.

A. R. Judah b. Betera says, "*They unloose a vow for a man by reference to his own honor and by reference to the honor of his children*" [M. Ned. 9:9A].

B. R. Ishmael said to him, "You have acquired possession of her and of her clothing [possessions] on her back" [M. 9:10J].

C. When he died, what did they say before his bier?

D. "*Israelite girls,* weep over R. Ishmael, *who clothed you in scarlet delicately, who put ornaments of gold upon your apparel*" (11 Samuel 1:24) [M. 9:10L-M].

T. 5:6 L pp. 115-116, ls. 26-30

T. attributes M. 9:9A to Judah b. Betera and augments M. 9:10.

CHAPTER ELEVEN

NEDARIM CHAPTER TEN

This chapter is remarkably unified. While it seems to be in two parts, M. 10:1-3 + 4, M. 10:5-7 + 8, in fact it forms a smoothly unfolding discourse, moving from some general points to specific and problematic cases relying for their solution on those same general points. The first part—M. 10:1-3—speaks of a girl who is betrothed and raises the important question of who has the power to annul her vows in line with Numbers 10:14. (As we look back, we notice, therefore, how M. 9:10 has prepared the present theme for consideration.) Since both the father of the girl less than twelve years and six months and one day old and the husband who has betrothed that girl have power over her, both annul her vows. The real question comes at M. 10:2. If one or the other party dies, who retains power to abrogate her vows? If the husband died, the father has full power. But if the father dies, the husband does not acquire the father's power. M. 10:3 raises the expected question of a sequence of marriages and divorces on a given day. In such an unlikely case the father and the last husband annul the vows of the day (in line with M. 10:8: vows are to be annuled within a day, from sundown to sundown). M. 10:4 is a suitable interlude, telling us that sages' daughters are sent out by their prudent fathers with all vows annuled.

M. 10:5-7 lay out a triplet of three formally and conceptually tightly joined opinions of Eliezer and others. In all three instances Eliezer argues in favor of the husband's power to abrogate the vows of his wife. The first involves an adult girl who has awaited twelve months and not been taken in marriage. Now, we know, the husband must support her. He therefore has power to abrogate her vows, so Eliezer. Sages say that is so only when the marriage is fully consummated. In the second case, M. 10:6, we have the deceased childless brother's widow awaiting consummation of the levirate marriage. Eliezer holds that the levir may abrogate her vows, a position quite consistent with his overall view. ʿAqiba rejects this view and holds that the levir may not abrogate the vow. While the woman is bespoken, this is not equivalent to an act of betrothal in normal circumstances (an angle of interpretation important at T.). At M. 10:7, finally, Eliezer rules that, while the husband cannot *confirm* vows the wife will take before she actually takes them, he may *declare null* vows she will take before she actually takes them. This he argues is merely an exercise over her of power he has over his own vows, which he may declare null before he actually takes them. Sages hold that that is not the case. If he cannot confirm them, he also cannot annul them. M. 10:8, finally, gives some minor details of how the vow is abrogated, a fine conclusion to a chapter of remarkable consistency and unity.

10:1-3

A. A betrothed girl—
B. her father and her husband annul her vows.
C. [If] the father annulled her vow, but her husband did not annul her vow,
D. [or if] her husband annulled her vow, but her father did not annul her vow,
E. it is not annulled.
F. And it is not necessary to say, if one of them confirmed her vow [and the other did not, that it is not confirmed].

M. 10:1

A. [If] the father died, [his] authority does not pass to the husband.
B. [If] the husband died, [his] authority passes to the father.
C. In this regard the power of the father is greater than the power of the husband.
D. In another regard, however, the power of the husband is greater then the power of the father.
E. For the husband annuls the vows in the case of a grown-up woman, but the father does not annul the vows of a grown-up woman.

M. 10:2

A. [If] she took a vow while she was betrothed and was divorced on that very day [and] betrothed again on that same day [and repeated the process], even a hundred [times],
B. her father and her last husband annul her vows.
C. This is the general principle: In the case of any girl who has not gone forth to her own domain for a single moment, her father and her last husband annul her vows.

M. 10:3

We conclude the discussion begun at M. 10:1-2. The point is clear as given. The vow must be annulled on the day on which it is made (so M. 10:8).

The formal traits of M. 10:1-2 require little comment since the balance throughout is so carefully maintained. M. 10:1A-B introduce the main point, C, D + E, with the useful gloss at F. Then M. 10:2A and B stand in perfect balance, with a fine conclusion at C-E. The point is equally clear. The girl—between twelve years and twelve years, six months, and one day of age—is still within her father's domain. If, however, she is betrothed, she enters that of the husband. The man who has betrothed her has partial rights to invalidate or validate the vow, and the father at this point retains partial rights to do so. This gray area, so beloved of M., is nicely delineated at M. 10:1C, D. These statements then call for the clarification of M. 10:2A, B. The father's right to annul the vows does not pass upon his death to the husband. The husband has the right to annul his wife's vows only following consummation of the marriage. If the husband dies, however, the father regains the full right to annul the vows. But a husband does have the right to annul his wife's vows, even when she is an adult, while the father does not retain that right once the daughter becomes an adult, M. 10:2C-E.

A. Under what circumstances did they rule that *[if] the husband died, his power passes to the father* [M. 10:2B]?
B. When he [the husband] did not hear it, or heard it and was silent and died on that very day.
C. But [if] he [the husband] heard the vow and remained silent, heard it and confirmed it, and died on the text day, he [the father] has not got the power to annul it.
D. [If] the husband heard the vow and did not annul it, and the father did not suffice to hear the vow before the husband died,
E. this [too] is the case concerning which they ruled, *[If] the husband died, his power [to annul the vow] passes to the father.*

T. 6:2 L pp. 116-117, ls. 6-9

A. [If] her father heard the vow and did not annul it for her, and the husband did not suffice to hear the vow before the father died,
B. this is the sort of case concerning which they ruled, *[If] the father died, his authority [to annul her vows] does not pass to the husband* [M. 10:2A].
C. [If] her husband heard the vow and annulled it, but the father did not suffice to hear the vow before he died, lo, this is a case in which annulment is prohibited.
D. For the husband has the power to annul the vow only in conjunction with the father [M. 10:2C].
E. [If] her father heard the vow and annulled it for her, but the husband did not suffice to hear the vow before he died, let the father go back and annul the share of the husband.
F. Said R. Nathan, "This indeed represents the opinion of the House of Shammai.
F. "The House of Hillel say, 'He has not got the power to annul the vow.' "

T. 6:3 L p. 117, ls. 9-15

My text for T. 6:2B follows Lieberman's revisions, pp. 116-117 to ls. 7. If the husband had no chance to annul the vow, either because he did not know about it, or because he heard about it but died, then the father has the right to cancel the vow all by himself. In this circumstance the husband's right cannot have been exercised in any circumstances. But if the husband heard the vow and remained silent or confirmed it, and then died, the father cannot on his own cancel what the husband at least partially has confirmed. D then reverses matters, reverting to the case of B. So the answer to the question at A is at B and C, and the point is clear. T. 6:3 then proceeds to M. 10:2's correlative proposition: cases in which the husband by himself cannot annul the vow. If the father did not exercise his right, and the husband had no chance to do so before the father died, then the vow is not susceptible of annulment. C then reverses the case of A, with the same result. E allows a procedure by which the father takes over the right of the husband by annulling the husband's share upon his death. Surely M. contemplates just this sort of procedure in its statement at M. 10:2B. Nathan, however, maintains that this procedure accords only with the Shammaite opinion. The Hillelites maintain that in this case the father cannot annul the vow. Once the father has annulled his share, he cannot act on the share of the late husband.

A. *A betrothed girl—her father and her husband annul her vows* [M. 10:3].

B. [If] the father heard the vow and annulled it for her, but the husband did not suffice to hear the vow before he died,

C. and she then was betrothed, even to ten [further] men—

D. this is the case which they ruled, *Her father and her last husband annul her vows.*

E. [If] her father heard the vow and annulled it, but the husband did not suffice to hear the vow before he died,

F. and she was betrothed to another,

G. let her second husband go and annul the share [in the vow] of the first husband.

H. Said R. Nathan, "This indeed is the opinion of the House of Shammai.

I. "The House of Hillel say, 'He has not got the power to annul the vow.'"

J. Under what circumstances?

K. When he divorced her that day and remarried her that day [M. 10:3C], or he divorced her that day, and she was betrothed to someone else.

L. But if she reached maturity and was married,

M. or if she awaited consummation of the marriage for twelve months [and was not then married],

N. he [the father] has not got the power to annul her vows any longer.

T. 6:4 L pp. 117-118, ls. 16-22

T. 6:4, finally, brings us to the end of M.'s discussion. It supplies an example of how the father and the final husband exercise the power to annul the girl's vows, A-D. Then we turn to apply M. 10:2 to the considerations of M. 10:3. E-G treat matters as expected. That is, if the first husband cannot annul the vow in sequence with the father, the second husband may go along and annul the share of the first. The slight variation in the situation—the father annuls the vow, but the husband of that moment drops dead before he can do so, so the next husband instead does so—makes no difference whatsoever. Nathan once more assigns this view to the House of Shammai. Hillelites maintain that that is not possible any longer, even with the help of the second husband. J-N simply state the obvious fact that once the girl is mature and married or has passed the twelve-month-waiting-period and is not married, she wholly leaves the father's domain, and the father now loses his power to annul her vows.

10:4

A. The way of a disciple of sages [is this]:

B. Before his daughter goes forth from his home, he says to her, "All vows which you vowed in my house, lo, they are annulled."

C. And so the husband, before she enters his domain, says to her, "All vows which you vowed before you came into my domain, lo, they are annulled."

D. For after she enters his domain, he cannot annul [those prior] vows any more.

M. 10:4

M. provides for a clean slate and so avoids the sorts of problems laid out at M. 10:1-3.

10:5-7

I A. A grown-up woman who waited twelve months, and a widow who waited thirty days—

B. R. Eliezer says, "Since her husband is liable to support her, he annuls her vows."

C. And sages say, "The husband does not annul her vows until she enters his domain."

M. 10:5

II A. A deceased childless brother's widow awaiting levirate marriage, whether with a single levir or with two levirs—

B. R. Eliezer says, "He annuls her vows."

C. R. Joshua says, "That is the case with one, but not with two."

D. R. ʿAqiba says, "That is the case neither with one nor with two."

E. Said R. Eliezer, "Now if in the case of a woman whom he acquired for himself, lo, he annuls her vows, a woman who is acquired for him by Heaven, is it not logical that he should annul her vows?"

F. Said to him R. ᶜAqiba, "No. If you have so stated the rule in regard to a woman whom he has acquired for himself,

"the fact is that others have no claim on her.

"But will you say the same in the case of a woman acquired in his behalf by Heaven, in whom others [other levirs] have a claim?"

G. Said to him R. Joshua, " ᶜAqiba, your argument applies in the case of two levirs. What will you say in the case of one levir?"

H. He said to him, "A deceased childless brother's widow is not wholly [betrothed] to the levir [alone] in the way in which a betrothed girl is wholly [betrothed] to her husband."

M. 10:6

III A. He who says to his wife, "All vows which you will vow from this time until I return from such-and-such a place, lo, they are confirmed," has said nothing whatsoever.

B. [If he says], "Lo, they are annulled"—

C. R. Eliezer says, "It is annulled."

D. And sages say, "It is not annulled."

E. Said R. Eliezer, "If he annulled vows which have the force of a prohibition, will he not annul vows which do not have the force of a prohibition?"

F. They said to him, "Lo, Scripture says, *Her husband will confirm it and her husband will annul it* (Num. 30:14)—

G. "That which enters the category of confirmation enters the category of annulment. That which does not enter into the category of confirmation does not enter into the category of annulment."

M. 10:7

The three relevant rulings of Eliezer, joined in the present complex, exhibit shared conceptual and formal traits. In form all are disputes, set up in apocopation from the topic sentence. Each presents its own exegesis, a semblance of a debate at M. 10:5, and fully articulated ones at M. 10:6 and M. 10:7. A shared tendency also unites the pericopae, since Eliezer consistently rules in favor of the husband's authority to annul the vows of a wife in some ambiguous relationship, M. 10:5A, M. 10:6A, and M. 10:7A-B. So, in all, the hand which united them did fairly well. The provision of the debates, moreover, once more makes the exegesis of the disputes rather simple.

The problem of M. 10:5 is that the woman who has waited twelve months or the widow who has waited thirty days, both of whom have a claim for support on the man who betrothed them (M. Ket. 5:2), now may turn to the man to annul their vows. Sages reject this view, for the stated reason.

M. 10:6A brings us to the next gray area, the woman awaiting levirate marriage. The gloss, *whether with one or two*, means, whether the deceased is survived by one or more brothers, and serves Joshua's saying, since neither Eliezer nor ʿAqiba cares whether there are many or one. In line with his view that a widow awaiting marriage turns to her betrothed for abrogation of her vows, Eliezer consistently rules here that the levir, before he has consummated the marriage, also annuls the vows. (T. will add that the levir has bespoken the widow.) Joshua maintains that if there is one surviving brother, he may annul her vows, along the lines of Eliezer's reasoning. But if there are more than one, there is no power of abrogation. And, as we see, ʿAqiba says that in no circumstance may the levir or levirs annul the vows. Eliezer's argument is complete at E, and it is not a very strong one, since F refutes it without difficulty. If the husband had "acquired the woman for himself," meaning betrothed her under normal circumstances, he might annul her vows (e.g., along with the father in the case worked out at M. 10:1-3, or under the circumstances described at M. 10:5). Now Heaven has given him this sister-in-law. Surely he should have the same right to abrogate her vows. ʿAqiba's answer, F, is so strong, that it appears to me E is phrased solely to permit ʿAqiba to say what he has to say. A woman whom a man has acquired as his betrothed may not then be betrothed by anyone else. But all levirs have an equal right to take in levirate marriage the widow of their deceased childless brother. Without Joshua, C, G-H, the matter would come to a neat conclusion. Joshua simply invokes at G the issue introduced in his behalf at A, C. So once more the whole leads to providing ʿAqiba with a stunning reply. The sister-in-law is not wholly in the domain of the levir, for one who has sexual relations with her even after she is betrothed ("bespoken") to the levir is not liable to the death penalty. But the one who has sexual relations with a betrothed girl is liable to the death penalty (Deut. 22:24). The widow is not deemed so wholly betrothed to the levir as the betrothed girl is wholly betrothed to her husband. This is simply a more subtle formulation of what ʿAqiba says at F.

The third and final case is set up by A. If the woman has not made a vow, the husband obviously cannot confirm it. He has nothing to confirm. But what about his *annulling* in advance any vows she may make, B? Eliezer says the husband may annul those vows in advance. His reasoning is given at E. The husband has the power to annul vows which the woman actually makes, and these are already in force ("with the force of a prohibition"). Surely he should have power to annul vows which are not yet in force at all, that is, which do not yet have the force of a prohibition.

Sages reject this view, invoking A. If the husband cannot confirm, he also cannot annul, the vow. This essentially is an argument for consistency, nothing more profound than that.

    A. *A deceased childless brother's widow awaiting levirate marriage, whether with a single levir or with two levirs—*
    B.   R. Eliezer says, "He annuls her vows."
    C.   R. Joshua says, "That is the case with one, but not with two."
    D.   R. ʿAqiba says, "That is the case neither with one nor with two" [M. 10:6A-D].
    E.   Said R. Eliezer, "Now in the case of a woman in whom I have no part before she enters my domain, once she enters my domain, she is wholly in my power [so that I may annul her vows]. In the case of a woman in whom I have some part before she comes into my domain [in that the woman cannot marry anyone other than the levir in the event that her childless husband dies, and that is the case while she is still married to her first husband], once she enters my domain [since I have bespoken her], is it not logical that she should be wholly in my power [so that I may annul her vows]?"
    F.   Said to him R. ʿAqiba, "No. If you have so stated matters in the case of a woman in whom I have no part before she comes into my domain, while once she enters my domain, she is wholly within my power, the fact is that, just as I have no part in her, so others have no part in her.
    G.   "But will you say the same of a woman in whom I have a part before she enters into my domain, and who, once she enters my domain, is wholly within my power? For just as I have a part in her, so others [at that point] have a part in her."
    H.   *Said to him R. Joshua, " ʿAqiba, your argument applies to a case of two levirs. What will you reply in the case of one levir* [M. 10:6G]?"
    I.   He said to him, "Just as you have not made a distinction for us between a case in which there is a single levir and one in which there are two levirs,
    J.   "or in a case in which he bespoke the widow and one in which he did not bespeak the widow,
    K.   "so in the case of vows and oaths you should make no distinction."
    L.   He said to him, "It would have been too bad for you had you been around in the time of R. Eleazar b. ʿArakh and given an answer of this sort!"
    M.   He said to R. Eliezer, "The case of an immersion pool will prove the matter as I see it [M. 10:7]. It raises things which have become unclean from their status of uncleanness, but it does not rescue things which are clean from becoming unclean."
    N.   R. Eliezer went and offered a different mode of argument, which is as follows: "No. If in a situation in which he cannot annul his own vows once he has made them, lo, he has the power to annul his own vows before he has made them [by declaring them null in advance], in a situation in which he may annul the vows of his wife once she has made them, is it not logical that he should be able to annul the vows of his wife before she makes them?"
    O.   They said to him, "Now if he is able to annul his own vows before he

makes them, it is also true that if he wanted to confirm his vows [by actually making] them, he does confirm them. But may he annul the vows of his wife before she actually vows? For if he wanted to confirm them, he has not got the power to do so."

T. 6:5 L pp. 118-119, ls. 23-40

A. "Another matter: *Her husband will confirm it and her husband will annul it* (Num. 30:14)—
B. "*A vow which enters the category of confirmation enters the category of annulment. A vow which does not enter into the category of confirmation does not enter into the category of* annulment" [M. 10:7F-G].

T. 6:6 L p. 119, ls. 40-41

Eliezer's argument, E, is essentially a restatement of what he says in M. ʿAqiba at F distinguishes the case of the widow from ordinary women. In the case of an ordinary woman, "While I have no part in her, so others have no part in her too." But in the case of the sister-in-law, the levir has had a presumptive claim on her even before she entered his domain. But so too others—other brothers—also have had a claim on her. This is nothing more than what ʿAqiba has said in M. The answer to Joshua, I-K, also is familiar. So far as the death penalty is concerned, even if there is only one levir who bespoke her, she is exempt from the death-penalty in the case of her having sexual relations with another party. It follows that, in vows and oaths, it does not matter whether there is one levir or many, just as in the case of her having sexual relations that fact makes no difference. ʿAqiba therefore assumes that the bespeaking of the levirate bride is not equivalent to an act of betrothal of an ordinary woman. Joshua's answer, L, is external to the course of argument, because he simply points out that while ʿAqiba does not regard the act of bespeaking in the case of levirate marriage as equivalent to a complete act of betrothal, Eleazar b. ʿArakh maintains that bespeaking most certainly does effect a complete act of acquisition.

M moves us on to M. 10:7. Eliezer has argued that if the husband can annul vows which are in force, he surely can annul vows vows which are not yet in force. The contrary argument, N, is a strong one. The immersion-pool purifies what already is unclean but cannot prevent something which is clean from *becoming* unclean. Eliezer's argument thus is a curious one. He points out that the husband can annul his own vows before he has made them but not afterward. This he does by declaring them null in advance. Surely if he can annul his wife's vows after she has made them, he also can annul them before she makes them. That is, he has the power equally to declare that all his and her coming vows are null.

90   NEDARIM CHAPTER TEN 10:5-8

Sages at O simply invoke the facts, on which all parties concur, of M. 10:7A. T. 6:6 then concludes by citing M. 10:7F-G. N's argument is neatly rephrased and clarified at B. Ned. 75b: "If an immersion-pool, though it raises the unclean from uncleanness, cannot nevertheless save the clean from becoming unclean, then a man, who cannot raise the uncleanness from uncleanness, how much the more can he not save the clean from becoming unclean."

10:8

A. The annulment of vows [may be done] all day long.
B. There is in this matter a basis for a lenient ruling and for a stringent ruling.
C. How so?
D. [If] she vowed on the night of the Sabbath, [the husband] annuls the vow on the night of the Sabbath and on the Sabbath-day, down to nightfall.
E. [But if] she vowed just before nightfall, he annuls the vow only until it gets dark.
F. For if it should get dark and he should not annul the vow, he cannot annul the vow [any longer].

M. 10:8

The long discussion about special cases of the abrogation of vows ends with a general rule on when this is to be done. The explication of A at D-F is clear as given.

A. [If one said], "This ox will be sanctified once I have purchased it,"
"This house will be sanctified once I have purchased it,"
"This ox will be sold to you, once I have purchased it,"
"This house is sold to you, once I have purchased it,"
"Give this divorce to my wife, once I have betrothed her,"
B. he has said nothing.
C. [If he said], "The ox which I shall inherit from father is sold to you,"
"What will come up in my trap is sold to you,"
D. he has said nothing.
E. [If he said,] "What I shall inherit from father today is sold to you,"
"What will come up in my trap this day is sold to you,"
his statements are confirmed [and put into force].

T. 6:7 L pp. 119-120, ls. 42-46

The difference between A-D and E is that, in the former instances, the man speaks of something which is not yet his property. The sale is not validated by what happens after the sale, which is to say, the acquisition of what, in fact, is up for sale. At E the man speaks of what in fact is within the same day of becoming his own. It would therefore represent a rather subtle illustration of M. 10:8, vows are available for annulment an entire day, to darkness, but not for longer than that time.

 A. R. Yosé b. R. Judah and R. Eleazar b. R. Simeon say, "The annulment of vows is done over a twenty-four hour period" [*vs.* M. 10:8A].
 B. How [do they annul vows]?
 C. [If] his wife was subject to five vows, or he had five wives and each had taken a vow,
 D. and he said, "It is annulled,"
 E. all of them are annulled.
 F. [If] he said, "It is annulled for you," he has annulled the vow only pertaining to her.
 G. [if he said,] "*This vow* [is annulled]," he has annulled only that particular vow."
 H. [If he said,] "Now why did you take a vow?" "I don't want you to take a vow!" "This is not a vow!" he has said nothing whatsoever.
 I. [If he said,] "This is annulled!" "This is cancelled!" lo, this is cancelled.
 J. [If he said,] "It is confirmed for you!" "You did very nicely!" "So may I be like you!" "If you had not vowed as you did, I should have imposed a vow upon you!"
 K. he has no power to annul that vow.

T. 6:1 L p. 116, ls. 1-6

A's authorities reject M. 10:8A and allow a different period. B-K explain details of how vows are abrogated.

CHAPTER TWELVE

NEDARIM CHAPTER ELEVEN

In the background of the present chapter is Num. 30:6-15, which provides for the husband's right to confirm or abrogate the vows of his wife. Num. 30:13 specifies, *Any vow and binding oath to afflict herself her husband may confirm or her husband may annul.* On this basis M. comes to the reasonable conclusion that there is a particular sort of vow which the husband abrogates, and that there are other sorts of vows which the husband may not annul. The former type, further, falls into the category of a vow to *afflict herself,* as specified at Num. 30:13 and M. 11:1. M. 11:1 defines such vows of self-affliction as vows whether or not to bathe or get dressed up. Yosé rejects this definition and offers as an example vows not to eat a given sort of produce. How this differs from the foregoing is by no means clear. T.'s rephrasing (if that is what we have) of the dispute at M. 11:1-2 greatly improves matters, but in no way clarifies the issues stated within the limits of M. For T. introduces the issue, which M. does not express, of vows affecting relationships between the husband and the wife, as against vows affecting the wife's relationship to other people. The former the husband abrogates, but not the latter. M. 11:3, 4 specify vows the husband may have no power to abrogate, and they are precisely of that sort; and M. 11:11 specifies a vow affecting the husband, which of course he may abrogate. But this is not made explicit at the outset, and the independent exegesis of M. 11:1-2, while persuasively reshaped at T. 7:1-3, from our perspective must remain obscure.

Once the discussion of vows the husband may or may not abrogate is concluded, the chapter moves in a closely related direction: circumstances in which the husband may exercise his right. M. 11:5-8 deal with that matter, defining the context and means for abrogation, as well as the situation in which the husband has not got the right to annul his wife's vow. M. 11:8 is a singleton, in no clear relationship to what comes fore or aft—just as is the case with M. 11:11, already referred to.

M. 11:9 and 10 then present cases in which there is no one able to effect the abrogation of a woman's vows, along the lines specified at Num. 30:10. M. 11:9 presents a rather handsome triplet on that matter. M. 11:10, equally well-formed, treats nine sorts of girls who have no one to annul their vows.

M. 11:12, at the end, specifies something quite irrelevant: claims which, at the outset, a woman might make to effect collection of her marriage-contract upon her own initiative, but which, later on, were subjected to revision. The point of relevance comes at the end: aforetimes, if a woman vowed that she would have nothing to do with any Jew, she would be given her divorce and also collect her marriage-contract. Later on, however, it was ruled that the husband might annul that part of the vow touching upon his relationship with the wife, even though the vow remained valid in regard to all other Jews—that is, the operative consideration of M. 11:1-4. With this only tangentially relevant, but formally elegant, construction the tractate draws to a close.

11:1-2

A. And these are the vows which he annuls:
B. matters of inflicting self-punishment [*"afflicting the soul,"* Num. 30:13]—
C. "...If I shall wash," or, "If I shall not wash," "...If I shall adorn myself," or, "...If I shall not adorn myself."
D. Said R. Yosé, "These are not vows which inflict self-punishment.

M. 11:1

A. "And what are those vows which do inflict self-punishment?
B. "[If] she said, '*Qonam* to me be the produce of the world,' lo, this [sort of vow] he does have the power to annul.
C. "[If she said, '*Qonam*] be to me the produce of this province,' let him bring her produce from another province.
D. "[If she said, '*Qonam*] be the produce of this stall for me,' he cannot annul that vow.
E. "But if he derived his provisions from that particular store alone, lo, this one may annul the vow," the words of R. Yosé.

M. 11:2

The husband annuls vows of a particular sort, that is the presupposition of A. But the promised list is remarkably brief (B-C). Yosé rejects the definition, not the principle, and, at M. 11:2, spells out vows of self-punishment to be annulled as against those not to be annuled, B as against C, then D as against E; E duplicates the attribution. This slightly refocuses the discussion, from a definition of vows which inflict self-punishment, to vows which the husband has the power to annul as against those which the husband has not got the power to annul, as clearly phrased at M. 11:2B, C, then D, E. Nor is it self-evident why Yosé would not regard the vows of C as suitable examples of vows which inflict self-punishment. In all, this is a conglomerate of distinct, but related issues. T. will try its hand at straightening it all out.

A. Any matter in which there is inflicting of self-punishment [M. 11:1B],
B. whether it involves something between him and her,
C. or between her and other people,
D. he annuls.
E. But as to a matter in which there is no inflicting of self-punishment,
F. [if it is] between him and her, he annuls it.
G. [If it is] between her and other people, he does not annul it.
H. How so?
I. [If] he said, "Qonam if I work for father," "...for your father," "...for my brother," "...*for your brother*" [M. 11:4A],
J. "if I feed your cattle,"
K. *he has not got the power to annul* [such vows], because these are between her and other people.
L. [If she said, "*Qonam*] if I put on eye-shadow," "...if I put on rouge," "...if I adorn myself," "...if I have sexual relations with you,"
M. lo, this one annuls such vows as these, because they relate to matters which are between him and her [M. 11:1C].
N. [If she said, "*Qonam*] if I lay out the bed," "if I wash your feet," "...if I mix the cup for you,"
O. he does not have to annul [such a vow] but forces her to do these services against her will.
P. Rabban Gamaliel says, "He annuls such vows as these, since it is said, *He shall not profane his word* (Num. 30:2)" [cf. M. 11:4].

T. 7:1 L p. 120, ls. 1-7

A. [If] she vowed not to taste a particular sort of produce,
B. whether it is inedible or edible,
C. even if she had never in her life tasted that sort of produce [which she had vowed not to taste],
D. he annuls the vow.
E. [If] she said, "*Qonam* be pepper which I taste," "...be white bread which I taste,"
F. even if she had never had that sort of thing in her entire life,
G. he annuls that vow.

T. 7:2 L p. 120, ls. 7-10

A. [If] she said, "*Qonam* be the produce of the Land of Israel for me,"
B. if he has a share in them, he annuls that vow.
C. But if not, let him provide produce for her from other countries.
D. [If she said,] "*Qonam* be the produce of this hyparchy for me,"
E. if he has a share in them, he annuls that vow.
F. But if not, *let him provide produce for her from some other province* [M. 11:2C].
G. *[If] she said, "Qonam be the produce of this stall for me,"*
H. if there is there another stall, he does not annul that vow. But if not, he does annul that vow [M. 11:2D].
I. R. Yosé says, "Even if there were there a hundred other stalls, *if he derived provisions only from that stall, lo, this one annuls that vow,*

J. "since this is a vow which affects the relationship between him and her" [M. 11:2B-E].

T. 7:3 L pp. 120-121, ls. 10-16

T. 7:1 gives a clear and excellent account of the potentialities of M. 11:1A-B by making distinctions about the applicability of vows. If a vow applies to matters between the husband and wife or between the wife and other people, *and* it also involves inflicting self-punishment (in line with Num. 30:13), he has the power to annul it. If there is no inflicting of self-punishment, E, he may still annul the vow if it is between him and her. If there is no self-punishment and it is between her and others, he has not got that power. I-K illustrate E + G. L-M illustrate A-B + D, that is, self-punishment in matters relating to him and her. N-O do not require annulment, because these are duties which by Torah-law she is required to perform. Gamaliel wants the vow annulled simply to underline the solemnity of vows. All of this, then, will accord with the view of M. 7:1A-C that the things listed at L are matters of self-punishment (B. Ned. 81a). T. 7:2-3 take up the matter of M. 11:2B-E. T. 7:2 deals with a matter which has no affect upon the husband, yet the husband annuls that vow. The authority of M. 7:1A-C surely will concur in this view. T. 7:3 then goes over the ground of M. 11:2C, D, E, introducing its own considerations. In the view of sages, the man annuls the vow because it involves inflicting self-punishment, as at M. 7:1A-C. In the view of Yosé, the man will annul it, as specified at J, because it affects the relationships between husband and wife.

11:3

A. [If she said,] "*Qonam* if I derive benefit from anybody," he has not got the power to annul that vow.
B. But she may derive benefit from Gleanings, the Forgotten Sheaf, and the Corner of the Field (Lev. 19:9, Deut, 24:19).
C. [If she said], "*Qonam* be the benefit priests and Levites derive from me," they collect their dues by force.
D. [If she said,] "*Qonam* be the benefit these [particular] priests and Levites derive from me," others collect [the priestly dues from her].

M. 11:3

A-B are separate from C-D. The point of the former is that this vow is not one which inflicts self-punishment, for the woman can support herself from the poor-taxes. C-D treat as null to begin with a vow not to give tithes and heave-offerings to Levites and priests, since these are things which priests have a right to take. But if she will not give to a specific group of priests, others collect the taxes and these particular ones are prohibited from doing so.

    A. *[If she said,] "Qonam if I derive benefit from anybody,"* he has not got the power to annul that vow. But she can derive benefit from Gleanings, the Forgotten Sheaf, and the Corner of the Field [M. 11:3A-B],
    B.   and [from the tithe set aside for the poor.
T. 7:4 (continued) L p. 121, ls. 16-17

T. adds B to M.'s list.

11:4

    A.   [If she said,] "*Qonam* if I work for father," or, "For your father," or, "…For your brother," he cannot annul that vow.
    B.   [If she said, "*Qonam*] if I work for you," he need not annul [that vow, which is null to begin with].
    D.   R. ʿAqiba says, "Let him annul it.
    E.   "lest she place a burden upon him more than is appropriate for him."
    F.   R. Yoḥanan b. Nuri says, "Let him annul it,
    G.   "lest he divorce her, and she be prohibited from returning to him."
M. 11:4

There is no possibility of annuling the vow of A since this is not a vow inflicting self-punishment. The vow of B is null, because the Torah requires the wife to perform work for the husband. But ʿAqiba and Yoḥanan b. Nuri concur that he should annul it anyhow, for the reasons of E, G. E's point is that the woman may produce more than she owes the husband, and that additional production is subject to her vow, unless he annuls it (= M. Ket. 5:4, Meir). So he must annul the vow, contrary to B. F-G's point is that if the man divorces the woman, the vow will come into force. Then, if he wants to remarry her, he will be unable to, for he will be unable to derive benefit from her wages. He had best annul the vow now.

11:5

  I   A.   [If] his wife took a vow and he thought that his daughter had taken a vow,
    B.   [if] his daughter took a vow and he thought that his wife had taken a vow,
  II   C.   [If] she vowed a Nazirite vow and he thought she had vowed by *Qorban,*
    D.   [if she vowed by] *Qorban,* and he thought that she had vowed a Nazirite-vow,
  III   E.   [if] she vowed not to eat figs, and he thought she had vowed not to eat grapes,

F. [if] she vowed not to eat grapes and he thought she had vowed not to eat figs—
G. lo, this one should go back and annul [the vow again].

M. 11:5

The triplet makes a single point. If the man has annulled a vow in error, he has to go and annul it correctly. Abrogation done in error is null.

C. *If his wife took a vow* and he annulled it for her, and *he thought that his daughter had taken a vow,*
D. or *if his daughter took a vow* and he annulled it for her *and thought that his wife had taken the vow* [M. Ned. 11:5A, B],
E. lo, this one may confirm the vow.
F. But if he wanted to annul it, he annuls it.
G. [If] his wife took a vow and he confirmed it for her and he thought that his daughter had taken the vow,
H. [if] his daughter took a vow and he confirmed it for her and he thought that his wife had taken the vow,
I. lo, this one annuls the vow.
J. But if he wanted to confirm it, he confirms it.

T. 7:4 (continued) L p. 121, ls. 18-21

C-E merely expand and clarify M. If the husband has annulled a vow in error, he has the choice of either going back and annulling it properly or confirming it. He is not bound by his prior error, one way or the other. G-J make exactly the same point in reverse.

11:6

A. [If] she said, "*Qonam* be these figs and grapes if I taste [them],"
B. [if] he confirmed the vow concerning figs, the whole is deemed confirmed.
C. [If] he annulled the vow concerning figs, it is not deemed annulled until he annuls the vow concerning grapes too.
D. [If] she said, "*Qonam* be figs if I taste them, and grapes if I taste them," lo, these are deemed two distinct vows.

M. 11:6

We move from the husband's annulling, to his confirming, his wife's vows. The point has to do with treating a complex statement in its distinct elements. At A, the confirmation of one element of the statement serves for the whole. If he annulled the first of the two, the abrogation if ineffective. The reason is that a vow which is partially annulled is not annulled at all. He must explicitly annul the vow on both statements. D then qualifies A-B. If the vow treats figs and grapes as distinct linguistic elements, then it must be confirmed for each of its elements.

K. If she vowed not to eat figs and grapes, [and] he annulled the vow concerning figs but did not annul the vow concerning grapes,

L. she is prohibited from eating figs and grapes [M. 11:6C].

M. [If] he annulled the vow not to eat grapes but did not annul the vow not to eat figs, she is prohibited from eating grapes and figs.

N. [If] he annulled the vow concerning figs and it got dark [M. 10:8], she is prohibited from eating figs and grapes.

O. [If] he annulled the vow concerning grapes and it got dark, she is prohibited from eating grapes and figs.

P. *[If] she said, "Qonam be a fig if I taste it,* and furthermore *[Qonam] be grapes if I taste them,"* lo, *these are deemed two distinct vows* [M. 11: 6D].

Q. He annuls whichever one he wants and confirms whichever one he wants,

R. since it is said, *Her husband will confirm it* [regarding this one], *and her husband will annul it* [regarding the other one].

T. 7:4 (concluded) L pp. 121-122, ls. 21-26

K-M merely spell out M. 11:6C. At N the time for annulling the vow passed before the husband got around to the whole of it. The abrogation is null. All T. here does is read into the problem of M. 11:6 the considerations of M. 10:8. Finally, P-R cite and amplify M. 11:6D, as indicated.

A. A more strict rule applies to confirming vows than applies to annulling vows, and a more strict rule applies to annulling vows than applies to confirming vows.

B. For silence [on the part of the husband who hears a vow] is tantamount to confirmation but it is not tantamount to annullment.

C. The husband may confirm a vow in his heart, but he may not annul the vow in his heart [but must say so explicitly].

D. There is a rule governing confirmation of vows which does not apply to annulling them, and there is a rule applying to annulling vows which does not apply to confirming vows.

E. Once the husband has confirmed a vow, he cannot annul it.

F. Once he has annulled a vow, he has not got the power to confirm it.

T. 7:5 L p. 122, ls. 26-29

B and C say the same thing, to illustrate A, and E-F treat D.

11:7

A. [If he said,] "I was aware that there are vows, but I was not aware that there is the possibility of annulling them," he may annul [the vow].

B. [If he said], "I was aware that there is the possibility of annulling vows, but I was not aware that this particular statement was a vow,"

C. R. Meir says, "He may not annul the vow."

D. And sages say, "He may annul the vow."

M. 11:7

Continuing M. 11:5 at A and M. 11:6 at B-D, we conclude the set. The claim at A is acceptable, and the husband may annul the vow on the day on which he learns that he has the power to do so. At B he says, he was not aware that this statement which his wife made required abrogation. Meir says that, later on, he may not go and annul it, and sages invoke the same procedure as at A. Meir's thesis is that, since the husband knew that he could annul vows in general, he should have annulled this one, even though he did not think he had to (along the lines, I suppose, if Gamaliel's view, T. 7:1P).

11:8

A. He who was prohibited by vow from imparting any benefit to his son-in-law but who wants to give his daughter some money

B. says to her, "Lo, this money is given to you as a gift, on condition that your husband has no right to it, but you dispose of it for your own personal use."

M. 11:8

The condition, B, is deemed valid. Compare M. 4:2-3.

11:9

A. *But the vow of a widow or a divorcee shall stand against her* (Num. 30:9)—

B. How so?

C. [If] she said, "Lo, I shall be a Nazir after thirty days,"

D. even though she was married during the thirty days, he [whom she married] has not got the power to annul her vow.

E. [If] she took a vow and she was in the domain of the husband, he annuls the vow for her.

F. How so?

G. [If] she said, "Lo, I shall be a Nazir after thirty days,"

H. [if] the husband abrogated the vow], even though she was widowed or divorced within thirty days, lo, this [vow] is annulled.

I. [If] she took a vow on that very day and was divorced on the same day and remarried to the same man on the same day, he cannot annul the vow.

J. This is the general principle: [In the case of] any woman who has gone forth into her own domain for a single moment [M. 10:3C]—he has not got the power to annul the vows.

M. 11:9

The working out of Num. 30:9 is in three parts, B-D, E-H, and I, with J repeating the whole. At B-D, the vow is confirmed while the woman is still a widow or a divorcee and cannot then be annulled. At E-H, if the husband abrogated the vow and then died, it is suitably abrogated and not in effect.

At I, the woman takes a vow, and, instead of abrogating it, her husband divorces her. Then she remarries him. Even though, M. 10:8, all this has happened on the same day, it does not matter. Once the woman has been divorced, the possibility of annulling the vow has ended, even though, within the same time-span, there is a remarriage. It is this fact which is explained at J, which invokes the conception of M. 10:3.

    A. A married woman who said, "Lo, I am a Nazirite when I shall have been divorced"—
    B. R. Ishmael says, "He does not annul such a vow."
    C. R. ʿAqiba says, "He annuls such a vow."
    D. A widow who said, "Lo, I am a Nazirite when I shall have been married"—
    E. R. Ishmael says, "He annuls such a vow."
    F. R. ʿAqiba says, "He does not annul such a vow."
    G. For R. Ishmael says, "*But any vow of a widow or of a divorcee, anything by which she has bound herself, shall stand against her* (Num. 30:9)—so long as it be a prohibition which takes place at the moment at which she is a widow or a divorcee."
    H. R. ʿAqiba says, "*By which she has bound herself shall stand against her*—so long as it be a prohibition binding at the moment at which she binds herself."
    T. 7:6 L p. 122, ls. 30-35

T. provides a much more subtle treatment of Num. 30:9. At A the woman, who is married, says, she will be a Nazirite once her husband divorced her. Does he have the right to annul a vow which will take effect only when he no longer has the right to annul her vows? Ismael says that he does not. She is not in his domain. ʿAqiba, that he does. In ʿAqiba's view the prohibition is validated or invalidated at the moment at which the woman binds herself, that is, while she is yet married, even though the restrictions attendant thereon apply only after the divorce. If a widow says the same to take effect when she will be married, however, the positions, obviously, are reversed. ʿAqiba says the husband has no power to annul this vow. Why not? Because at the moment at which she takes the vow, he has no authority over her. Ishmael treats as decisive the time at which the prohibition will take effect. M. then accords with ʿAqiba, judging the vow in terms of the situation prevailing when it is made, B-D, E-H (B. Ned. 89a, Hisda).

11:10

    A. In the case of nine [sorts of] girls, their vows are valid [and not subject to abrogation]:

B. (1) a girl [who vowed when] past maturity who is an orphan [in her father's lifetime];

(2) a girl who [vowed as] a minor-girl and then passed maturity and is an orphan [in her father's lifetime];

(3) a girl who [vowed] before she reached maturity and is an orphan [in her father's lifetime];

C. (4) a girl [who vowed] past maturity whose father died;

(5) a girl who [vowed as] a minor and then passed maturity whose father died;

(6) a girl who [vowed] before she reached maturity and whose father died;

D. (7) a girl whose father died, and [who vowed and] after the death of her father, she passed maturity;

(8) a girl [who vowed] past maturity whose father is alive;

(9) a girl who passed maturity [and then vowed] and whose father is alive.

E. R. Judah says, "Also: He who marries off his minor daughter and she was widowed or divorced and came back home to him—she is still deemed a girl [subject to the abrogation of her vows by the father]."

M. 11:10

We continue M. 11:9: girls whose vows stand. The "nine" are in three groups of three, as indicated. In the first lot, we have a girl deemed an orphan while the father is yet alive. That is, this girl has been married off by her father and so has left his domain. Then she was widowed or divorced. She is deemed subject to her own authority and therefore her vows are not subject to abrogation. The father has no authority, and there is no husband. (1) is a girl who vowed when she was already past maturity; (2) is one who vowed while she was a girl and then passed maturity; and at the (3) one who vowed when she was a girl and still is a girl. In all three instances the father has no power to annul the vows. C's group then has a girl who vowed after she has passed maturity and whose father then died. She is an adult and no one is available to annul her vows. (5) is a girl who vowed before maturity and who then loses her father. (6) is a girl short of maturity whose father died. The point is that in the case of girls less than twelve years, six months and one day and girls beyond that age whose father died, that is, the girls at D, there is no one to annul the vows. D's girls have passed maturity, and in all three cases, the father has no authority over them. Judah rejects B's conception out of hand.

11:11

A. [If she said,] "*Qonam* be any benefit I have of father...," "Of your father..., if I do any work for you,"

B. "...if I derive benefit from you, if I work for my father," "...if I work for your father,"

C. lo, this one he annuls.

M. 11:11

At M. 11:4, the husband cannot annul such a vow. But here the vow is so phrased that it affects relationships between husband and wife.

    A. [If she said,] "*Qonam* be what I do at your instruction if it benefits my father"—
    B. R. Nathan says, "He annuls such a vow."
    C. And sages say, "He does not annul such a vow."
T. 7:7 L pp. 122-123, ls. 35-36

T. goes over M.'s case at A and assigns M. to Nathan.

11:12

    A. Aforetimes they did rule: Three sorts of women go forth and collect their marriage-contract:
    (1) she who says, "I am unclean for you,"
    (2) "Heaven [knows] what is between you and me [namely, your impotence],"
    (3) "I am removed from [having sexual relations with] all the Jews."
    C. They reverted to rule:
    D. so that a woman should not covet someone else and spoil [her relationship with] her husband,
    E. but: (1) she who says, "I am unclean for you," must bring proof for her claim.
    (2) [She who says], "Heaven [knows] what is between you and me,"—let them find a way to appease her.
    (3) [She who says], "I am removed from all the Jews,"
let him annul his share [in the vow], so that she may have sexual relations with him,
but let her be removed from all the other Jews.
M. 11:12

The formal perfection of the pericope is self-evident. The sole gloss is D. The woman at A1 is a priest's wife who claims that she was raped, so is prohibited from remaining wed to him; the one at A2 claims irreconcilable differences, e.g., impotence; and the one at A3 vows that she will have no sexual relationships with Jews. For the reason given in D, the provisions listed at E are decreed. The sole relevant point is at E3: the husband has a right to annul a vow affecting relationships between him and his wife (= M. 11:1-2). When he dies, however, the woman cannot then remarry.

    A. *She who says, "I am removed from the Jews if I serve you"*—
    B. *let him annul his share in the vow so that she may serve him* [M. Ned. 11:12H].
    C. R. Nathan says, "He does not annul such a vow."
    D. And sages say, "He annuls such a vow."
T. 7:8 L p. 123, ls. 36-38

T. repeats its dispute of Nathan and sages.

NAZIR

CHAPTER THIRTEEN

INTRODUCTION TO NAZIR

The right of the husband to annul his wife's vows encompasses the Nazirite-vow which she may take. That is the insignificant, essentially formal reason for placing this tractate in sequence with its predecessor. From the viewpoint of the interests of the tractate itself, it is not a very important one. For Mishnah works out its ideas on the theme of the Nazirite-vow without reference to the larger redactional setting of the tractate in the order of Women, although, in the formulation of some of its problems, e.g., M. 4:4-7, pericopae which can have been phrased in terms of a man's sudden death are stated in terms of a husband's annulling the vows of his wife, showing that Mishnah so phrases matters as to fit into the larger division. M. 1:1 for its part clearly wishes to draw the tractate into tandem with M. Nedarim Chapter One. But these observations do not bring us toward a recognition of the generative problematic of our tractate, therefore of its fitting position in this division. It is only when we shall have contrasted Scripture's and Mishnah's conceptions of how our tractate's theme is to be laid out—of what it is important to say *about* the Nazir—that we shall come to a clearer and more accurate conception of why Nazir is in the order of Women rather than in the order of Holy Things. Indeed, in the end we shall, I believe, come to a striking conception of why Mishnah joins Nazir, Nedarim, and Ketubot, and (self-evidently) how Sotah is a worthy companion as well. The generative problematic of Nazir contains the key to much beyond the frontiers of the Nazirite and his or her taboo-encumbered existence. Let us undertake the require exercise of comparison and contrast.

To discern how Mishnah proposes to analyze the theme, we have to turn first to Scripture and see how it lays out the matter. Only then shall we gain clear perspective upon the points of concern, the elements of critical tension, in our tractate. The relevant Scriptural passage is as follows:

> And the Lord said to Moses,
> "Say to the people of Israel, When either a man or a woman makes a special vow, the vow of a Nazirite, to separate himself to the Lord, he shall separate himself from wine and strong drink; he shall drink no vinegar made from wine or strong drink, and shall not drink any juice of grapes or eat grapes,

fresh or dried. All the days of his separation he shall eat nothing that is produced by the grapevine, not even the seeds or the skins.

"All the days of his vow of separation no razor shall come upon his head; until the time is completed for which he separates himself to the Lord, he shall be holy; he shall let the locks of hair of his head grow long.

"All the days that he separates himself to the Lord he shall not go near a dead body. Neither for his father nor for his mother, nor for brother or sister, if they died, shall he make himself unclean; because his separation to God is upon his head. All the days of his separation he is holy to the Lord.

"And if any man dies very suddenly beside him, and he defiles his consecrated head, then he shall shave his head on the day of his cleansing; on the seventh day he shall bring two turtledoves or two young pigeons to the priest to the door of the tent of meeting, and the priest shall offer one for a sin-offering and the other for a burnt-offering, and make atonement for him, because he sinned by reason of the dead body. And he shall consecrate his head that same day, and separate himself to the Lord for the days of his separation, and bring a male lamb a year old for a guilt-offering; but the former time shall be void, because his separation was defiled.

"And this is the law for the Nazirite, when the time of his separation has been completed; he shall be brought to the door of the tent of meeting, and he shall offer his gift to the Lord, one male lamb a year old without blemish for a burnt-offering, and one ewe lamb a year old without blemish as a sin-offering and one ram without blemish as a peace-offering, and a basket of unleavened bread, cakes of fine flour mixed with oil, and unleavened wafers spread with oil, and their cereal-offering and their drink-offerings. And the priest shall present them before the Lord and offer his sin-offering and his burnt-offering, and he shall offer the ram as a sacrifice of peace-offering to the Lord, with the basket of unleavened bread; the priest shall offer also its cereal-offering and its drink-offering. And the Nazirite shall shave his consecrated head at the door of the tent of meeting, and shall take the hair from his consecrated head and put it on the fire which is under the sacrifice of the peace-offering. And the priest shall take the shoulder of the ram, when it is boiled, and one unleavened cake out of the basket, and one unleavened wafer, and shall put them upon the hands of the Nazirite, after he has shaven the hair of his consecration, and the priest shall wave them for a wave-offering before the Lord; they are a holy portion for the priest, together with the breast that is waved and the thigh that is offered; and after that the Nazirite may drink wine.

"This is the law for the Nazirite who takes a vow. His offering to the Lord shall be according to his vow as a Nazirite, apart from what else he can afford; in accordance with the vow which he takes, so shall he do according to the law for his separation as a Nazirite."

What we see is that, from the perspective of Scripture, what must be said about the Nazirite is that, once he or she takes such a vow, certain prohibitions are invoked, taboos against (1) wine, (2) hair-cutting, and (3) corpse-uncleanness. All are laid out very neatly. The second point of special interest to the Priestly author is the sacrificial process provoked by the

Nazir's being made unclean with corpse-uncleanness, Num. 6:9-12, and by the Nazir's completing his vow in a state of cleanness, Num. 6:13-20. All this is natural to the Priestly perspective—and carefully ignored in Mishnah.

Now if we may ask, what is it that Scripture deems to require no detailed analysis, it is of course that process by which the man or woman becomes a Nazirite—*the vow itself*. The first five chapters of our tractate are devoted to that topic. More interesting still: it is in the treatment of the vow that Mishnah expresses its fresh and interesting ideas and produces fruitful points of contention and dispute. The analysis of the triple taboo-restrictions on the Nazir, by contrast, simply restates various facts, none of them generative of fructifying conflict. The last four chapters then trail off into a set of conundrums of one kind or another. In this second half—unit III of the following outline—Mishnah truly serves as a kind of complement to Scripture. It is dull, factual, and derivative. Its service to Scripture is hardly impressive. It is in the first half—units I and II—that we see a fresh and original contribution to the exposition of the theme introduced by, and shared with, Scripture. Before pursuing this topic to its natural conclusion, let us then review the way in which Mishnah dissects and lays out its ideas on the topic of the Nazirite.

The tractate opens with its important statement, on the character of the Nazirite vow. This is the matter which, as we saw, is of limited interest to Scripture. But, as usual, Mishnah takes for granted a sizable corpus of facts and forthwith turns its attention to secondary and subtle matters. Its intention to deal with gray areas is underlined by the opening unit, which does not trouble to define what one says to become a Nazir but turns directly to ask about language similar in sound or in meaning to the known formularies. Its next range of problems concerns stipulations which one might make alongside taking the Nazirite-vow, conditions under which the vow is or is not invoked, the taking of sequences of Nazirite-vows at a single moment. This last item then forms a transition to the next subdivision of the unit, the duration of the vow, left, curiously, undefined in Scripture. The final topic is the intervention of the husband into the applicability of the vow to his wife—in this context, a special case.

The second unit is so formulated as to carry forward the topic introduced in this last part of the first, the husband's control of the wife's Nazirite-vow. In fact, the unit is autonomous of the foregoing. It deals with designating diverse animals for the Nazirite's offerings at the end of his or her vow, and dealing with situations in which they are not used as planned. The main point is made in several different ways. There is, at the end, a concluding conundrum, and it is certainly within reason to regard the opening two units as a single, extended one. Indeed, I think the redactor wanted them to be seen in just that way.

I. *Becoming a Nazirite: The Vow.* 1:1-4:3

    A. *The Language of the Vow to be a Nazirite.* 1:1-7·

1:1	All euphemisms for a Nazirite-vow are equivalent to a Nazirite-vow.
1:2	He who says, "Lo, I shall be an abstainer [Nazir] from grape-pits or grapeskins"—lo, this one is a Nazir in all regards. If he says, "I shall be like Samson," he is a Nazir in the status of Samson.
1:3	A Nazirite-vow not specified as to length is for thirty days. If he said, "I shall be a Nazir and for one day," he is a Nazir for two spells of thirty days.
1:4	If he said, "I will be a Nazir like the hairs of my head," he is a lifetime Nazir.
1:5-7	Triplet: If he says, "Lo, I am a Nazir a jugful,"—they examine his intention. If he said, "I intended one long period," he is a Nazir for thirty days. But if it is without specification, he is a Nazir for the rest of his life.

    B. *Stipulations and the Nazirite-Vow.* 2:1-10

2:1-2	If he said, "Lo, I am a Nazir as to dried figs and pressed figs," the House of Shammai say, "He is a Nazir." And the House of Hillel say, "He is not a Nazir." (Doublet)
2:3	If they mixed a cup for someone, and he said, "Lo, I am a Nazir from it," lo, this one is a Nazir.
2:4	Triplet: "If he said, "Lo, I am a Nazir on condition that I may drink wine and contract corpse-uncleanness," he is a Nazir, but may not do these things.
2:5-6	If one said, "I am a Nazir and I take upon myself to bring the hair-offering of another Nazir," and his friend heard and said, So am I," if they are smart, they bring the hair-offering for one another.
2:7-8	If one said, "I will be a Nazir when a son is born to me," and a son is born to him, he is a Nazir. If there is a daughter, he is not. If he said, "When I see that a child is born to me," even if a daughter is born to him, he is a Nazir. If his wife miscarried, he is not a Nazir. Simeon differs.
2:9-10	Triplet: "Lo, I am a Nazir, and again a Nazir, if a son is born to me," and he began counting out the Nazir days covering his own vow, and afterward a son was born to him, he completes the days of his own vow, and afterward he counts out the days of the vow pertaining to his son. Transition.

C. *The Duration of the Vow.* 3:1-7

3:1 He who said, "Lo, I am a Nazir," cuts his hair on the thirty-first day. But if he cut it on the thirtieth, he has fulfilled his obligation. If he said, "Lo, I am a Nazir for thirty days," if he cut his hair on the thirtieth day, he has not fulfilled his obligation.

3:2 He who took a Nazirite-vow for two spells cuts his hair for the first on the thirty-first day and for the second on the sixty-first day. And if he cut his hair for the first on the thirtieth day, he cuts his hair for the second on the sixtieth day.

3:3-4 He who said, "Lo, I am a Nazir," if he was made unclean on the thirtieth day, he loses the whole thirty days he already has observed. Eliezer: Only seven. If he said, "Lo, I am a Nazir for a hundred days," if he was made unclean on the hundredth day, he loses the whole. Eliezer: He loses only thirty. If he was made unclean on the hundred and first, he loses thirty. Eliezer: Seven.

3:5 He who vowed to be a Nazirite while in a graveyard, even if he was there for thirty days—those days do not count for him toward the number of days owing under the vow.

3:6 He who took a vow [while overseas] for a long spell and completed the vow and afterward came to the Land—the House of Shammai: He is a Nazir for thirty days. House of Hillel: He is a Nazir as from the very beginning.

3:7 He concerning whom two groups of witnesses gave testimony—these say, Two spells, those, five—the House of Shammai say, The testimony is at variance, and no Naziriteship applies here at all. House of Hillel: In the sum of five are two spells, so let him serve out two spells of Naziriteship.

D. *Annulling the Vow.* 4:1-3

4:1-2 He who said, "Lo, I am a Nazir," and his friends heard and said, "Me too," "Me too"—all of them are Nazirs. If the vow of the first is declared not binding, those of the others are not binding. Pair of doublets: If he said, "Lo, I am a Nazir," and his wife heard and said, "Me too"—he annuls her vow, but his stands.

4:3 A woman who took a vow as a Nazir and nonetheless went around drinking wine, etc.: lo, this one receives forty stripes. If her husband annulled the vow for her but she did not know it and violated it, she does not receive forty stripes.

II. *The Nazirite's Offerings.* 4:4-5:7

A. *Designation and Disposition of the Offerings.* 4:4-5:4

4:4 A woman who took a vow to be a Nazir and set aside her beast and her husband annulled her vow for her—if the beast belonged to him, it goes forth and pastures in the corral. If it belongs to her, the animal designated as a sin-offering is left to die; the one designated as a burnt-

	offering is offered as a burnt-offering; the one designated as a peace-offering is offered as a peace-offering, etc.
4:5	Once the blood of any one of the offerings has been tossed in her behalf, the husband can no longer annul her vow.
4:6	A man imposes a Nazirite-vow upon his son, but a woman does not impose a Nazirite-vow upon her son.
4:7	A man brings a hair-offering with offerings set aside for the Naziriteship of his father, but a woman does not bring a hair-offering with the Nazirite-offerings set aside for her father.
	N.B. M. 4:6 and M. 4:7 go over the ground of the disposition of unneeded animal-offerings which have been set aside for the hair-offering of a Nazirite and repeat M. 4:4.
5:1-3	The House of Shammai: An act of consecration done in error is binding [= consecrated]. And the House of Hillel say, It is not binding. + Triplet of examples, debate. Point of relevance: If one vowed to be a Nazir and sought absolution of a sage, who declared the vow to be binding, he counts out the days from the moment at which he took the vow.
5:4	He who vowed to be a Nazir and went to bring his beast for a sacrifice and found it was stolen, if before the beast was stolen he took the vow, he is a Nazir. If after the beast was stolen he took the vow as a Nazirite, he is not a Nazir—in line with Hillelite position above.

    B. *Concluding Conundrum.* 5:5-7

5:5-7	If people were going along the way and someone was coming toward them, and one said, "Lo, I am a Nazir if this is so-and-so," and another said, "Lo..., if it is not," etc., the House of Shammai say, All of them are Nazirs. The House of Hillel: A Nazir is only the one whose statement was not confirmed.

The third and final unit of the tractate works out the restrictions imposed on the Nazirite during the duration of the vow. Mishnah has nothing important to contribute and at best presents fairly routine clarifications. These work systematically through the restrictions on wine, III. A, cutting the hair, III. C, and contracting corpse-uncleanness, III. D, carefully following the order of Scripture's agendum. What is left out by Scripture is the disposition of cases of doubt that a Nazir has been made unclean, dealt with at III. E. There are some intruded pericopae, e.g., M. 9:1 does not clearly carry forward the interests of M. 8:1-2, which do continue at M. 9:2. M. 9:3-4, of course, are in place only because of a shared formula, and M. 9:5 is tacked on as a needless, *aggadic* conclusion.

III. *Restrictions on the Nazirite.* 6:1-8:2 + 9:1-5

    A. *The Grape.* 6:1-4

6:1	Anything which exudes from the grapevine joins together with anything else which exudes from the grapevine to form a volume prohibited for use.

6:2	One is liable for wine by itself, grapes by themselves, grape-pits by themselves, and grape-skins by themselves.
6:3	A Nazirite-vow for an unspecified period of time applies for thirty days. If a Nazir cut his hair, in whatever way, he is liable.
6:4	Triplet: A Nazir drinking wine all day long is liable only on one count. If he was warned through the day, he is liable on each count.

B. *Transition.* 6:5

6:5	Nazir is prohibited to cut hair, contract corpse-uncleannes, or use anything which goes forth from the grapevine. Triplet comparing each to the other two.

C. *Cutting Hair.* 6:6-6:11

6:6	Cutting the hair on account of contracting corpse-uncleanness: under what circumstances? Dispute of ʿAqiba and Ṭarfon.
6:7	Cutting the hair in the case of completing the vow in a state of cleanness: how is it done? Sacrifice brought, peace-offering slaughtered, then hair is cut, so Judah. Eleazar: After sin-offering is slaughtered.
6:8	If one brought three beasts, and did not specify their purposes etc., so Simeon b. Gamaliel.
6:9	He would cook the peace-offering or seethe it. The shoulder of the ram and one unleavened cake and wafer are waved. Then the Nazir can drink wine and contract corpse-uncleanness.
6:10	If he cut off his hair after a sacrifice and it turned out to be invalid, the cutting of the hair is invalid. Triplet.
6:11	He in whose behalf one of the drops of blood has been properly tossed and who then was made unclean [= corpse-uncleanness], Eliezer says, loses the whole set of offerings. Sages: He may bring the rest of the offerings when he is clean, and does not lose the earlier one. Transition.

D. *Corpse-uncleanness.* 7:1-4

7:1	A high priest and a Nazir do not contract corpse-uncleanness on account of burying even close relatives, but they do on account of a neglected corpse.
7:2-3	On account of what sorts of uncleanness does the Nazir cut his hair and bring an offering for having become unclean?
7:4	Eleazar in the name of Joshua: For every form of corpse-uncleanness on account of which a Nazir cuts his hair are people liable on account of entering the sanctuary. Meir: Let this matter not be less stringent, etc. Double appendix to M. 7:2-3.

E. *Doubt in the Case of the Nazir.* 8:1-9:2 + 3-5

8:1	Two Nazirs, to whom someone said, "I saw one of you made unclean, but I don't know which one of you it was"—they cut their hair and bring

	an offering, etc. If one of them died + Joshua *vs.* Ben Zoma on the required procedure.
8:2	A Nazir who was subject to doubt as to being made unclean and subject to doubt as to being a confirmed victim of ṣaraʿat. Conundrum.
9:1	Gentiles are not subject to the Nazirite vow. Women and slaves [of Israelites] are. Comparison of rules applicable to one and to the other.
9:2	A Nazir who cut his hair and then, before he made his offerings, learned he had been unclean, if it was a known uncleanness, loses all the days he counted in cleanness. If it was one subject to doubt, he does not lose the days he has counted. If before he cut his hair he learned he had been made unclean, one way or the other, he loses the days he already has observed. Formula: For there are grounds for such a decision.
9:3-4	Further triplet of constructions built on that formula, none relevant to the topic of the tractate.
9:5	Aggadic conclusion: Samuel was a Nazir, so Nehorai. Yosé: He was not a Nazir.

Now that we have seen the evidence for the stated proposition, that what makes Mishnah distinctive and important for our theme is its fructifying inquiry into the Nazirite-vow, its language, applicability, annulment, duration, conditions, and stipulations, we may return to our original observation. If we must locate that element in our tractate which both draws together its discrete units and defines its generative problematic and its points of critical tension, we see that it is located precisely where Nedarim would have led us to expect to find it: the meaning and affects of language. To restate the main point: On the basis of the substance of Scripture, we should have expected to find this tractate among its topical companions in the order of Holy Things. On the basis of the exposition of Mishnah, we may hardly be surprised to find it where it is: among its companions in the order of Women, devoted as is that order to the affects of language upon the relationship of men and women, with continual reference to the interest of Heaven in those relationships.

If a man or woman says a certain set of words, he or she thereby adopts certain restrictions and prohibitions—whether, as in Nedarim, not to eat certain foods of any sort or derive benefit from a given person, or, as in Nazir, not to eat grapes in particular, cut hair, or attend funerals. These restrictions serve to provoke Heavenly interest in, and intervention into, the conduct of that man or woman. Having stated matters in this way, we may hardly be amazed at the inclusion of the theme of the Nazir in the larger framework of the order of Women. For there is no important difference in substance between the stating of a certain formula or the writing down of a certain formula into a document, which drastically restricts the relationship of a woman to the generality of mankind, on the one side, and radically opens up a range of relationships of that same woman to a particular man, on the other side, and the stating of other formulas of words, which effect important changes, permitting and prohibiting relationships. The vow in general, and the vow to be a Nazirite in particular, share a common conception of the enchanted power of words to affect relationships and to change the world.

But the source of the power of language is Heavenly confirmation of earthly affirmation. It is by using formulary language in invoking the response of Heaven—more really, by throwing up words toward Heaven and so by provoking a response in Heaven—that the patterns of behavior and relationship defined by vow, Nazirite-vow, or marriage-contract, equally though in different ways, are subjected to Heaven's concerned response. Relationships and deeds by words are made subject to taboo and sanctified. Mishnah in our division patiently and stolidly investigates the effects of words. So it answers the question, What can a man and a woman say and so become obliged to do or not to do? And the answers to that question reply to yet another, deeper one: How is Heaven mindful of man and woman on earth? The ornate and filigreed essay into the trivialities of language and its use, of which the last and present tractates form an important and engaging part, in the end speaks large and simple truths. It conveys a remarkable vision of humanity in God's image, able to provoke and even encumber God's caring and concern, because it knows how to say those ordinary words which make an extraordinary difference on earth and in Heaven.

CHAPTER FOURTEEN

NAZIR CHAPTER ONE

The tractate opens with the definition of the basic rules for the Nazirite-vow: how the vow is expressed, how it is defined, and for how long a period it remains in force. There are two subdivisions: M. 1:1-2 and 1:3-7, dealing with each of these subjects respectively. M. 1:1 is a rerun of M. Ned. 1:1: substitutes and euphemisms for Nazirite-vows are deemed equivalent to Nazirite-vows and are enforced. M. 1:2 makes the same point about vows to be "like Samson," which may be expressed in diverse euphemisms but with a single result. This introduces the second notion, that there are Nazirites for a single spell of thirty days, for a multiple sequence of such spells, and for a lifetime, just as Samson was a lifetime Nazir of a given order.

The second subdivision then takes up the possibilities of multiple spells and uninterrupted lifetime spells of Naziriteship. M. 1:3 announces that Nazirite spells without further specification last for thirty days. Diverse formulations are examined, to see which produce a single thirty-day spell, and which yield two or more such spells. At M. 1:4 we have a dispute about multiple spells. If someone says he will be a Nazirite "like the hair on my head," that means an unending sequence of individual periods of thirty days, lasting for a lifetime. Rabbi says that that spell lasts a lifetime but is uninterrupted. An interrupted sequence of spells, permitting the cutting of hair every thirty days, will be expressed in different language. M. 1:5-7 take up the interpretation of the language which may be used, a triplet of possibilities, e.g., "I am a Nazir for as long as it takes to go from here to there" will mean for thirty days if it is less than that time to make the trip, or for the length of the trip if it exceeds thirty days.

1:1

A. All euphemisms for [the form of words for] a Nazirite-vow are equivalent to a Nazirite-vow [and binding].
B. He who says, "I will be [such],"—lo, this one is a Nazir.
C. Or: "I shall be comely,"—he is a Nazir.
D. [If he says,] "Naziq," "Naziaḥ," "Paziaḥ,"—lo, this one is a Nazir.
E. [If he says,] "Lo, I shall be like this one,"
"Lo, I shall curl [my hair],"

"Lo, I shall tend [my hair],"
"Lo, it is incumbent on me to grow [my hair] long,"
lo, this one is a Nazir.
F. [If he says,] "Lo, I pledge myself [to offer] birds"—
G. R. Meir says, "He is a Nazir."
H. And sages say, "He is not a Nazir."

M. 1:1

The generalization at A is not illustrated by B-C. For A refers to substitute-language found at D. B-C, E present euphemisms or allusions—not substitute-language—which are spelled out (B. Naz. 2b). F-H deal with an expression which may or may not be meant as a euphemism for a Nazirite vow. A Nazir offers a bird-offering if he becomes unclean (Num. 6:10). But sages' view is that not only the Nazir may be liable for a bird-offering. The comeliness at C refers to the beauty of long hair. D present imitations of the sound of the word. E refers to the growing of long hair.

A. The House of Shammai say, "Euphemisms for euphemisms are binding."
B. And the House of Hillel say, "Euphemisms for euphemisms are not binding."
C. The House of Shammai say, "They do not give testimony [that a woman's husband has died] on the basis of what is heard merely through an echo."
D. And the House of Hillel say, "They give testimony on the basis of what is merely heard through an echo" [*Cf.* M. Yeb. 16:6].

T. 1:1 L p. 124, ls. 1-3

A-B augment M. 1:1A, and the matter continues at M. 2:1.

1:2

A. [He who says,] "Lo, I shall be an abstainer [Nazir] from grape-pits," or, "From grape-skins," or, "From hair-cuts, or "From uncleanness [of corpses]"—lo, this one is a Nazir [in all regards].
B. And all the details of a Nazirite-vow pertain to him.
C. [He who says,] "Lo, I shall be like Samson," "Like the son of Manoaḥ," "Like the husband of Delilah," "Like the one who tore down the gates of Gaza," "Like the one whose eyes the Philistines plucked out,"—lo, this one is a Nazir in the status of Samson.
D. What is the difference between a life-long Nazirite and a Nazirite in the status of Samson [also a Nazirite for life]?
E. A life-long Nazirite: [If] his hair got too heavy, he lightens it with a razor and brings three [offerings of] cattle [Num. 6:14].

F. And if he is made unclean, he brings an offering on account of uncleanness.

G. A Nazirite in the status of Samson: [If] his hair got too heavy, he does not lighten it.

H. And if he is made unclean, he does not bring an offering on account of uncleanness.

M. 1:2

The pericope is in two distinct parts, A-B, and C-H, itself divided between C and a secondary expansion, D-H. The point of A-B is that if one vows to do only part of what is incumbent upon a Nazir, he is subject to all of the restrictions of the Nazirite-vow. B makes clear what A has not left in obscurity.

C goes back over the ground of M. 1:1: euphemisms and substitute-language for a vow to be a Nazir in the status of Samson are effective. D-H ask a question not invited by C. There are two types of life-long Nazirs, one in the status of Samson, one not. The difference between them is spelled out at E-F, G-H. Samson-Nazirs do not cut their hair under any circumstances, E/G, but life-long Nazirs are not to suffer corpse-uncleanness, while Samson-Nazirs are not restricted in that regard.

A. Just as euphemisms for Nazirite-vows are equivalent to Nazirite-vows, so euphemisms for Samson-vows are equivalent to Samson-vows [M. 1:2C].

B. R. Judah says, "A Nazir in the status of Samson is permitted to become unclean with corpse-uncleanness.

C. "For Samson himself became unclean with corpse-uncleanness" [M. 1:2H].

D. R. Simeon says, "He who says, 'Lo, I am like Samson,' has said nothing.

E. "For the language of Naziriteship has not gone forth from his lips [to encumber] him" [*vs.* A and M. 1:2C].

F. Naziriteship applies in the Land and abroad,

G. whether the man has hair or does not have hair,

H. even though it is said, *[And the Nazirite shall shave his consecrated head at the door of the tent of meeting] and shall take the hair from his consecrated head [and put it on the fire]* (Num. 6:18).

I. And it applies whether or not he has hands,

J. even though it is said, *[And the priest shall take the shoulder of the ram...and one unleavened cake out of the basket, and one unleavened wafer,] and shall put them upon the hands of the Nazirite* (Num. 6:19).

T. 1:5 L p. 125, ls. 20-25

A. A totally hairless Nazirite—

B. the House of Shammai say, "He [nonetheless] has to pass a razor across his whole body."

C. And the House of Hillel say, "He does not have to do so."

D. And so is the dispute concerning the *meṣoraʿ*, and so is the dispute concerning Levites.

E. A more strict rule applies to the Nazir than applies to the *meṣoraʿ*, and to the *meṣoraʿ* that does not apply to the Nazirite.

F. A Nazirite, if he shaved on the day of completion of his vow, incurs forty stripes, which is not the case with the *meṣoraʿ*.

G. A *meṣoraʿ* shaves his head, his beard, and his eyebrows, which is not the case with the Nazirite.

T. 1:6 L pp. 126-127, ls. 25-29

A. A more strict rule applies to Nazirite-vows than applies to oaths, and to oaths than to Nazirite-vows.

B. For a Nazirite-vow may be found within another such vow, but an oath is not contained within another oath [M. Ned. 2:3].

C. A more strict rule applies to oaths, for an oath made inadvertently is binding, but a Nazirite-vow made inadvertently is not binding.

T. 1:7 L p. 127, ls. 29-31

Only T. 1:5A-D are relevant to M. A spells out what M. 1:2C implies. B-C explain M. 1:2H. Simeon rejects the view of M. 1:2C. T. 1:5G-H, I-J, and T. 1:6A-C, all treat as inconsequential the fact that a Nazir may be unable to carry out every detail of the law. If this is because of natural conditions, e.g., baldness, absence of hands, absence of hair, it does not matter in the first two cases, and by the Hillelites is treated as of no consequence in the third. Perhaps the rationale for including this set here in the general relevance to M. 1:2A-B: just as a person cannot deliberately exclude a detail of the Nazirite-vow, but the whole is binding, so if he, by nature, cannot do some element of the vow, that does *not* mean the whole is not binding. Then the inclusion of the comparison of the Nazir to the *meṣoraʿ* is a secondary expansion of the D, that is, inclusion of materials not directly relevant but thematically connected.

1:3

A. A Nazirite-vow which is unspecified [as to length] is for a period of thirty days.

I B. [If] he said, "Lo, I shall be a Nazir for one long spell," "Lo, I shall be a Nazir for one short spell," [or] even, "From now until [for as long as it takes to go] the end of the world,"—

C. he is a Nazir for thirty days.

II D. [If he said,] "Lo, I shall be a Nazir and for one day [more]," "Lo, I shall be a Nazir and for one hour [more]," "Lo, I shall be a Nazir for one spell and a half,"—

E. lo, he is a Nazir for two spells [of thirty days].
III F. [If he said], "Lo, I shall be a Nazir for thirty days and for one hour," he is a Nazir for thirty days and for one day,
G. for Nazirite-vows are not taken by the measure of hours.

M. 1:3

Our attention now turns to the length of a vow to be a Nazir. A is the foundation of what follows. Then we have a triplet, B-C, D-E, and F-G. B presents specifications which are meaningless and add nothing to the normal thirty days. At D-E, the man says, "I shall be a Nazir *and one day*," and so on, interpreted to require two distinct spells. If the man specified, F, a normal Nazirite period of thirty *days*, plus one hour more, he keeps a whole day, for the reason given at G. But the contrast which is important is between D and F, and the difference clearly is that at the latter point the specification involves different language: "*Nazir and one*" as against "*thirty days and one.*"

A. He who says, "Nazirite-vows"—
B. Rabban Simeon b. Gamaliel says, "Lo, this one is a Nazir for two spells."
C. [If he said,] "Lo, I am a Nazir and one," lo, this one is a Nazir for two spells [M. 1:3D].
D. [If he said,] "...and more," lo, he is a Nazir for three spells.
E. [If he said,] "...one and more and again," lo, this one is a Nazir for four spells.
F. Symkhos says, "[If he said,] 'Lo, I am a Nazir *tetragon*,' lo, this one is a Nazir for four spells. '...*digon*,' lo, three Nazirite-spells [are incumbent on him], '...*Drigon*,' lo, two Nazirite-spells [are incumbent on him]."

T. 1:2 L p. 124, ls. 3-6

The complement to M. 1:2 is in three parts, A-B, C-E, and F. The points are clear as given.

1:4

A. [He who said], "I will a Nazir like the hairs of my head," or, "...like the dust of the earth," or, "...like the sand of the sea,"—lo, this one is a lifetime Nazir.
B. But he cuts his hair once every thirty days.
C. Rabbi says, "Such a one as this does not cut his hair once every thirty days.
D. "But who is the one who cuts his hair once every thirty days?
E. "It is he who says, 'Lo, I pledge myself to as many [distinct] Nazirite-vows as the hairs of my head,' or '...as the dust of the earth,' or, '...as the sand of the sea.' "

M. 1:4

This is a fine example of an amplified dispute, in which all elements are kept in perfect balance, best shown at A/E. The real issue then is B as against C. Do we deem the saying at A to invoke an interrupted spell of Naziriteship, that is, an unending succession of thirty day periods? If we do, then B follows. Rabbi asks for different language, as at E, which specifies not a single spell, but an unending sequence of individual spells.

A. [If he said], "Lo, I will be a Nazir like the hairs of my head," "...like the dust of the earth," "...like the sand of the sea," lo, this one is a lifetime Nazirite.
B. And he cuts his hair in thirty days.
C. Rabbi says, "Such a one as this does not cut his hair once every thirty days.
D. "For this is not a lifelong Nazir" [M. 1:4A-C].
E. [If he said,] "Lo, I am a Nazir from now until the border," "...from the earth to the firmament," lo, this one is a lifelong Nazir.
F. [If he said,] "Lo, I am a Nazir all my days," "Lo, I am a lifelong Nazir," lo, this one is a lifelong Nazir.
G. [If he said, "Lo, I am a Nazir] for a hundred years," or "...for two hundred years," this one is not a lifelong Nazir.

T. 1:4 L p. 125, ls. 15-20

A-C cite M. D's point is that one who cuts his hair every thirty days is not a lifetime Nazir. One who is is defined at E, F.

1:5-7

I A. [He who says,] "Lo, I am a Nazir, a jugful," or "...a basketful"—
B. they examine his intention.
C. And if he said, "I intended to take a Nazirite-vow for one long period," he is a Nazir for thirty days.
D. But if he said, "I took a Nazirite-vow without specification," they regard the basket as if it is full of mustard-seeds.
E. And he is a Nazir for the rest of his life.

M. 1:5

II A. [If he said,] "Lo, I shall be a Nazir from here to such-and-such a place,"
B. they make an estimate of how many days it takes to go from here to such-and-such a place.
C. If it is less than thirty days, he is a Nazir for thirty days.
D. And if not, he is a Nazir is accord with the number of days [required to go to such-and-such a place].

M. 1:6

III A. [If he said,] "Lo, I shall be a Nazir according to the number of days of the solar year,"
B. he counts his Nazirite-spell in accord with the number of days of the solar year.

C. Said R. Judah, "There was a case of this sort, and once he had fulfilled [his Nazirite-vow], he dropped dead."

M. 1:7

The triplet is joined by the introductory language, M. 1:5A, 1:6A, 1:7A. But there is no effort at tightly repeated patterns. The point of M. 1:5 is clear in the contrast between C and D-E. The former recalls M. 1:3B. The connection to M. 1:4 will be in whether or not we see the man as subject to an endless sequence of distinct vows or to one unending, single vow. M. 1:6 and M. 1:7 are clear as given. Judah's precedent has a man serve out more than thirty years of Nazirite vows, that is, three hundred sixty consecutive months.

A. [He once said,] "Lo, I am a Nazir, if I do not [reveal] the families [which are impure]," let him be a Nazir and let him not reveal the famlilies [which are impure].
B. "Lo, I am a Nazir in accord with the hours of the day," "...in accord with the months of the year," lo, this one is a Nazir for twelve spells.
C. "...in accord with the days of the week," "...in accord with the years of the septennate," "...in accord with the years of release of a Jubilee," lo, this one is a Nazir for seven spells.
D. "Lo, I am a Nazir in accord with the days of the sun," he is a Nazir for three hundred sixty-five spells of Naziriteship, in accord with the number of days of the solar year [M. 1:7A-B].
E. "...in accord with the days of the moon," "...in accord with the number of the days of the moon,"—he is a Nazir for three hundred fifty-four spells of Naziriteship, in accord with the number of the days of the lunar year.
F. Rabbi says, "[This is valid] only if he will say, 'Lo, I am a Nazir for the number of Nazirite-spells equivalent to the days of the solar year,' '... equivalent to the number of the lunar year,' '...equivalent to the number of days of the lunar year.' "
G. R. Judah says, "[If] he said, 'Lo, I am a Nazir in accord with the sheaves of the summer-harvest,' and, '...the paths of the year of release,' lo, this one is a lifetime Nazir.
H. "And he shaves once in thirty days."
I. *[If he said, "Lo, I am a Nazir], '...a jugful,' or '...a basketful,' "* [M. 1:5A]
lo, this one is a lifetime Nazir.
J. And he shaves once in thirty days.
K. [That is so] unless he says to them, "It was not to that purpose [that I intended in taking a vow]" [cf. M. 1:5D-E].

T. 1:3 L pp. 124-125, ls. 6-15

The complement to M. 1:5-7 poses few problems. Rabbi will not concur with M.'s formulation at M. 1:7, since he wants the man to use more specific language, F. Otherwise he will regard the man as subject to a lifelong vow of Naziriteship.

CHAPTER FIFTEEN

NAZIR CHAPTER TWO

The preferred formulary pattern of our tractate, "Lo, I am a Nazir...," occurs in the present construction six times: M. 2:1A, 2:4A, 2:5A, 2:7A, 2:9A, 2:10A, and its appearance formally marks the advent of the principal units of the chapter. But this picture is somewhat misleading, since, from the perspective of themes and principles, M. 2:9-10 take up the problem of Chapter Three, even though, as we shall see, M. 2:9 looks as if it proposes to carry forward the topic and problem of M. 2:7-8. It follows that, as is often the case, M.'s ultimate redactor has made up materials to provide formal and even thematic bridges between essays on what are in fact discrete and even diverse principles. The main issue of the primary unit, M. 2:1-8, is whether or not we interpret the language used in making a Nazarite-vow, and, if we do interpret it, how we do so. There are three principal units worked out in M., so T. makes clear, Judah's Meir's, and Simeon's.

Judah's position is worked out at M. 2:1-2, using pseudoattributions to the Houses to underline unanimous concurrence in his view. Judah maintains that if a person vows with the language of the Nazirite vow but in details not particular to the Nazirite vow, the vow is null so far as his becoming a Nazir is concerned. This opinion he assigns to the Hillelites. He further insists that the Shammaites concur in that principle and differ only on whether or not the man's particular vow of abstinence (now: *nazir* with a small n) is imposed upon him. M. 2:7-8 repeat his view that Nazirite-vows are valid only when clearly stated and totally free of doubt.

The second unit is Simeon's, M. 2:3-4, with a further unit of Simeon at M. 2:7-8. The point of the former is that in Simeon's view, a vow made in a manner contrary to normal procedure is not valid and not binding. Sages reject this view and hold that, if a man vowed in a manner contrary to accepted form, the vow is binding.

M. 2:5-6, which are Meir's, place Meir on the opposite side of that issue. If a man vows in an unusual way, e.g., to bring half of the required offerings of a *Nazir*, he must bring *all* of the required offerings. Simeon, T. shows, has him owe nothing. Sages here have him bring just what he said.

The second unit of Simeon, M. 2:7-8, sets him into opposition to Judah on a quite distinct point. If we have a matter of doubt in dealing with a

Nazirite vow, Simeon rules that the vow is binding, and therefore will make provision for enforcing it. Judah (as T. shows) maintains that the vow is not binding if it is subject to doubt. It must be stated clearly and beyond doubt to be effective. So we have Judah, M. 2:1-2, Simeon, M. 2:3-4, Meir *vs.* Simeon, M. 2:5-6 and Judah *vs.* Simeon, M. 2:7-8 (!).

M. 2:9-10 take up the specific problem by which the foregoing unit expresses its principles, but turn to the matter of counting out the days of several related vows of Naziriteship. If a person vows to be a Nazirite and adds another such vow to take effect later, he first keeps the one, then the other. If he vows to be a Nazirite at a given point in the future, and also vows to be a Nazirite from this time and for a long period of days, he starts the one as scheduled, and then sets the counting aside for that vow, keeps the second when it falls due, and, having cut his hair and brought the hair-offering for the second, resumes counting for the former vow and completes that one. The one important provision, which will be vital in the coming chapter, is that for each vow, he must observe at least one spell of thirty days' growth of hair before he brings the hair-offering.

2:1-2

A. [He who says,] "Lo, I am a Nazir as to dried figs and pressed figs"—
B. the House of Shammai say, "He is a Nazir."
C. And the House of Hillel say, "He is not a Nazir."
D. Said R. Judah, "Also: When the House of Shammai made this ruling, they made it only with reference to him who says, 'Lo, they are unto me as a *Qorban*.' "

M. 2:1

A. [If] one said, "This cow says, 'Lo, I am a Nazir if I stand up,'
B. "This door says, 'Lo, I am a Nazir if I am opened' "—
C. the House of Shammai say, "He is a Nazir."
D. And the House of Hillel say, "He is not a Nazir."
E. Said R. Judah, "Also: When the House of Shammai made this ruling, they made it only with reference to him who says, 'Lo, this cow is unto me as a *Qorban* if it stands up.' "

M. 2:2

The point of the matched pair of disputes, in perfect form, is the Shammaites' view that as soon as the man has uttered the words, "I am a Nazir," further qualifications are null (Rashi, B. Ned. 9a). The Hillelites are prepared to read the man's words in context (B. Naz. 9a). Judah brings the Shammaites to the Hillelite position: the man is not a Nazir, except in the general sense of abstainer, that is, he must not eat dried figs or pressed figs; and, if the cow stands up, it is sanctified. But this obviously reverses the clear position of the Shammaites, who maintain that when the man refers to the figs or the cow or door, he explains his decision to become a Nazir.

    A. The House of Shammai say, "Euphemisms for euphemisis are binding."
    B. How so?
    C. [If] he said, "Lo, I am a Nazir from dried figs and from pressed figs,"
    D. the House of Shammai say, "He is a Nazir" [M. 2:1A-B].
                                      T. 2:1 L p. 126, ls. 1-2

T. links our disputes to M. 1:1 and so supplies a different exegesis of the dispute from Judah's. Even C is a euphemism for a Nazirite-vow.

The Shammaites and Hillelites differ at M. Ned. 3:4 on whether a vow which is partially unloosed remains valid as to details not covered by absolution. The Hillelites maintain that that is the case. This view then is repeated at M. Ned. 9:7. Now when we consider the matter before us, the Hilleites take up the consistent position that a vow which is not wholly in force is not in force at all. There is no absolution which is only partially effective; what is in part in force in wholly in force. There is no binding force of a vow which is only partially effective. What in part is not in force is wholly not in force. This seems to me a single position, expressed in diverse ways in accord with different contexts. But compare Albeck, pp. 371-2, for a different angle, based on M. 5:1.

2:3

    A. [If] they mixed a cup for someone, and he said, "Lo, I am a Nazir from it,"
    B. lo, this one is a Nazir.
    C. MʿŚH B: A woman was drunk, and they filled a cup for her, and she said, "Lo, I am a Nazirite from it."
    D. Sages ruled, "She intended only to say, 'Lo, it is unto me as a Qorban.'"
                                             M. 2:3

The pericope forms a transition between the foregoing set and, as we shall see, what follows. For the issue is now more subtle: the woman declares herself a Nazir from that particular cup of wine. She is a Nazir for all purposes, so A-B. C-D reject A-B. The ruling of sages follows the principle of Judah. It furthermore carries forward the method of the Hillelites, in that it examines the context of the vow. Consequently, sages rule that the woman has vowed to abstain from that cup of wine alone, but not from all wine for the period of a Nazir-vow. The position at A-B contains no surprises from the Shammaite viewpoint. But that of C-D shows how extreme is the Hillelite view, for, after all, we deal now not with something quite irrelevant to the Nazir—the cow, the door, the figs—but something to which the statement pertains. Yet we continue to insist that the vow must be expressed in a wholly appropriate manner or to deem the vow to be null. B. Ned. 11a recognizes the obvious fact that the "precedent" rejects the stated rule and proposes a harmonization, which we may safely ignore.

2:4

I A. [If one said,] "Lo, I am a Nazir on condition that I shall drink wine and become unclean with corpse-uncleanness,"
B. lo, this one is a Nazir.
C. But he is prohibited to do all of these things [which he has specified as conditional upon his vow].
II D. [If he said,] "I recognize that there is such a thing as Naziriteship, but I do not recognize that a Nazir is prohibited from drinking wine,"
E. lo, this one is bound [by the Nazirite oath].
F. And R. Simeon declares him not bound.
III G. [If he said,] "I recognize full well that a Nazir is prohibited to drink wine, but I was thinking that sages would permit me to do so, because I cannot live without wine,"
H. or, "...because I am in the work of burying the dead,"
I. lo, this one is not bound.
J. And R. Simeon declares him bound.

M. 2:4

The three constituents of this triplet, A-C, D-F, and G-J, make two points. The first is that one may not make a vow of the sort described at A, because he has made the vow conditional upon the violation of the rules contained therein and specified in the Torah. This, of course, is not possible. The twin-dispute, D-F and G-J, however, is separate. Its issue is the vow made in error. The man has taken a Nazirite-vow. He claims not to have known its conditions. Simeon sees this as a vow made in error and therefore null. The second version shifts the two positions. If the man knew the conditions, then Simeon finds no grounds to declare the vow to be one made in error. Sages treat the statement at G as suitable pretext to annul the vow. But B. Naz. 11a-b presents the view that the positions of I and J should be reversed.

A. *[If he said], "Lo, I am a Nazirite on condition that I shall drink wine and become unclean with corpse-uncleanness,"*

B. *lo, this one is a Nazir* [M. 2:4A-B].
C. But his prior condition is null.
D. For he has made a stipulation contrary to what is written in the Torah and whoever makes a stipulation contrary to what is written in the Torah—his condition is null.

T. 2:2 L p. 126-127, ls. 2-4

A. *"I recognize that there is such a thing as Naziriteship, but I do not recognize that Nazirs are prohibited from drinking wine"* [M. 2:4D]
B. "that it is prohibited to drink wine and to become unclean with corpse-uncleanness"—
C. R. Simeon says, "You have no greater pretext than such a statement [for annulling the vow]" [Cf. M. 2:4F].

T. 2:3 L p. 127, ls. 4-6

T. supplies reasons for M.'s positions.

2:5-6

A. [If one said,] "Lo, I am a Nazir, and I take it upon myself to bring the hair-offering of a[nother] Nazir," and his friend heard and said, "So am I, and I take upon myself to bring the hair-offering of a[nother] Nazir,"
B. if they are smart, they bring the hair-offering of a[nother] Nazir,
C. And if not, they bring the hair-offering of other Nazirs.

M. 2:5

A. [If one said,] "Lo, I pledge myself to bring half of the hair-offering of a Nazir," and his friend heard and said, "And I too pledge myself to bring half the hair-offering of a Nazir,"
B. "this one brings the whole hair offering of a Nazir and that one brings the whole hair-offering of a Nazir," the words of R. Meir.
C. And sages say, "This one brings half the hair-offering of a Nazir, and that one brings half the hair-offering of a Nazir."

M. 2:6

When the Nazir completes the time of his separation, he shaves his consecrated head and takes the hair and puts it on the fire, along with a sacrifice of a peace-offering (Num. 6:18). The language used in these pericopae refers to that "cutting of the hair"-*offering*. The two pericopae are related only in theme, since the problem at M. 2:5 and the one at M. 2:6 are not the same. The former has a man take the Nazirite-vow and in addition pledge to bring the hair-offering of another Nazir. B, C simply provide good advice. The dispute at M. 2:6, by contrast, has a distinct vow to bring half of the offerings owed by a Nazir. Meir's view is that the man must provide a whole hair-offering. He has said, "Lo, incumbent on me...," so he owes the whole thing. Sages affirm that the man says what he means and does what he says. The man's oath carries its own condition, which is valid. The inclusion of the words of the friend here make no difference at all, so M. 2:6 has been rephrased for conglomeration with M. 2:5. The fundamental issue is the same as at M. 2:1-4, namely, whether or not we take seriously qualifications and revisions of a vow. Sages here are consistent with the House of Hillel at M. 2:1-2, sages at M. 2:3, and sages at M. 2:4G-J: explanatory language is taken into account and is validated. Meir of course is consistent with the House of Shammai.

    A. *"Lo, I pledge myself to offer half of a Nazir's hair-offering, lo, this one offers the whole of a Nazir's hair-offering," the words of R. Meir* [M. 2:6A, B].
    B. R. Simeon declares him exempt.
    C. For he has not volunteered to do so in the normal way in which people make such voluntary pledges.
T. 2:4 L p. 127, ls. 6-8

    A. *[If he said], "Lo, I am a Nazir, and I take it upon myself to offer the hair-offering of a[nother] Nazir"* [M. 2:5A],
    B. and if he [first] offered his own hair-offering, he has not fulfilled the terms of his pledge.
T. 2:5 L p. 127, ls. 8-9

    A. "Lo, I pledge myself to offer half of the hair-offering of a Nazir," and he further said, "Lo, I am a Nazir,"
    B. if he [first] offered his own hair-offering, he has not fulfilled the terms of his pledge.
    C. [If he said], "These are the offerings on account of which I shall separate [myself as a Nazir],"
    D. he has said nothing,
    E. since it says, *His offering for the Lord on account of his Nazirite-vow* (Num. 6:2), and not his Nazirite vow on account of his offering.
T. 2:6 L p. 127, ls. 9-11

    A. "Lo, I pledge myself to offer the sin-offering or the guilt-offering owed by Mr. So-and-so"—
    B. if he said so with the other's knowledge, the other has fulfilled his obligation.
    C. If he said so not with the other's knowledge, he [the other] has not fulfilled his obligation.
    D. "Lo, this is the sin-offering or the guilt-offering owed by Mr. So-and-so"—
    E. and the other went and brought offerings in his own behalf—
    F. lo, these [brought by the first party] are in the status of a sin-offering or a guilt-offering, the owner of which has effected atonement through some other animal.
T. 2:7 L p. 127, ls. 11-14

T. 2:4 phrases the issue of M. 2:6 without the matter of the friend. It provides us now with yet a third position, in addition to Meir's, as given, and M.'s sages' view. Simeon says the man owes nothing, for the stated reason, familiar from M. Men. 12:3, 13:10 (*Holy Things* II, pp. 172ff.). M. 2:6 does not deal with Simeon's perspective on the present issue. What we appear to have is several sets of essays on a common theme, Judah's at M. 2:1-2, Simeon's at M. 2:4, and Meir's at M. 2:5-6. T. 2:5 restates M. 2:5 without attention to the fellow and makes the obvious point that the man must bring his own hair-offering as well as that of the other Nazir. The point of T. 2:5 is that if the man first of all brought the hair-offering of his own, he has not yet carried out the terms of his vow. He already owed the Nazirite hair-offering for himself before he made to vow to provide the hair-offering of another Nazirite. The offerings carry out his own obligation, not the obligation for his vow. That is, the first-hair-offering covers the one which he owes for himself, not the one he has pledged for some other Nazir—a rather minor qualification of M. 2:5. T. 2:6 then reverses matters, A-B, and the point is equally clear. T. 2:6C-E are closely relevant to our passage. If the sets aside, that is, designates animals as, offerings *before* he has made his Nazirite-vow (= T. 2:6A-B) the designation is null, because at the moment the animals were so designated, the man did not owe them. T. 2:7 is a rather general illustration of a further conception about designating animals for offerings, when the man who does the designating does not owe them.

2:7-8

I A. [If one said,] "I will be a Nazir when a son is born to me," and a son was born to him, lo, this one is a Nazir.

B. [If] a daughter, a child of unclear sexual traits, a child bearing the sexual traits of both sexes, is born to him, he is not a Nazir.

II C. If he said, "When I see that a child is born to me, [I shall be a Nazir],"

D. even if a daughter, a child bearing unclear sexual traits [or] a child bearing the sexual traits of both sexes, is born to him, lo, he is a Nazir.

M. 2:7

III A. [But if] his wife miscarried, he is not a Nazir.

B. R. Simeon says, "He should say, 'If it was a viable foetus, lo, I am a Nazir out of obligation. And if not, lo, I am a Nazir by free choice.' "

C. [If] she went and gave birth again, lo, this one is a Nazir.

D. R. Simeon says, "He should say, 'If the first was a viable foetus, the first [Nazirite-spell which I observed] is done out of obligation, and this one is by free choice. And if not, then the first was by free choice, and this one is out of obligation.' "

M. 2:8

128   NAZIR CHAPTER TWO 2:7-8

The contrast at M. 2:7A + B, C + D, contains no surprises and merely serves, at C-D, to introduce M. 2:8. The important points come with Simeon's views. The wife of the man who said, "I shall be a Nazir when my wife gives birth," has a miscarriage. We do not know whether or not the foetus was viable. If it was viable, then he owes a Nazirite vow. If not, he does not. The anonymous position at M. 2:8 is that in a case of doubt, we rule leniently. The man does not have to keep a spell as a Nazir. Simeon's view is expressed at B. The man is to keep a Nazir-vow by reason of doubt, and A-B specify the matter as Simeon spells it out. C is important only from Simeon's viewpoint. If the woman gives birth, sages obviously will maintain that the man now must keep the Nazirite-vow. But Simeon has to explain how we manage affairs in the light of B, which he does in the expected way at D.

A. *"Lo, I am a Nazir if I have a son,"* and a son was born to him [M. 2:7A]—
B. it is a matter of doubt whether or not the foetus is viable—
C. R. Judah declares him exempt.
D. For in Nazirite-vows a vow subject to unclarity is not binding.
E. R. Simeon declares him liable.
F. For in Nazirite vows a vow subject to unclarity is binding.
G. *"He therefore should say, 'If it was a viable foetus, lo, I am a Nazir out of obligation. And if not, lo, I am a Nazirite by free choice'"* [M. 2:8B].

T. 2:8 L pp. 127-128, ls. 14-17

A. "Lo, I am a Nazir, on condition that in this pile of wheat there should be a hundred *kor*,"
B. and he went and found it had been stolen or got lost—
C. it is a matter of doubt whether or not there was that volume of wheat in the mound—
C. R. Judah declares him exempt.
D. For in Nazirite vows, a vow subject to unclarity is not binding.
E. R. Simeon declares him liable.
F. For in Nazirite vows, a vow subject to unclarity is binding.
G. He therefore should say, "If matters were as I said, lo, I am a Nazir out of obligation. And if not, lo, I am a Nazir out of free will."

T. 2:9 L p. 128, ls. 17-20

T. 2:8A has no difficulty in phrasing the issue in terms of M. 2:7A, that is, the man wants a son, and there is a still-birth, male, which may or may not have been viable. T.'s contribution is to phrase the point at dispute. Judah's view is that if there is doubt in matters of Nazirite-vows, we rule leniently. Simeon insists the vow subject to doubt is valid and has to be negotiated as he proposes.

2:9-10

I A. [He who said], "Lo, I am a Nazir, and [again] a Nazir if a son is born to me,"

B. [if] he began counting out the Nazir days covering his own vow, and afterward a son was born to him,

C. he completes the days of his own vow and afterward counts out the days of the vow pertaining to his son.

II D. [If he said], "Lo, I am a Nazir when a son will be born to me, and [again] a Nazir,"

E. [if] he began to count out the days covering his own vow, and afterward a son was born to him,

F. he puts aside [the observance of the days of] his own [vows] and counts out the days covering the vow he made for his son.

G. And afterward he completes the days required for his own vow.

M. 2:9

III A. [If he said], "Lo, I am a Nazir when a son will be born to me and a Nazir for a hundred days,"

B. [if] a son was born to him before seventy days [had passed], he has lost nothing.

C. [If the son was born] after seventy days, he loses the seventy days he has observed,

D. for there is no cutting of hair in less than thirty days [from the beginning of the observance of the vow].

M. 2:10

Once more M.'s redactor has shown how he can link two essentially disparate themes, the opening units of our chapter, down through M. 2:8, and Chapter Three, which follows. From M. 2:7-8, he has taken up the circumstance of a man's vowing to be a Nazir if he has a son. From Chapter Three he introduces the problem of counting out days covering more than a single Nazirite-vow. And the whole is so deftly done that we scarcely feel the transition until it is completed, since the simple cases of M. 2:9 hardly suggest the real point at hand, M. 2:10, which is not, as indicated, that of our subdivision at all.

The first two cases require little explanation. The man has two vows on his hands. The first is his own, the second, that which takes effect when the son is born. Obviously he completes the first and then the second. If the order is reversed, he still begins his own spell. If then a son is born, he stops counting days to carry out his own spell as a Nazir and counts out the days covering the vow he made for the son. Then he completes the days of his own vow. The interesting problem comes at M. 2:10. He repeats the procedure of M. 2:9D-G. It follows that he counts out days covering his own vow—a hundred. But if the son is born, he has to set aside counting for the hundred days and count out the thirty he owes for the son. Now if the son was born before seventy days have passed, he simply counts thirty days for the son, cuts his hair and brings the offering, then goes back to counting his own vow's days. What happens, however, if seventy days (or more) have passed, and then the son is born? He has to count out thirty days and cut his hair—for the son's vow. If then he already has observed, let us say, eighty days of his own vow, that leaves only twenty days. That cannot do, for the reason given at D. Therefore the man has to start counting all over again. This means he loses the eighty days and starts the hundred afresh. An alternative view is that the man loses the days in excess of seventy, but the days up to seventy remain to his credit.

> A. "Lo, I am a Nazir after twenty days, [and] a Nazir from now for hundred days,"
> B. he counts twenty and afterward he counts thirty and stops,
> C. and he counts eighty to complete his first Nazirite-vow.
>
> T. 2:10 (continued) L p. 128, ls. 20-22

The man owes two vows. He first has to be a Nazir for a hundred days. He second has to be a Nazir after twenty days have passed. And, of course, we have to provide for thirty days growth of hair, M. 2:10D. How do we arrange matters. He observes twenty days of the hundred-day vow. He then counts out thirty days for the vow he owed at that point. He has now kept fifty. He stops, cuts his hair and brings the offering covering that thirty-day vow. Then he keeps another eighty days, and the twenty plus the eighty fulfill the first of the two vows, the one for the hundred days.

Maimonides (*Naziriteship* 4:3-5) states matters as follows:

> If a person says, "I intend to become a Nazirite now, and a Nazirite again if I should have a son," and a son is born to him after he has begun to reckon his own Naziriteship, he must complete his own and then reckon the one occasioned by his son. If he says, "I intend to become a Nazirite if I should have a son; and I also intend to be a Nazirite for a certain number of days," and a son is born to him after he has begun his own Naziriteship, he must interrupt his own Naziriteship, reckon the one occasioned by his son, and then resume his own and complete it. Both are regarded as if they were one Naziriteship. Consequently, if he becomes unclean during the Naziriteship for his son, this renders the whole void. If he becomes unclean upon commencing the completion of his own Naziriteship and after the termination of his Naziriteship for his son, this renders void only the period preceding the Naziriteship for his son. In how many days does he complete his own? Should thirty or more days of his own Naziriteship remain when the son is born, he must reckon the Naziriteship for his son, and then complete the remaining days of his

own. If less than thirty days of his own Naziriteship remain, he must reckon thirty days after the Naziriteship for his son. For there can never be less than thirty days between one polling and the next.

For instance, if a person says, "I intend to become a Nazirite if I should have a son, and I also intend to be a Nazirite for one hundred days," and after beginning his own Naziriteship has a son born to him, the rule is as follows: If, when the son is born, thirty or more days of the hundred remain, he loses nothing. For he need only interrupt his own Naziriteship and begin reckoning the one for his son, after which he must poll his head and offer his sacrifices. He may then complete the remaining thirty or more days of his own Naziriteship and poll his head for it. If less than thirty of the hundred remain, those after seventy are canceled.

For instance, if the son is born on the eightieth day, he must reckon the Naziriteship for his son, complete it, and poll. After polling, he must begin counting thirty days more. He thus loses ten days from before the birth—that is, from the seventieth day until the birth. This holds good in all similar cases.

CHAPTER SIXTEEN

NAZIR CHAPTER THREE

We now know that either one may declare himself a Nazir without specification, so the spell is for thirty days, or he may commit himself to a longer period, divided into several spells. In the latter case, how do we treat the day on which one spell is completed and another begun? The chapter raises that question and yet one more: What happens if a man observes a period of Naziriteship but becomes unclean at the point at which the period is concluded? So in both units of the chapter—M. 3:1-2 and M. 3:3-4 + 5-6 (+ 7)—we dispose of the status of the day on which the vow is completed and the offerings brought.

The rule of M. 3:1-2 is that if the thirtieth day marks the end of an unspecified vow, then, once the purification-process is complete, the remaining part of the day will be credited to the coming spell, which commences at that point. But if the man specified he will be a Nazir for thirty (whole) *days,* then the purification-rite is done on the thirty-first day. The whole of the thirtieth day is assigned to the first of two successive vows.

The point of M. 3:3-4 is rather subtle. We know that if a Nazir has kept some days in a state of cleanness but is then made unclean, he loses the days he has observed and starts a new count. This, after all, is Scripture's own view. But what happens if he completes the required period, e.g., thirty days, but on that very day he becomes unclean? Now we have a dispute. Sages simply invoke Scripture's rule. Eliezer's position is that, if the man is made unclean on the day on which he is able to bring his offerings, he loses not the whole period already observed, but only the seven days required for a purification rite.

Because of Eliezer's triplet at M. 3:3-4, a further unit of materials in which Eliezer figures is appended, M. 3:5, to which are added M. 3:6, relevant for its issue, and M. 3:7, joined to M. 3:6 because it cites the same authorities. So M. 3:3-4 carry in their wake a sizable supplement. The point of M. 3:5 is that if someone vows to be a Nazir and is unclean, he commences counting the clean days only after he has become clean. Eliezer glosses this rule. M. 3:6 is relevant because of its common theme: someone who vows to be a Nazir while abroad. Since the dirt of foreign countries is unclean as is a graveyard in the Holy Land, the vow takes effect only when the man comes up to the Land and enters a state of cleanness. The Houses then dispute how long a spell must be observed if the man has vowed a sizable period. The Shammaites rule he keeps only a standard thirty-day period, and the Hillelites hold the man to his originally specified period. M. 3:7 then presents another Houses' dispute, this time on conflicting testimony about how long a period a man has vowed to be a Nazir. This item is relevant, as is clear, only because the Houses figure in the apodosis. At this point, with this sequence of singleton-appendices, the present unit draws to a close and a new problem will come into view.

3:1

A. He who said, "Lo, I am a Nazir," cuts his hair on the thirty-first day.
B. But if he cut it on the thirtieth day, he has fulfilled his obligation.
C. [If he said], "Lo, I am a Nazir for thirty days,"
D. if he cut his hair on the thirtieth day, he has not fulfilled his obligation.

M. 3:1

The cutting of the hair takes place once the vow has been fulfilled. If one vows to be a Nazir without further specification of the length of his spell, he is assumed to be a Nazir for thirty days. Therefore if he cuts his hair on the thirty-first, he has done his duty. If he cut it on the thirtieth, he also has fulfilled his obligation, since part of the thirtieth day—before the haircut—is deemed equivalent to the whole. C-D then are the operative clause. If the man vowed to observe thirty (whole) days, he has to keep the whole of the thirtieth day, so that we do not invoke the principle operative at B. The purpose of the pericope therefore is effected in the contrast of B with D.

D. Said R. Simeon b. Eleazar, "The House of Shammai and the House of Hillel did not differ concerning one who vowed to be a Nazir for thirty days,
E. "that *if he cut his hair on the thirtieth day, he has not fulfilled his obligation* [M. 3:1C-D].
F. "Concerning what did they dispute?
G. "Concerning a case in which one vowed without further specification [M. 3:1A].
H. "For: The House of Shammai say, 'If he cut his hair on the thirtieth day, he has not fulfilled his obligation.'
I. "And the House of Hillel say, '*If he cut his hair on the thirtieth day, he has fulfilled his obligation*' " [M. 3:1B].

T. 2:10 (concluded) L P. 128, ls. 23-26

Simeon b. Eleazar phrases matter in terms of a Houses' dispute.

3:2

A. He who took a Nazirite-vow for two spells cuts his hair for the first on the thirty-first day and for the second on the sixty-first day.

B. And if he cut his hair for the first on the thirtieth day, he cuts his hair for the second on the sixtieth day.

C. But if he cut his hair on the sixtieth day less one, he [nonetheless] has fulfilled his obligation.

D. This testimony did R. Pappyas present concerning one who took a vow to observe two spells as a Nazir, that:

E. if he cut his hair for the first spell on the thirtieth day, he cuts his hair for the second on the sixtieth [B].

F. But if he cut his hair for the second on the sixtieth day less one, he has fulfilled his obligation [C].

G. For the thirtieth day counts for him among the number [of days of the second Nazirite vow].

M. 3:2

The principle, M. 3:1A-B, that part of a day is equivalent to the whole of a day is spelled out yet a second and third time. The pericope goes over the matter twice, A-C, D-G. Cutting the hair on the thirty-first day, A, is in line with M. 3:1A. Why then on the sixty-first day? Because the thirty-first day, on which the hair was cut for the first oath, also counts as the first day for the oath, so the sixty-first day then is the thirty-first day of the second oath. C merely invokes M. 3:1B; this is the thirtieth day of his second vow's spell. Pappyas's testimony states the same principle spelled out in B at E. If we invoke that rule, then we further repeat F, and G explains the whole.

A. He who took two successive vows to be a Nazir, the first a vow to be a Nazir without specification [as to length], and the second a vow to be a Nazir for thirty days

cuts his hair for the first oath on the thirty-first day and for the second on the sixty-first day.

B. *But if he cut his hair for the first on the thirtieth day, he cuts his hair for the second on the sixtieth day* [M. 3:2B],

C. [and] he has fulfilled his obligation.

D. [If the time specified for] for the first Nazirite-vow was thirty days and for the second was not specified,

E. he cuts his hair for the first vow on the thirty-first day and for the second on the sixty-first day.

F. And if he cut his hair on the sixtieth day, he has not fulfilled his obligation.

T. 2:11 L pp. 128-129, ls. 26-32

A simply repeats the point of M. 3:2. Both vows, after all, are thirty-day-ones, just as M. assumes. The problem of the second case, D-F, is that thirty whole days are required for the first. So he cuts his hair for the first vow on the thirty-first day, and for the second on the sixty-first, that is, giving him thirty days from the thirty-first. But, F, the sixtieth day is only twenty-nine days from the thirty-first, so he cannot fulfill his obligation until the sixty-first.

3:3-4

I A. He who said, "Lo, I am a Nazir,"
    B. [if] he was made unclean on the thirtieth day,
    C. he loses the whole [thirty days he already has observed].
    D. R. Eliezer says, "He loses only seven days."
    E. [If he said,] "Lo, I am a Nazir for thirty [whole] days," [and] was made unclean on the thirtieth day, he loses the whole [thirty days he already has observed.]

M. 3:3

II A. "Lo, I am a Nazir for a hundred days,
    B. [if] he was made unclean on the hundredth day,
    C. he loses the whole [hundred days already observed].
    D. R. Eliezer says, "He loses only thirty days."
III E. [If] he was made unclean on the hundred and first day, he loses thirty days.
    F. R. Eliezer says, "He loses only seven days."

M. 3:4

The triplet of disputes of Eliezer and sages follows the same simple dispute form. After specifying the number of days we count for a vow, we come to the problem of a Nazir's being made unclean willy-nilly, Num. 6:9: *If a man dies suddenly beside him and he defiles his consecrated head.* Now Num. 6:12 specifies, *And the former time shall be void, because his separation was defiled.* The issue is not how much of this former time is void, or lost to the Nazir, but how much is lost if the vow has been fulfilled but the offerings not completed, a typically secondary issue. The view of M. 3:3A-C, M. 3:4A-B, is that the whole of the period already observed is lost to the Nazir, who begins the count of thirty days afresh. Eliezer says he loses only seven days. Eliezer's position is that once the vow is fulfilled, contracting uncleanness voids only seven days—that is—imposes the requirement to observe seven clean days before bringing the hair-offering. The man was in a suitable state to bring his offerings on the thirtieth day (M. 3:1). He loses not the whole preceding period. He simply cuts his hair on the seventh day after he was made unclean. Then he counts seven days and grows new hair. This he cuts off in a state of cleanness. He therefore loses only seven of the clean days which he already has observed. Eliezer cannot differ at M. 3:3E, for reasons clear from M. 3:2. The man is required to keep thirty complete days and has not done so, so we have no remedy for him.

The second version of the dispute, M. 3:4A-D, makes the same point, now about a hundred-day-vow. Since the man was made unclean on the day on which his vow was completed, he loses thirty days, D. If he had completed the vow, M. 3:4E-F, but had not brought the offerings, he loses only seven days, in Eliezer's view, just as at M. 3:3. Here it is the anonymous view which is fresh. The point of M. 3:4E is that the man has to observe an unspecified vow, that is, thirty days, all over again.

> A. *He who said, "Lo, I am a Nazir," and was made unclean on the thirtieth day loses the whole [thirty days which he already has counted in accord with the rules of being a Nazir].*
> B. *R. Judah says in the name of R. Eliezer, "He has lost only seven days."*
> C. *[If] he said, "Lo, I am a Nazir for thirty days," and was made unclean on the thirtieth day, he loses the whole [thirty days already observed]* [M. 3:3].
>
> T. 2:12 L p. 129, ls. 32-34

> A. *"Lo, I am a Nazir for a hundred days," and he was made unclean on the hundredth day, he loses the whole [period already observed].*
> B. *R. Judah says in the name of R. Eliezer, "He has lost only thirty days."*
> C. *[If] he was made unclean on the hundred and first day, he loses thirty days.*
> D. *R. Judah says in the name of R. Eliezer, "He has lost only seven"* [M. 3:4].
> E. This is the general principle which R. Judah said in the name of R. Eliezer, "Whoever was made unclean on the day on which it is [not] suitable to bring his offering and who has to count [more days of Naziriteship] [loses all. If he does not have to count], he loses thirty days.
> F. "And whoever was made unclean on a day on which it is suitable to bring his offering and who does not have to count [more days of his Naziriteship] has lost only seven days,
> G. "exclusive of the days on which he is unclean only."
>
> T. 2:13 L p. 129, ls. 33-40 (Reading of E-F: *TK*, p. 523-4)

After citing M., T. supplies E-G, which spell out Eliezer's principle. If the man is made unclean while he still has more days of his Naziriteship, he loses all that he has observed, just as Scripture has said. But if he is made unclean on the day on which it is suitable to bring his offering, that is, when he no longer has to count days of being a Nazir, then he loses only seven days.

3:5

> A. He who vowed to be a Nazirite while in a grave yard,
> B. even if he was there for thirty days—

C. those days do not count for him toward the number [of days owing under the vow].

D. Nor does he bring an offering for his uncleanness [for being in the graveyard].

E. [If, however] he went out and then came back [into the graveyard], they do count for him toward the number [of required days].

F. And he does bring an offering for his uncleanness.

G. R. Eliezer says, "That is not the case if it is on the very same day, since it says, *But the former days shall be void* (Num. 6:12)—[the offering for uncleanness is brought] only when the former days apply to him."

M. 3:5

The point of the contrast between the neatly balanced statements, A-D, E-F, is that the period of Naziriteship does not commence until the man has left the graveyard. But the man also does not bring an offering for his uncleanness as is required at Num. 6:9-10, because he never has been a Nazir to begin with. E-F then complete the picture, and G qualifies E-F. All of this is obvious.

A. He who was unclean and took an oath as a Nazir is prohibited from cutting his hair and from drinking wine and from contracting corpse-uncleanness.

B. And if he cut his hair, drank wine, or contracted corpse-uncleanness, he receives forty stripes.

C. He is sprinkled and repeats the process [on the third and seventh days of becoming unclean with corpse-uncleanness].

D. The days on which he is unclean do not count toward the fulfillment of his vow.

E. But also: the seventh day does count toward the fulfillment of his vow.

F. All cases concerning which they have said, "He does not begin to count [the clean days for the purposes of his Nazirite-vow] until he becomes clean"—the seventh day [of purification] does not count toward the fulfillment of the vow.

G. All cases concerning which they have said, "He begins to count [the clean days for the purposes of his Nazirite-vow] forthwith"—the seventh day does count toward the fulfillment of his vow [M. 7:2].

H. [If] he counted out the days in fulfillment of his Nazirite-vow but did not bring his offerings, he is prohibited from cutting his hair, from drinking wine, and from contracting corpse-uncleanness.

I. And if he cut his hair, drank wine, or contracted corpse-uncleanness, lo, this one receives forty stripes.

J. R. Simeon says, "Once the blood of one of his sacrifices has been tossed in his behalf, he is released from his vow as a Nazir and may drink wine or contract corpse-uncleanness" [M. 6:9].

T. 2:14 L pp. 129-130, ls. 40-48

138   NAZIR CHAPTER THREE 3:5-6

T.'s case runs parallel to M.'s. The man was unclean and declared himself a Nazir. The vow is binding, A-B, even though the days he observes are null, a very valuable addition to M. Then he undergoes a process of purification from corpse-uncleanness, C. This is a seven-day process. These days do not count toward the fulfillment of the vow. But the seventh day, from the moment at which he is purified, does count toward the vow, just as partial days count at M. 3:1ff. F-G refer to M. 7:2. The point of F is that when we say, "He begins to count only when he has become clean," we refer to cleanness completed by sunset or the bringing of the sacrifices. In such a circumstance, the counting begins from the eighth day. But if "he counts forthwith," the reference is to the seventh day, after the sprinkling and immersion on that day, or to a situation in which he does not bring an offering. Then he counts the remainder of the seventh day as a clean day. H-J then specify the point at which the vow is deemed to come to an end, as at M. 6:9.

3:6

A. He who [while overseas] took a vow to be a Nazir for a long spell and completed his spell as a Nazir, and afterward came to the Land [of Israel]—
B. the House of Shammai say, "He is a Nazir for thirty days."
C. And the House of Hillel say, "He is a Nazir as from the very beginning."
D. M'ŚH B: Helene the Queen—her son went off to war, and she said, "If my son comes home from war whole and in one piece, I shall be a Nazir for seven years." Indeed her son did come home from war, and she was a Nazir for seven years. Then at the end of the seven years she went up to the Land. The House of Hillel instructed her that she should be a Nazir for another seven years. Then at the end of the seven years she was made unclean. So she turned out to be a Nazir for twenty-one years.
E. Said R. Judah, "She was a Nazir only fourteen years."

M. 3:6

The foregoing has specified that if one vows to be a Nazir in the graveyard, the vow takes effect only when he leaves it. The lands outside of the Holy Land are deemed to be unclean with corpse-uncleanness. Shall we then invoke the same rule? The Houses concur that we do. The issue is, How long a spell is required once the man comes to the Land? The Shammaites require a standard period, thirty days. The House of Hillel hold him to his word and require him to observe the vow he has specified. D of course is meant to serve as a precedent for C. Judah has a different view of the facts of the case.

3:7

A. He concerning whom two groups of witnesses gave testimony—
B. these testify that he took a vow to be a Nazir for two spells,
C. and these testify that he took a vow to be a Nazir for five spells—
D. the House of Shammai say, "The testimony is at variance, and no Naziriteship applies here at all."
E. And the House of Hillel say, "In the sum of five are two spells. So let him serve out two spells of Naziriteship."

M. 3:7

The dispute is clear as stated. The Shammaites see the two groups as contradicting one another. The Hillelites stress the facts on which they agree. The pericope is relevant to the foregoing in only a tenuous way.

A. Said R. Ishmael b. R. Yohanan b. Beroqah, "The House of Shammai and the House of Hillel did not differ concerning a case
B. "in which there were two sets of witnesses,
C. "in which there were two sets of witnesses giving testimony concerning him,
D. "that he is a Nazir for the shortest period [specified in their joint testimony].
E. "Concerning what sort of case did they differ?
F. "Concerning a case in which there were two individual witnesses giving testimony concerning him.
G. "For: *The House of Shammai say, 'The testimony is divided, so that there is no obligation to be a Nazir here at all.'*
H. "*And the House of Hillel say, 'In the sum of five are two spells. So let him serve out two spells of Naziriteship'* " [M. 3:7].

T. 3:1 L p. 131, ls. 1-5

C appears to repeat B. Otherwise the case is clear as restated.

CHAPTER SEVENTEEN

NAZIR CHAPTER FOUR

This rather odd chapter takes up two distinct problems, but as we have already seen, M. has a way of phrasing the closing pericope of one unit in such a way that the statement of its *principle* introduces the *theme* of the unit which is to follow, while the statement of its *theme* or problem preserves the concerns of the unit which is drawing to a close. This is so, in Chapter Four, at M. 4:4. The opening unit, M. 4:1-3, treats the problem of several persons affirming that they take upon themselves the status of Nazir adopted by others. The important point is that if a man adopts his wife's vow while at the same time annuling it, the vow is binding on him and not binding on her. This point is made twice over, in nearly the same language, at M. 4:1 and M. 4:2. M. 4:3, finally, has a man annul his wife's vow without her knowledge. If she violates the terms of the vow, thinking that she is violating those terms when in fact she is free of the vow, she is not punished.

The second unit wants to discuss the disposition of animals set aside but not actually needed in fulfillment of the requirement that the Nazir bring as an offering along with his hair ("hair-offering") a sin-offering, burnt-offering, and peace-offering. Now if the animals are set aside but then no longer needed, e.g., because the Nazir dies during the vow, the sin-offering is allowed to die. The others are given as freewill-offerings. If coins are set aside and not designated for specific purposes, all are used for a freewill-offering. If they are designated for their particular animals, then the ones for the sin-offering are disposed of, and the others are used as specified. Now this point may well be expressed (and T. so states it) in terms of the sudden death of the well-prepared Nazir. But M. expresses it in terms of a *woman* who has vowed to be a Nazir and set aside an animal, and then whose husband annuls her vow. The problem is the same. But the case now serves as a continuation of the superficially overriding theme of the chapter, the control exercised by the husband over the vows of the wife. Moreover, M. 4:5 carries this same theme forward, asking to what point in the offering up of the hair-offering does the husband lose the right to annul the vow, as from the beginning.

The shift which in a rather subtle way has taken place is best seen at M. 4:6 and M. 4:7, which concern themselves with the disposition of animals set aside for a Nazir but not needed by him or her. These pericopae now ignore the case of the wife entirely, even while repeating, at M. 4:6, the language of M. 4:4 specifying the disposition of various items in the collection of animals. The interest of M. 4:6 is in how we deal with animals set aside by a father for the fulfillment of a son's hair-offering, in a case in which the father has imposed the oath of Nazir upon the son, and the son has rejected or deliberately violated the oath. So here too the animals are not needed. At M. 4:7 we ask about whether a son may make use of the animals set aside for his father's hair-offering in place of his father. So in all, M. 4:4 + 6, 7 take up one problem and M. 4:1-3 + 5, another, and the two problems are woven together at M. 4:4-5, a masterpiece of formulation for the purposes of tight and smooth redaction.

4:1-2

A. He who said, "Lo, I am a Nazir," and his friend heard and said, "Me too," "Me too"—
B. all of them are Nazirs.
C. [If] the vow of the first was declared not binding, the vows of all of them are deemed not binding.
D. [If the vow of the] last of them was declared not binding, the last of them is not bound, but all the rest of them remain bound.
E. [If] he said, "Lo, I am a Nazir," and his friend heard and said, "Let my mouth be like his mouth, and my hair like his hair," lo, this one is a Nazir [= M. 1:1A].
I F. [If he said], "Lo, I am a Nazir," and his wife heard and said, "Me too"—
G. he annuls her vow, but his stands.
II H. [If the wife said,] "Lo, I am a Nazir," and her husband heard and said, "Me too," he cannot annul [her vow].

M. 4:1

I A. "Lo, I am a Nazir,—and you?"
B. and she said, "Amen,"
C. he annuls hers, but his stands.
II D. [If she said,] "Lo, I am a Nazir, and you?"
E. and he said, "Amen,"
F. he has not got the power to annul her vow.

M. 4:2

We have two units, closely related in general theme but distinct in specific problem, M. 4:1A-E and M. 4:1F-G, which is repeated by M. 4:2. I cannot point to another instance in M. when two pericopae so completely repeat the points and language of one another as M. 4:1F-G and M. 4:2. M. 4:1A-E are divided into two parts, a triplet at A-B, C, and D, and a supplement at E, which simply supplies other acceptable language for the procedure indicated at A. The main point throughout, then, is that if one Nazirite-vow depends upon another, then the unbinding of the principal one serves the loosen all the others, just as at M. Ned. 9:7. But the contrary is not the case, so C as against D.

The same point is then made at M. 4:1F-G and H. If the husband vows first and the wife follows suit, then, while he has the power to annul her vow, he can do nothing about his own. If he follows suit when she takes a vow, this is tantamount to confirming her vow, H. As we see, M. 4:2A-C repeats M. 4:1F-G, and M. 4:2D-F, M. 4:1H. All that shifts is the language acceptable for the procedure indicated at M. 4:1F-H, and that means that M. 4:2 is formally and functionally parallel to M. 4:1E (!).

A. He who took two vows as a Nazir, counted out the first but did not bring his offerings, and afterward sought absolution for the first from a sage to declare it not binding for him—

B. the second vow to be a Nazir goes forth with the loosening of the first.

C. [If] he counted out the days required for both of them, and brought the offerings for both of them at one time,

D. he gets credit only for one of them.

E. [If] he set aside the offerings for one of them by itself and the offering for the other by itself and went and offered this one in place of that one, he has not fulfilled his obligation.

T. 2:15 L p. 130, ls. 48-52

T. makes two points, one of them tangentially relevant to M. 4:1. If a man has taken two vows to be a Nazirite, that is, in two successive spells, the second depends upon the first. If the first is declared not binding, so is the second—a notion familiar from M. T.'s second point, C-D and E, is that the vows are distinct from one another and each has to be carried through to its final sacrifices. The man therefore may not bring the offerings for both together. Nor may he use offerings set aside in fulfillment for one vow for the conclusion of the other, which says the same point again. So the dependence of the two vows is at the outset, not at the end, and the reason is that the motive for the one, if proved to be invalid, also annuls the other. But, as is clear, each must be served out to its own conclusion.

A. *He who said, "Lo, I am a Nazir,"* and then hesitated for a time sufficient for a break in conversation,

B. *and his friend heard and said, "And me too"* [M. 4:1A]—

C. he is bound by the oath, but his friend is not bound by it.

D. And how long as a time sufficient for a break in conversation?

E. Sufficient time to ask after someone's welfare.

T. 3:2 L p. 131, ls. 5-7

NAZIR CHAPTER FOUR 4:1-2

A. *"Lo, I am a Nazir,"*

B. and his friend heard and said, *"Let my mouth be like his mouth, and my hair like his hair,"* lo, this one also is a Nazir [M. 4:1E].

C. [If he said], "Let my hand be like his hand," "My foot like his foot," lo, this one is a Nazir.

D. [If he said], "My hand is a Nazir," "My foot is a Nazir," he is not a Nazir.

E. "My head is a Nazir," "My liver is a Nazir," lo, this one is a Nazir.

F. This is the general principle: [If he spoke of] something upon which life depends, he is a Nazir. [If he spoke of] something on which life does not depend, he is not a Nazir.

T. 3:3 L p. 131, ls. 7-10

A. He who says to his wife, "Lo, I am a Nazir, and you?"

B. if she said, "Yes," both of them are bound [by his oath].

C. If he wanted to annul her vow, he annuls her vow, because the vow [of his] came before the confirmation [of her vow].

D. If not [B], he is bound by his vow, and she is not bound [by his vow].

E. He who says to his wife, "Lo, I am a Nazir, and [if] you [are]?"

F. if she said, "Yes," both of them are bound by his oath.

G. And if not, both of them are not bound,

H. because he makes his vow contingent upon her vow.

T. 3:4 L pp. 131-132, ls. 10-14
(Lieberman lists no T. 3:5 on pp. 131-132)

A. [If] his wife said to him, "Lo, I am a Nazir, and you?"

B. [if] he said, "Yes," both of them are bound by her oath.

C. If he wanted to annul her vow, he cannot annul it,

D. because [his] confirmation [of her vow] came before his vow.

E. If not, she is bound and he is permitted.

T. 3:6 L p. 132, ls. 14-16

A. [If] his wife said to him, "Lo, I am a Nazir, [if] you are?"

B. if he said, "Yes," both of them are bound by her vow.

C. If not, both of them are not bound,

D. because she made her vow depend upon his vow.

T. 3:7 L p. 132, ls. 16-18

A. He said to his friend, "Lo, I am a Nazir, and you?"

B. if he said, "Yes," both of them are bound.

C. If not, he is bound, and his friend is not bound.

T. 3:8 L p. 132, ls. 18-19

A. He who says to his friend, "Lo, I am a Nazir, [if] you are?"

B. if he said, "Yes," both of them are bound.

C. And if not, both of them are not bound,

D. because he made his vow depend upon the vow of his [friend].

E. [If] his friend said to him, "Lo, are you a Nazir?"

F. [if] he said to him, "You?"
G. if he said to him, "Yes," he is bound, and his friend is not bound.
H. [If] his friend said to him, "Lo, are you a Nazir?"
I. if he said to him, "And you?"
J. if he said to him, "Yes," then both of them are bound.
K. And if not, both of them are not bound,
L. because he made his vow contingent upon the vow of his [friend].

T. 3:9 L p. 132, ls. 19-23

T. 3:2's gloss of M. is clear and required. The friend is bound by the oath only if he applied it to himself at the instant at which it is first expressed. T. 3:3's complement is equally useful. After augmenting the repertoire of acceptable formularies, C, it makes a familiar distinction. If someone declares his extremities to be "Nazir," it is meaningless. But if he refers to an essential part or organ, that means he speaks of himself, and so he becomes a Nazir. T. 3:5 augments M. 4:2. At A-D, the man asks his wife whether or not she wishes to join him in the Nazirite-vow. If she affirms that she does, he may still annul her vow, just as at M. If she does not consent, D, then she is not a Nazir, because a man cannot force a Nazirite-vow upon his wife. At T. 3:5E-H, the man makes his vow contingent upon the wife's joining him, as H specifies, and the rest follows. T. 3:6 continues this line of thought. When the husband says, "Yes," it is deemed to be his confirmation of the wife's vow, before his following suit. If he does not wish to follow suit, E, she is in any case bound by his having said, "Yes." T. 3:8 is obvious and prepares the way for T. 3:9, which goes over entirely familiar ground.

A. The woman who took a vow and her girl-friend heard and said, "And I too," and afterward the husband of this one [who originally took the vow] came and annuled it for her—
B. she is not bound by her vow, but her girl-friend is bound by it.
C. R. Simeon says, "If she [the girl-friend] had said, 'Also I intended only to be like her,' then both of them are not bound by the vow."

T. 3:10 L p. 132, ls. 23-27

Once more M.'s principle, that a vow made contingent upon another is released along with that upon which it depends, is worked out. It is Simeon's view which is the important qualification, for if, A-B, the friend made the vow without such a specification, then the husband's annulling the vow of his wife has no affect upon that of the other.

A. [If she said], "By an oath that I not enter this house,"
B. and she made a mistake and went into it—
C. she is not bound as to the past but is bound as to the future.

T. 3:11 L p. 132, ls. 26-27

The interpretation of A may be this: she said, "By oath, I have not gone into that house," but she erred and actually had gone in. The oath is null, since she is treated as one who does so under constraint. But if she prohibited herself by such an oath from entering the house in the future, and by error she went in, the oath is valid (*TK* p. 530). The relevance to our context is unclear.

    A. A woman who took an oath to be a Nazir and her husband heard and did not annul the vow for her—
    B. R. Meir and R. Judah say, "He has put his finger between her teeth."
    C. "If he wanted to annul the vow, he may do so.
    D. "And if he said, 'I do not want a wife who is a Nazir,' he puts her away and pays off her marriage-contract."

T. 3:12 L p. 132, ls. 27-29

    A. R. Yosé and R. Simeon say, "She has put her finger between her teeth.
    B. "For if the husband wanted to annul the vow, he cannot do so.
    C. "And if he said, 'I do not want a wife who is a Nazir,' she goes forth without receiving payment of her marriage-contract."

T. 3:13 L pp. 132-133, ls. 29-31

Since the husband has the power to annul the oath and does not do so, if he divorces her on its account, he pays off the marriage-contract, so Meir and Judah. Yosé and Simeon say that since he cannot annul her Nazirite vow, if he divorces her on its account, he also does not have to pay off the contract.

4:3

    A. A woman who took a vow as a Nazir but nonetheless went around drinking wine and contracting corpse-uncleanness—
    B. lo, this one receives forty stripes.
    C. [If] her husband annulled the vow for her, but she did not know that her husband had annulled it for her and nonetheless continued to go around drinking wine and contracting corpse-uncleanness,
    D. she does not receive forty stripes.
    E. R. Judah says, "If she does not receive forty stripes, nonetheless, she should receive punishment for disobedience."

M. 4:3

A-B are obvious and are stated only to set up C-D, as well as Judah's gloss, E.

    A. *A woman who took a vow as a Nazir—*
    B. *her husband annuled the vow for her, but she did not know that her husband had annuled [the vow] for her,*

C. *she went around drinking wine and contracting corpse-uncleanness* [M. 4:3A, C]
D. lo, this one receives forty stripes [*vs.* M. 4:3D].
E. And when R. ʿAqiba would reach this matter, he would cry, saying, "Now if someone who intended to take up in his hand pig-meat and took up in his hand lamb-meat and who ate it has to effect atonement, he who intends to take up in his hand pig-meat and who actually does take up in his hand pig-meat—how much the more so that he require atonement and forgiveness!"

T. 3:14 (continued) L p. 133, ls. 31-36

A. He who took a vow to be a Nazir but went around drinking wine and contracting corpse-uncleanness,
B. and afterward he sought absolution from a sage, and the sage absolved him of the vow,
C. does not receive forty stripes.
D. Said R. Judah, "If he does not receive forty stripes, he receives stripes for rebellion against the law."

T. 3:15 L p. 133, ls. 39-41

T. goes over M.'s ground. If T. 3:14D does not refer to stripes for rebelling against the law, as at T. 3:15, then T. differs from M.'s ruling.

4:4

A. A woman who took a vow to be a Nazir and set aside her beast [for the required sacrifice], but afterward her husband annulled her vow for her—
B. now if the beast set aside for her belonged to him,
C. it goes forth and pastures in the corral.
D. But if the beast set aside for her belonged to her,
E. the animal designated as a sin-offering is left to die. And the animal designated as a burnt-offering is offered as a burnt-offering. And the animal designated as a peace-offering is offered as a peace-offering. It is eaten for one day [like a Nazir's peace-offering] but it does not require bread-offering [unlike a Nazir's offering].
F. [Now if] she had coins which she had not designated for any specific purpose, they fall to a freewill-offering.
G. [If the] coins [were] designated [for a specific purpose]—
H. those designated for a sin-offering are to go off to the Salt Sea.
I. They are not available for benefit, but the laws of sacrilege to not apply to them.
J. The coins set aside for the purchase of a burnt-offering are used for the bringing of a burnt-offering.
K. And they are subject to the laws of sacrilege.
L. The coins set aside for the purchase of a peace-offering are used for the bringing of a peace-offering.
M. And [the animal] is eaten for one day and does not require a bread-offering.

M. 4:4

M. now wishes to raise the question of the disposition of the Nazir's offering in the event that it cannot be sacrificed. M.'s way to introduce this problem is to tie it to the foregoing. That is, since the husband may annul the wife's vow, his doing so also may permit us to treat the disposition of the wife's animals, or the money set aside for the purchase of those animals, in the event that he does annul the vow. We could have formulated the same problem with reference to a Nazir who sets aside animals or money for their purchase and then dies. But if we stated matters in that framework, we should have no suitable point of continuity with M. 4:1-3. That is why the redactor has formulated the problem in the terms which are before us. Let us proceed to the details.

The woman vowed to be a Nazir and set aside animals for the purpose of the sacrifices due at the end of her vow. But inbetween times, her husband annuled her vow. What is the status of the animals? The answer to the question is given in two parts, B-C, and D-E. The pattern set then generates a sizable, distinct counterpart. The basic point is worked out at B-C. If the animal belonged to the husband, then it was not sanctified and returns to the fold, unconsecrated. The wife cannot consecrate what is not hers, and the husband has obviously not made that beast over to her.

D then sets up the pericope's more compelling interest, which is expressed at D-E, F, and G-M, with the important point repeated at E and G-M. If the beast was hers, then it was indeed consecrated, even though the vow turns out to be null. The sin-offering has been designated for a particular purpose and can serve no other (M. Zeb. 1:1). It is therefore left to die. The burnt-offering and the peace-offering are offered up as freewill-offerings—just as at F. The peace-offering is treated in accord with the law covering the peace-offering of a Nazir, so it is eaten only for a day and a night. If it were an ordinary peace-offering, it would have been available over a period of two days and the intervening night following the sacrifice (M. Zeb. 5:6-7). A bread-offering accompanies the Nazirite's peace-offering. But because the vow has been nullified, in this instance we drop that requirement. So at one point we follow the Nazir's offerings' rule, *viz*, the time at which the peace-offering is eaten, and at the other we do not. The second case, F, is self-evident. If the woman has not designated the several coins for the purchase of animals for the several required offerings, all the money is used for a freewill-offering. If the coins are designated for their several purposes, then we purchase animals with them and designate the animals and then treat them as at E.

A. He who set aside coins for the purchase of offerings for his Naziriteship—

B. they are not available for benefit but are not subject to the laws of sacrilege.

C. For all of them [the coins which have been set aside] are suitable to serve for bringing peace-offerings.

D. [If] he died, coins which have not been designated for the purchase of a particular sacrifice fall for the purchase of a freewill-offering [M. 4:4F].

E. Coins which have been designated for the purchase of a particular sacrifice [are dealt with as follows]:

F. *Those which have been set aside for the purchase of a sin-offering go off to the Salt Sea. They are not available for benefit but are not subject to the laws of sacrilege.*

G. *Those which have been set aside for the purchase of a burnt-offering are used for the bringing of a burnt-offering. And they are subject to the laws of sacrilege.*

H. *Those which are set aside for the purchase of a peace-offering are used for the bringing of a peace-offering, which is eaten for one day and which does not require a bread-offering* [M. 4:4H-M].

I. [If he said,] "These are for my burnt-offering, and the rest of the money is for the purchase of the rest of the offerings for my Naziriteship," and then he died—

J. with the money set aside for the purchase of a burnt-offering, let one bring a burnt-offering. And the rest of the money falls for the purchase of a freewill-offering.

K. [If he said that] these are for his peace-offering and the rest is for the remainder of the offerings for his Naziriteship and then died,

L. with the money set aside for the purchase of a peace-offering, let one bring a peace-offering. And the rest of the money falls for the purchase of a freewill-offering.

M. [If he said,] "These [coins] are for the purchase of my burnt-offering, and these for the purchase of my sin-offering, and the rest are for the purchase of the rest of the offerings for my Naziriteship," and then he died—

N. the coins set aside for the sin-offering go off to the Salt Sea. They are not available for benefit but are not subject to the laws of sacrilege.

O. [If he said,] "These are for my sin-offering, and these are for my burnt-offering, and these are for my peace-offering," and the coins got mixed up together,

P. lo, this one should purchase with them three beasts, whether from one point [of the mixture of coins] or from three distinct points [of the mixture].

Q. He renders the coins set aside for the purchase of a sin-offering unconsecrated on account of the animal to be used for the sin-offering [which he now has purchased], and the coins set aside for the purchase of a burnt-offering [are rendered] unconsecrated on account of the burnt-offering, and the coins set aside for the purchase of a peace-offering [are rendered] unconsecrated on account of the peace-offering.

R. And he pays the coins over to the owners of the several animals.

S. He should not pay out the money to the owners until he renders the coins unconsecrated by means of each of the animals [which he is purchasing].

T. 3:16 L pp. 133-134, ls. 41-51

A-C make the important point that, since any or all of the coins may be used for bringing peace-offerings, the laws of sacrilege do not apply, for those laws do not apply to peace-offerings. T.'s further development of the problem confirms the view that M. could as well have spoken of a Nazir who set aside coins and who died as the woman whose husband annuled her vow. T.'s fresh points come at Iff. What T. does is simply to extend M.'s basic principle at M. 4:4F, so I-L. If the coins which have been designated get mixed up with one another, O-Q + R-S invoke the standard procedure.

4:5

A. Once the blood of any one of the offerings has been tossed for her, he cannot any longer annul the vow.
B. R. ʿAqiba says, "Even if any one of the beasts had been slaughtered in her behalf [but the blood not yet tossed], he cannot annul her vow."
C. Under what circumstances?
D. In the case of the hair-offering of a woman who had remained clean.
E. But if it was the hair-offering of a woman who had become unclean, he may annul her vow.
F. For he has the power to say, "I don't want a disgraceful wife."
G. Rabbi says, "Even in the case of a hair-offering brought by a woman who had remained clean, he may annul the vow.
H. "For he has the power to say, 'I don't want a wife whose hair is shaved off.' "

M. 4:5

The dispute, A vs. B, concerns the point at which the vow is deemed fulfilled and therefore no longer subject to the husband's abrogation. A places that time at the tossing of the blood of any of the offerings. ʿAqiba sets the time back to the act of slaughtering of the beast. This dispute, C-F maintain, is at the sacrifices brought upon the completion of the Nazirite-vow in a state of cleanness. But if the Nazirite-woman has to bring sacrifices on account of her having becoming unclean, the husband still may annul the vow for the reason given, E-F. For in any event she has more days to observe. Rabbi invokes the same kind of reasoning in a case in which the sacrifices are those marking the absolute fulfillment of the vow. He may annul the vow right down to the point at which her hair is shaved off, for the reason specified at H.

F. *Under what circumstances?*
G. *In the case of the hair-offering of a woman who had remained clean.*
H. *But if it was the hair-offering of a woman who had become unclean, he may annul the vow* [M. 4:5C-F].

I. For it is as if he annuls the vow for the future.
J. *For he has the power to say, "I do not want a disgraceful wife."*
K. *Rabbi says, "Also in the case of a hair-offering brought by a woman who had remained clean, he may annul the vow.*
L. *"For he has the power to say, 'I do not want a wife whose hair is shaved off' "*
[M. 4:5G-H].

T. 3:14 L p. 133, ls. 36-39

T. glosses M. as indicated.

4:6

A. A man imposes a Nazirite-vow upon his son, but a woman does not impose a Nazirite-vow upon her son.
B. How so?
C. [If] he cut his hair, or his relatives cut his hair,
D. he objected [and would not keep the vow] or his relatives objected—
E. [if] he had a beast set apart [for his offering],
F. the beast set aside as a sin-offering is left to die.
G. And the beast set aside as a burnt-offering is offered as a burnt-offering, and the one set aside as a peace-offering is offered as a peace-offering and eaten on one day and does not require a bread-offering.
H. [If] he had set aside coins [for the purchase of his offerings, and they] had not yet been designated, they fall to the purchase of a freewill-offering.
I. [If] the coins had been set aside and designated for particular purposes,
J. the coins set aside for the purchase of a sin-offering go off to the Salt Sea. They are not available for benefit, but they are not subject to the laws of sacrilege.
K. The coins set aside for the purchase of a burnt-offering are used for the bringing of a burnt-offering, and they are subject to the laws of sacrilege.
L. The coins set aside for the purchase of a peace-offering are used for the bringing of a peace-offering, which is eaten on one day and does not require a bread-offering.

M. 4:6

The point of the pericope is not quite obvious. It is not to say that against his will the son must keep the vow if the father imposes it upon him. The point is that, if the father imposes such a vow, and if the son chooses not to keep it, then the vow nonetheless is deemed valid so far as the designation of animals for sacrifice, or of money for the purchase of animals for sacrifice, is concerned. That is a quite different matter. What is proved by C is that the son may decline to observe the Nazirite-vow, and by D, the son may object to the vow. So without the son's concurrence, A is not valid. But the validity of the vow, as is clear, is tested by the disposition of the animals or money, E-L, verbatim at M. 4:4. Without B-L, A would have been rather misleading. But without B, C-L simply lay out a separate case, and A means what it says (!).

    A. The House of Shammai say, "A man does not impose a Nazirite-vow upon his son."
    B. And the House of Hillel say, "He does impose a Nazirite-vow on his son."
    C. [If] he imposed such a vow on him while he was a minor,
    D. if he then shaved,
    E. or produced two pubic hairs,
    F. the Nazirite-vow imposed on him by his father is null.
    T. 3:17 L p. 134, ls. 51-53

M. follows the Hillelites. If the son shaved his head (M. 4:6C), this nullifies the vow. Or if he reaches puberty, F, the vow is null—a separate point.

4:7

    A. A man brings a hair-offering [with offerings set aside] for the Naziriteship of his father, but a woman does not bring a hair-offering [with offerings set aside] for the Naziriteship of her father.
    B. How so?
    C. He who had a father who was a Nazirite, who had set aside coins for the purchase of his sacrifices, which had not been designated for his particular Naziriteship-offerings, and whose [father] died,
    D. and he said, "Lo, I am a Nazir on condition that I may bring a hair-offering with the coins [set aside by] father"—
    E. Said R. Yosé, "Lo, these coins fall to the purchase of a freewill-offering.
    F. "This one does not bring a hair-offering [with money set aside] for the Naziriteship of his father.
    G. "And what is the case in which one brings a hair-offering [with money set aside] for the Naziriteship of his father?
    H. "He who, along with his father, was a Nazir,
    I. "and his father set aside coins which were not designated for the purchase of particular animals for the fulfillment of his Nazirite-vow and [his father then] died—
    J. "this is a case which one brings a hair-offering [with offerings set aside] for the Naziriteship of his father."
    M. 4:7

At issue is whether the son may make use of the offerings set aside for the Naziriteship of his father. C-D lay matters out one way, E-I, the other. In the former case, the son has the right to become a Nazir in order to make use of the coins his father had put aside for the purchase of offerings (so long as these coins have not been designated for particular purposes, e.g., a sin-offering for the father). Yosé holds that the rule is invoked only for someone who already is a Nazir along with his father, that is, in the lifetime of the father.

    A. *Under what circumstances did they rule, A man brings a hair-offering [with offerings set aside] for the Nazirite-vow of his father* [M. 4:7A]?
    B. "When he took a Nazirite-vow in the lifetime of the father.
    C. "But if he took a vow to be a Nazir after the death of his father,
    D. "he does not bring a hair-offering [with offerings set aside] for the Nazirite-vow of his father," the words of R. Yosé and R. Eleazar and R. Simeon [= M. 4:7E-J].
    E. R. Meir and R. Judah say, "One way or the other, one does not bring a hair-offering [with offerings set aside] for the Nazirite-vow of his father.
    F. "Under what circumstances did they rule, *A man brings a hair-offering [with offerings set aside] for the Nazirite-vow of his father?*
    G. "When his father left him money which had not been designated [for particular animals in fulfillment] of his Naziriteship, and then his father died.
    H. "But if his father left money which had been designated, or a cow [designated in fulfillment of his Nazirite-vow], then he does not bring a hair-offering [with offerings set aside] for the Nazirite-vow of his father."

T. 3:18 L pp. 134-135, ls. 53-58

B-D repeat the view of M. 4:7E-I. E-G are the view of M. 4:7C-D.

CHAPTER EIGHTEEN

NAZIR CHAPTER FIVE

The applicability of a vow to be a Nazirite in a case in which one has taken such a vow in error is subject to a Houses' dispute, which provides the theme and substance of this brief, essentially unitary chapter. There are two units, M. 5:1-3 + 4, and M. 5:5-7. The House of Shammai maintain that a vow made in error is binding, and the House of Hillel hold that that is not the case (M. 5:1-3). This is stated in language distinctive to the issues of Nazirite-vows only at M. 5:3. But the construction is a unity, beginning to end, with a general statement of the dispute, three specific illustrations in perfect balance, then a debate. The Hillelite position, that a vow to consecrate something made in error is not binding, has then to be clarified. M. 5:4 therefore makes the point that the Hillelites refer to prevailing facts which happen not to be known at the time of the taking of the vow. But if the facts prevailing at the time of the vow change later on, the vow remains valid. There is no issue of treating the vow as null on account of things which happen later on, contrary to the position of Eliezer, M. Ned. 9:2.

The second unit goes over the same ground, which is why I regard the chapter as a single and unitary essay. Now we have a person coming toward a group of people. One says, "I am a Nazir if it is Mr. So-and-so," and the next, "...if it is *not* Mr. So-and-so," and so on down the line. The Shammaites, true to form, declare all to be Nazirs, in the theory that a vow made in error is binding, and the vow not made in error obviously is binding too. The Hillelites say that he is a Nazir who (in this context) turns out to be wrong. Tarfon maintains that none is a Nazir, since the issue of Naziriteship is not invoked in a case of mere exaggeration (= M. Ned. 3:1). T. shows that it is Judah who introduces Tarfon's saying, and of course, we are familiar with his position on this matter. The contrary view is Simeon's, which we know at M. 2:8: A Nazir-vow taken in a situation of doubt is binding, and we provide for that situation. M. 5:7, finally, outlines a situation on which all parties may concur, because the facts of the case are sufficiently ambiguous to treat all those who have taken conditional vows as having imposed a vow upon themselves. Clearly, it is the Hillelites who require this case. But, as we see, underlying the statement of the chapter as a whole are judgments on issues live in sayings assigned to Yavneans, and, especially, Ushans. So for substantive reasons it will appear that the work is the creation of authorities of Usha or their successors. In a moment we shall examine formal reasons for the same proposition.

5:1-3

A. The House of Shammai say, "[An act of] consecration done in error is binding [consecrated]."
B. And the House of Hillel say, "It is not binding [consecrated]."
C. How so?
I D. [If] one said, "The black ox which goes out of my house first, lo, it is consecrated,"
F. and a white one went out—
G. The House of Shammai say, "It is consecrated."
H. And the House of Hillel say, "It is not consecrated."

M. 5:1

II A. "The gold *denar* which comes into my hand first, lo, it is consecrated,"
B. and one of silver came up [into his hand]—
C. the House of Shammai say, "It is consecrated."
D. And the House of Hillel say, "It is not consecrated.
III E. "The jug of wine which comes up into my hand first, lo, it is consecrated,"
F. but one of oil came up—
G. the House of Shammai say, "It is consecrated."
H. And the House of Hillel say, "It is not consecrated."

M. 5:2

A. He who vowed to be a Nazir and sought absolution of a sage, who declared his vow to be binding
B. counts out the days from the moment at which he took the vow.
C. [If] he sought absolution from a sage, who declared him not bound,
D. [if] he had a cow set aside,
E. it goes forth and pastures with the herd [never having been consecrated].
F. The House of Hillel said to the House of Shammai, "Do you not concede in this case, which is [an example of] an act of consecration made in error, that the beast goes forth and pastures with the herd [so is not consecrated]?"
G. The House of Shammai said to them, "Do you not agree in the case of one who erred [in counting out the tithe of cattle] and called the ninth, tenth, and [called] the tenth, ninth, and [called] the eleventh, tenth, that it is [all three are] consecrated?"
H. The House of Hillel said to them, "It is not the staff [which he used for

counting out the cattle to name to tenth in sequence] which has rendered it consecrated.

I. "Now if he had laid the staff on the eighth or on the twelfth, do you think he has done anything of consequence at all? But the Scripture which declared the tenth consecrated has declared the ninth and the eleventh consecrated as well."

M. 5:3

This is a rather sophisticated pericope, since it takes for granted the reader will understand the importance of the case cited, as if out of nowhere, at M. 5:3A-E. That is, we are expected to understand that that independent pericope has been adduced in evidence in behalf of the position of the House of Hillel, as against the case of the tithe of cattle, which serves the Shammaites. Yet what appears to be external to the pericope as a whole in fact is its most important component, since, without M. 5:3A-E, we have nothing which accounts for the inclusion of the construction in this particular tractate and therefore also justifies its location in our chapter. It follows that the whole is unitary, and I am inclined to think, unitary from its very beginnings, since the redactional importance of M. 5:3A-E is matched by the formal importance of the tripartite example, M. 5:1D-G, M. 5:2A-D, and M. 5:2E-H, a perfectly matched set, clause for clause. Curiously, therefore, not only do we have a unitary construction, but, given the formal perfection of its central constituent, the formal, unitary character and its redaction in our tractate and chapter appear to coincide.

Once we recognize the formal and redactional traits, the exegesis of the pericope poses no problems. The dispute at the outset, M. 5:1A-B, is clear as given, and the three examples which follow show that the moot principle concerns a statement of consecration made in error. As at M. 1:1, 2:1, the Shammaites declare it binding, on the grounds that the qualifying language ("black") is secondary to the principal intent (to consecrate on ox). The Hillelites conceive that the whole statement forms one context, and therefore there is an error which nullifies it. The relevance at M. 5:3A-E is clear because the Hillelites tell us the meaning of the case, F. If the vow is not binding and the man had set aside a cow, then the cow is deemed not consecrated. This is evidently the position of all parties, for, if it were not, the Hillelites could not adduce it in support of their position. The Shammaites, for their part, invoke M. Bekh. 9:8 (*Holy Things* III, pp. 232-236). If one is counting out the tithe of his flock and errs by calling the ninth which comes out the tenth, then the tenth, ninth, and the eleventh, tenth, all three are deemed consecrated. Here is an error which is not null at all. The Hillelites hold that the reason that all three are consecrated cannot be that the man has made an error which is deemed null. For the same rule would not apply to the eight or twelfth, so the Shammaites' conclusions from this case are not a *propos*. Scripture, not the principle of the Shammaites, is invoked, M. 5:3I.

> A. *He who vowed to be a Nazir and sought absolution from a sage, who declared his vow to be binding* [M. 3:3A]—
> B. the House of Shammai say, "He counts out the days from the moment at which he made inquiry."
> C. And the House of Hillel say, "He counts out the days from the moment at which he [who took the vow] treated it as not binding."
> D. [If] he sought absolution from a sage, who declared his vow to be not binding, these and those concur that *if he had a beast set aside [for his offerings], it should go forth and pasture in the herd* [M. 5:2D-E].
>
> T. 3:19 (continued) L p. 135, ls. 58-61

The relevance to M. is clear at T. 3:19D. The pericope is shaped in a different direction at A-C. What we see is that M.'s case indeed flows from a distinct Houses' dispute. On the strength of this concurrence, D, M. is able to take for granted, as we surmised, that the Shammaites must concede the case invoked, in M., by the Hillelites. The reading at C is somewhat odd, but the point is clear. The Nazir has to observe those days which he treated as not subject to the Nazirite-vow prior to his consultation with the sage.

5:4

> A. He who vowed to be a Nazir and went to bring his beast [for the sacrifice] and found that it was stolen.
> B. if before his beast was stolen he took the vow as a Nazirite, lo, this one is a Nazir.
> C. And if after his beast was stolen he took the vow as a Nazirite, he is not a Nazir.
> D. And this error did Nahum the Mede make:
> E. When Nazirites came up from the Exile and found that the Temple had been destroyed, Nahum the Mede said to them, "Now if you had known that the Temple was destroyed, would you have taken vows to be Nazirs?"
> F. They said to him, "No."
> G. Nahum the Mede declared them unbound [by the Nazirite-vow].
> H. But when the matter came to sages, they said to him, "Whoever took a Nazirite-vow before the Temple was destroyed is a Nazir.
> I. "And whoever did so after the Temple was destroyed is not a Nazir."
>
> M. 5:4

We now explore the implications of the Hillelite position, that a Nazirite-vow taken in error is not binding. What sort of error is in mind? It must be an error of fact. That is, if one assumes that such-and-such is the case and in fact it is not the case, then the error nullifies the vow. But if one makes an assumption which is valid at the time of the vow but which is not valid at some later time, then the vow is valid, because, at the time it was made, it was not invalid. What is rejected is the position of Eliezer, M. Ned. 9:2, that one unlooses a vow on grounds of something which takes place after the vow is made. We have now two instances of the contrary view, M. 5:4A-E, E-I, joined by D. In the former, the man vows to be a Nazir, completes the vow, and then discovers the animal he had set aside in that connection has been stolen. If the beast was in hand when the vow was made, the man is a Nazir. If in fact he took the vow assuming that he owned a beast for the sacrifices at the end of the vow, and discovered that, at the time at which he took the vow, he was in error, owning no such beast, the vow was null at the outset. This rule is nicely stated in the balanced sentences at B, C. The second statement of the same conception is at E-I, which require no comment, since H, I, precisely parallel B, C.

5:5-7

A. [If people] were going along the way and someone was coming toward them—
D. one of them said, "Lo, I am a Nazir if this is so-and-so,"
C. and one of them said, "Lo, I am a Nazir if this is not so-and-so."
D. "Lo, I am a Nazir if one of you is a Nazir."
E. "Lo, I am a Nazir if neither one of you is a Nazir,"
F. "...if both of you are Nazirs,"
G. "...if all of you are Nazirs."
H. the House of Shammai say, "All of them are Nazirs."
I. And the House of Hillel say, "A Nazir is only one whose statement was not confirmed."
J. And R. Tarfon says, "None of them is a Nazir."

M. 5:5

A. [If] he turned away suddenly, he is not a Nazir.
B. R. Simeon says, "Let him say, 'If it was in accord with my statement, lo, I am a Nazir out of obligation, and if not, lo, I am a Nazir out of free will.'"

M. 5:6

A. [If] one saw a *koy* and said, "Lo, I am a Nazir if this is a wild beast."
B. "Lo, I am a Nazir if this is not a wild beast."
C. "Lo, I am a Nazir if this is a domesticated beast."

D. "Lo, I am a Nazir if this is not a domesticated beast."
E. "Lo, I am a Nazir if this is a wild beast and a domesticated beast."
F. "Lo, I am a Nazir if this is *not* a wild beast and a domesticated beast."
G. "Lo, I am a Nazir if one of you is a Nazir."
H. "Lo, I am a Nazir if none of you is a Nazir."
I. "Lo, I am a Nazir if all of you are Nazirs,"—
J. lo, all of them are Nazirs.

M. 5:7

The parallel cases, stated in apocopation, M. 5:5, 7, go over the ground of vows to be a Nazir made in error. The first case presents three pairs: M. 5:5B-C, D-E, F-G, and the second, four: M. 5:7A-B, C-D, E-F, G-I. Simeon's gloss, M. 5:6, makes its own point. The Houses' dispute is easy to interpret. In line with their view at M. 5:1-3, the Shammaites will deem all to be Nazirs, since we ignore the qualificatory language and affirm the principal statement. The Hillelites say that a vow made in error is null, but, here, turning things around, the one who is a Nazir if such-and-such is not the case indeed is a Nazir when his condition is met, I. Ṭarfon carries the Hillelite position to its extreme potentiality. Nazir-vows are valid only when one explicitly and unambiguously takes on the status of the Nazir. The intent of these people is only to make their opinions seem more credible, not to become Nazirs.

The issue of M. 5:6 is distinct. What happens if, in the end, we cannot ascertain the facts of the matter. The man turned away before the group could find out who he was. A holds that in a case of doubt, there is no Nazir-obligation. Simeon repeats his position of M. 2:8.

The second set, M. 5:7, speaks of a beast which is in a gray area. It may be any of the things the people say, and it may not. From the Shammaite position in any event there is no reason for the people not to be Nazirs. But now even the Hillelites are made to concede that the *koy* is in such a status that all of the statements may or may not be true. Now in this sort of doubt, the Hillelites are made to concede that all parties are Nazirs. Obviously, Simeon will derive a good bit of satisfaction from the formulation of M. 5:7. But his opposition in this case need not differ, and, it follows, M. 5:7's *koy* leaves all parties satisfied.

E. *This error did Nahum the Mede make* [M. 5:4D] when he declared a vow to be released.
F. *[If people] were walking on the way and some one was coming toward them,*
G. *one of them said, "Lo, I am a Nazir, if this is so-and-so,"*
H. *and one of them said, "Lo, I am a Nazir if it is not so-and-so,"*
I. *"Lo, I am a Nazir if one of you is a Nazir,"*
J. *and one of them says, "Lo, I am a Nazir if neither one of you is a Nazir,"*

K. *"Lo, I am a Nazir if both of you are Nazirs,"*
L. *and one of them says, "Lo, I am a Nazir if all of you are Nazirs,"*
M. *the House of Shammai say, "All of them are Nazirs."*
N. *And the House of Hillel say, "A Nazir is only one whose statement was not confirmed."*
O. And they bring an offering in partnership.
P. R. Judah says in the name of R. Tarfon, "Not a single one of them is a Nazir [M. 5:5], because a Nazirite-vow applies only when it is clearly and unambiguously expressed beyond a shadow of a doubt."
Q. Said R. Yosé, "The House of Shammai did say in the case of one who says, 'Lo, I am a Nazir if this is Joseph,' and it turned out to be Joseph, '...if this is Simeon,' and it turned out to be Simeon, that he is a Nazir."
R. If one saw an androgyne [a person with both male and female sexual traits] and said, "Lo, I am a Nazir if this is a man,"
S. and one says, "Lo, I am a Nazir if this is not a man."
T. "Lo, I am a Nazir if this is a woman,"
U. and one of them says, "Lo, I am a Nazir if this is not a woman,"
V. "Lo, I am a Nazir if this is not a woman,"
V. "Lo, I am a Nazir if this is both a man and a woman,"
W. and one of them says, "Lo, I am a Nazir if this is neither a man nor a woman,"
X. "Lo, I am a Nazir if one of you is a Nazir,"
Y. "Lo, I am a Nazir if none of you is a Nazir,"
Z. "Lo, I am a Nazir if both of you are Nazir,"
AA. "Lo, I am a Nazir if all of you are Nazirs,"
BB. all of them are Nazirs.
CC. And all of them count out nine vows of Naziriteship.

T. 3:19 L pp. 135-136, ls. 68-73

T. systematically cites and glosses M. 5:4, 5:5. The gloss of M. 5:4 is trivial. That of Tarfon at F is important, since the principle behind Tarfon's ruling now is supplied. R-CC provide a case parallel to M. 5:7. CC's point is that one may undertake nine successive Naziriteships in reference to a case such as this (B. Naz. 34a).

CHAPTER NINETEEN

NAZIR CHAPTER SIX

After having established the conditions under which a person is bound by the Nazirite-vow, we proceed to specify the restrictions imposed by that vow. These are three, repeated at M. 6:1A and M. 6:5A: not to contract corpse-uncleanness, not to cut the hair, and not to consume that which is produced by the vine, inclusive of grapes, grape-pits, and grape-skins. The chapter systematically treats the second and the third of these restrictions, not drinking wine at M. 6:1-2 and not cutting the hair at M. 6:3, 4-5; M. 6:6-11, then deal with cutting the hair at the end of the vow. Chapter Seven proceeds to the matter of contracting corpse-uncleanness. In all therefore, the materials are laid out with considerable attention to thematic cogency. But the contents are not very interesting. The prohibition against wine, grapes, grape-skins, and grape-pits is illuminated only slightly. What is the volume of these things on account of which the Nazir incurs liability? This matter is worked out at M. 6:1-2.

The rest of the chapter attends to issues of cutting the hair. At the outset, M. 6:3, some singleton declarative sentences state a few basic laws. M. 6:4 and M. 6:5, by contrast, constitute two very well-constructed and balanced pericopae, each making its own comprehensive points about wine, cutting the hair, and contracting corpse-uncleanness. The point of the former is that if one violates the rules many times without warning, then all of the violations together are expiated by a single offering. But if the violator is warned many times not to violate the rules of the Nazir, then he is liable for each and every violation. This point, of course, is hardly particular to our tractate. M. 6:5 presents rules which are distinctive to the Nazir: the ways in which the three prohibitions compare to one another. Both pericopae are elegantly laid out and could not be improved upon for their formal beauty.

M. 6:6 and M. 6:7 turn to the important questions of how one cuts his hair in a case of having contracted corpse-uncleanness, and how one does so at the end of a vow in which cleanness has been preserved throughout. M. 6:8 proceeds to the offerings which accompany the cutting and offering up of the thirty days' growth of hair, and, at M. 6:9, we pursue the topic of the offering up of the hair-offering: the hair and the animals which are sacrificed at the end of the period in which the Nazirite-vow is observed.

M. 6:10 and M. 6:11 deal with special problems in this same regard. If the offering on account of which the hair is cut off and offered up turns out to be invalid, then the hair-cutting also is invalid, and the Nazir has to observe the vow another thirty days. M. 6:11 finally asks about the case in which the blood of one of the Nazir's offerings is properly tossed, then the Nazir is made unclean (e.g., a priest drops dead while the Nazir is touching him). Eliezer says that the offerings which the man has already offered in a state of cleanness are lost, and when the man completes his new vow (for having contracted corpse-uncleanness), he has to replace these as well. Sages give the man credit for the offerings already prepared while the Nazir was in a state of cleanness.

6:1

A. Three things are prohibited to a Nazir: [corpse-]uncleanness, cutting the hair, and anything which goes forth from the grape-vine.

B. And: anything which exudes from the grape-vine joins together with anything else which exudes from the grape-vine [to form a volume prohibited for use].

C. And one is liable only if he will eat about an olive's bulk of grapes.

D. The first *mishnah:* Until he drinks a quarter-*log* of wine.

E. R. ʿAqiba says, "Even if he dunked his bread into wine and there is in what is sopped up enough to join together to be in the volume of an olive's bulk, he is liable."

M. 6:1

If we read the pericope as a connected series of sentences, then A introduces the whole, but is forthwith forgotten, only to be expounded at M. 6:5A. So the main point is B: Any product of the vine is equivalent to any other product to form the requisite volume of prohibited grapes. That volume is stated at C. If a person ate an olive's bulk of grapes, he is liable, and this is the case even if that volume does not contain, or yield, a quarter-*log* of wine. D then continues C, explaining what it is that C has excluded. The 'first Mishnah' then maintains that the liability is incurred only for drinking a quarter-*log* of wine. The force of E is to reject the volume of the quarter-*log* stated by D. ʿAqiba maintains that an olive's bulk of wine, in solid form, is sufficient to impose liability.

D. And what is the measure [to impose liability] for them?

E. In the volume of an olive's bulk [M. 6:1C].

F. And all of them join together to form the requisite volume of an olive's bulk [M. 6:1B].

G. Wine and vinegar follow suit.

162   NAZIR CHAPTER SIX 6:1-3

H. "What does he do? He brings a cup fulled with wine, and he brings a summer olive, and he puts it into the cup and lets it spill over.
I. "If he drank as much as spills out of the cup, he is liable, and if not, he is exempt," the words of R. ʿAqiba.
J. R. Eleazar b. ʿAzariah declares him exempt unless he drinks a quarter-*log* of wine [M. 6:1D]—
K. whether he mixed it and drank it or whether he drank it straight.

T. 4:1 (continued) L p. 136, ls. 3-6

T. goes over the ground of M. 6:1. H-I tell how we measure the liquid—volume of an olive, in line with M. 6:1C, E. Eleazar, J, is in line with the "first Mishnah."

6:2

A. And he is liable (1) for wine by itself, (2) for grapes by themselves, (3) for grape-pits (*harṣanim*) by themselves, and (4) for grape-skins (*zaggin*) by themselves.
B. R. Eleazar b. ʿAzariah says, "He is liable [in the case of (3) and (4)] only if he will eat two pits and their skin [that covers them]."
C. What are grape pits (ḤRṢNYM) and what are grape-skins (ZGYM)?
D. "*Harṣanim* are what is outside, and *zaggim* are what is inside," the words of R. Judah.
E. R. Yosé says, "That you not err:
F. "It is like the bell (ZWG) of cattle:
G. "What is outside is the hood (ZWG), and what is inside is the clapper."

M. 6:2

Even if one ate the requisite volume of any part of the vine, A, and not all parts together, he is liable. Eleazar rejects A3-4, insisting that one eat the pits and grapes together to the requisite volume. C-G present an explanation of A3, 4. Judah regards *harṣanim* as the skin, *zaggim* as the pits, and Yosé has the *zaggim* as the skin and the *harṣanim* as the pit. I have translated B in line with Yosé's view.

6:3

A. A Nazirite-vow for an unspecified period of time is [to apply] for thirty days.
B. [If] he cut his hair, or thugs forcibly cut his hair, he loses thirty days.
C. A Nazir who cut his hair, whether with scissors or with a razor, or who pulled out any hair whatsoever is liable.
D. A Nazir shampoos and parts his hair [with his fingers], but he does not comb his hair.

E. R. Ishmael says, "He should not shampoo his head in the dirt,
F. "because it makes the hair fall out."

M. 6:3

The topic now shifts to the matter of not cutting the hair. A (= M. 1:3) then is carried forward by B. C is autonomous of what precedes and follows, then D, E-F, present yet further independent rules on the same theme. So the whole is simply a set of mutually relevant, but independent declarative sentences. The points are clear as stated. The Nazir who is given a haircut has to allow his hair to grow for the thirty days more, in line with M. 2:10.

A. A Nazir who shaved or who rubbed his head or who pulled out a hair with a scissors in any amount at all, lo, this one is liable [M. 6:3C].
B. But he loses the days he already has observed only if he does so with a razor [cutting the hair of] the greater part of his head.
C. R. Simeon b. Judah says in the name of R. Simeon, "Just as to two hairs [if left] prevent him [from completing the Naziriteship], so two hairs cause him to lose the days he already has observed."

T. 4:3 L p. 137, ls. 12-14

T. presents a dispute between B and C. M. 6:3C's view is that liability for punishment is incurred if the Nazir removes any hair at all. M. 6:3B is silent on how much hair causes a loss of a month. So far as B is concerned, one loses a month only if he cuts off most of his hair. Simeon argues that just as, when the Nazir shaves, he is deemed not to have shaved sufficiently when two hairs remain, so, when the Nazir cuts off his hair, he is deemed to have violated the requirement of his vow when he cuts off only two hairs.

6:4

I A. A Nazir who was drinking wine all day long is liable only on one count.
B. [If] they said to him, "Don't drink it!" "Don't drink it!" and he continues drinking, he is liable on each and every count [of drinking].
II C. [If] he was cutting his hair all day long, he is liable only on a single count.
D. [If] they said to him, "Don't cut it!" "Don't cut it!" and he continued to cut his hair, he is liable for each and every count [of cutting].
III E. [If] he was contracting corpse-uncleanness all day long, he is liable on only one count.
F. If they said to him, "Don't contract corpse-uncleanness!" "Don't contract corpse-uncleanness!" and he continued to contract corpse-uncleanness, he is liable for each every count.

M. 6:4

The point of the perfectly executed triplet is clear as given.

A. A Nazir who ate anything which is prohibited to him or drank anything which is prohibited to him—
B. [if he was subject] to a single admonition not to do so, he is liable on only one count.
C. [But if] people admonished him and he nonetheless ate, people admonished him and he nonetheless drank, he is liable for each and every count [M. 6:4A-B].

T. 4:1 L p. 136, ls. 1-2

A. R. Eliezer says, "A Nazir who put his mouth over the mouth of a jug of wine and drank the whole thing up under a single admonition not to do so is liable only on one count.
B. "[But if] they were admonishing him not to do so and he nonetheless drank, admonishing him not to do so and he nonetheless drank, he is liable for each count."
C. And so did R. Eleazar rule, "[If] he took a single grapecluster and ate it while subject to a single admonition, he is liable only on one count.
C. "[But if] people were admonishing him and he ate, admonishing him and he ate, he is liable for each and every count."
D. If he ate from it [a grapecluster] fresh grapes and dried ones, ate from it two grape-pits and a single grape-skin, or squeezed from it an olive's bulk of wine and drank it [M. 4:1-2],
E. he is liable for each and every thing [he ate].

T. 4:2 L pp. 136-137, ls. 6-11

T. makes the same points as M.

6:5

A. Three things are prohibited to a Nazir: [corpse-] uncleanness, cutting the hair, and anything which goes forth from the grape-vine [= M. 6:1A].
I B. A more strict rule applies to corpse-uncleanness and hair-cutting than applies to that which comes forth from the grape-vine.
C. For corpse-uncleanness and hair-cutting cause the loss of the days already observed, but [violating the prohibition against] that which goes forth from the vine does not cause the loss of the days already observed.
II D. A more strict rule applies to that which goes forth from the vine than applies to corpse-uncleanness and hair-cutting.
E. For that which goes forth from the vine allows for no exception, but corpse-uncleanness and hair-cutting allow for exceptions,
F. in the case of [cutting the hair for] a religious duty and in the case of finding a neglected corpse [with no one else to provide for burial, in which case, the Nazir is absolutely required to bury the corpse].
III G. A more strict rule applies to corpse-uncleanness than to hair-cutting.

H. For corpse-uncleanness causes the loss of all the days previously observed and imposes the liability for an offering.

I. But hair-cutting causes the loss of only thirty days and does not impose liability for an offering.

M. 6:5

This elegant pericope, bearing a gloss only at F, follows a strict form to its logical fulfillment. The points are all clear as given. Only F refers to facts not immediately self-evident in the pericope—substantive evidence of its character as a gloss, parallel to the formal evidence. It may be a religious duty in the case of a Nazir who was afflicted with ṣaraʿat. He has to cut his hair in the purification-process (Lev. 14:9). One who finds a corpse with no one in attendance must bury it under all circumstances; even a Nazir must do so, as we see at M. 7:1. If the Nazir is made unclean, G, he loses all the days already observed. If he cuts his hair off, he loses only thirty days, H, a beautiful conclusion, since it brings us back to where we started at B-C.

A. A more strict rule applies to the cutting of the hair.

B. For the cutting of the hair is subject to no limit.

C. And the law treats the one who cuts the hair as equivalent to the one whose hair is cut,

D. which is not the case for the other two things.

E. How is it so that *for that which goes forth from the vine there is no exception* [M. 6:5E]?

F. A Nazir who drank wine in the status of heave-offering or in the status of second tithe—

G. one who said, "By an oath! I shall not drink wine," but drank it—

H. such as these are liable for each and every such action.

I. How is it so that *cutting of the hair is allowed an exception in the case of a religious duty* [M. 6:5F]?

J. A man who had been certified as a meṣoraʿ, lo, this one cuts his hair. One need not say that he cuts his hair in connection with his ṣaraʿat, but he even does so also to allow for the inspection-sign of his boil, to see whether or not it spread.

K. Whether he was made unclean or others made him unclean, whether inadvertently or deliberately, whether under constraint or willingly, he loses all the days already observed, and is liable for an offering [M. 6:5H].

L. Whether he cut his own hair or whether others cut his hair, whether inadvertently or deliberately, whether under constraint or willingly, he loses only thirty days [M. 6:5H].

T. 4:4 L pp. 137-139, ls. 14-22

A. Under what circumstances did they rule, *Hair-cutting causes the loss of thirty days [already observed]* [M. 6:5I]?

B. When he had no more days to count.
C. But if he had yet more days to count, lo, this one does not lose any days.
D. [If] he cut his hair on account of a sacrifice and it turned out to be invalid,
E. he loses thirty days.

T. 4:5 L p. 138, ls. 22-24

The meaning of B is that the man did not have thirty days remaining between the time of the hair-cut and the end of the vow. But, C, if there were thirty days left to grow a new head of hair for a proper hair-cut, he loses nothing.

6:6

A. Cutting off the hair on account of contracting corpse-uncleanness: how [is it done]?
B. "One would sprinkle [with purification-water] on the third and seventh day and cut off his hair on the seventh day and bring his offerings on the eight day.
C. "But if he cut off his hair on the eighth day, he brings his offerings on that same day," the words of R. ʿAqiba.
D. Said. R. Tarfon, "What is the difference between this one and a meṣoraʿ?"
E. He said to him, "In the case of this one, cleaning him is contingent on the passing of his [seven] days, but in the case of the meṣoraʿ, declaring him clean is contingent [in addition] upon his hair-cutting.
F. "And he [the Nazir] brings an offering only when the sun has set after conclusion of his purification-rite."

M. 6:6

The superscription at M. 6:6 inaugurates a saying of ʿAqiba, B-C, disputed by D, with a response at E-F. This is not the usual form of a dispute, and the opinion Tarfon should like to provide in place of B-C is not specified. The question is, if a Nazir is made unclean with corpse-uncleanness, and so, in accord with Scripture, has to cut off his hair and bring an offering on account of having been made unclean, how is the procedure worked out? The answer is given at B. The Nazir undergoes the purification-process, being sprinkled with purification-water on the third and seventh day after his contract with the corpse. He cuts off his hair on the seventh day. Then he brings his offering on the day following the completion of the purification-process, so B.

Now if, C, the man completed the purification-process but cut his hair off only on the day following, he brings his offering on the same day. We know that a *meṣoraʿ* undergoes a process of purification involving the cutting of the hair after a seven day spell of purification, then a bringing of offerings. Ṭarfon's question, D, is based on the correct assumption that a *meṣoraʿ* does precisely what the contaminated Nazir does. He then asks what is the difference between the procedures affecting the one and the other. Both are alike in that, C, if the hair is cut on the eighth day, the offerings are brought on the same day. E-F's reply is to differentiate the two in *other* respects. The process of purification of the Nazir is contingent upon the passing of seven days, even if he did not cut his hair. But in the case of the *meṣoraʿ* the process depends also upon the hair-cutting. A second difference, F, is that the Nazir has to await the completion of the purification-process—sunset—on the next day, whether he immersed on the seventh day or on the eighth day. The *meṣoraʿ* who immersed on the eighth day brings his sacrifice on the same day, having been declared clean on the basis of the first haircut and immersion (Lev. 14:8). That is, with reference to E, the *meṣoraʿ* takes a ritual bath only after the haircut (Lev. 14:8), while the Nazir takes it before the haircut. And the rest, F, follows.

6:7

A. The cutting of hair in the case of [completing the vow in a state of] cleanness: How is it done?
B. One would bring three beasts, a sin-offering, a burnt-offering, and a peace-offering [Num. 6:14].
C. "And he would slaughter the peace-offering and cut off his hair after their [slaughter]," the words of R. Judah.
D. R. Eleazar says, "He would cut his hair only after the sin-offering.
E. "For the sin-offering takes precedence under all circumstances."
F. But if he cut his hair after any one of the three of them, he has carried out his obligation.

M. 6:7

When the Nazir completes his vow in a state of cleanness, he brings three offerings, B. After slaughtering one of the three—C *vs.* D-E—he cuts his hair and offers it up. The dispute is clear as stated, with E, which refers to Lev. 5:8, supplying a reason for the position of D. There is no reason that both Judah and Eleazar should not concur on F.

6:8

A. Rabban Simeon b. Gamaliel says, "[If] one brought three beasts and did not specify [their purposes, respectively],
B. "that which is suitable to serve as a sin-offering [a ewe-lamb in its first

year] is offered as a sin-offering, [that which is suitable to serve as] a burnt-offering [a he-lamb in its first year] is offered as a burnt-offering, and [that which is suitable to serve as] a peace-offering [a ram two years old] is offered as a peace-offering."

C. He would take *the hair of the head of his separation* (Num. 6:18) and cast it under the cauldron [in which the peace-offering is cooked].

D. And if he cut it off in the provinces, he would [in any event] cast it under the cauldron [so Y.; B. Nazir 45a: *not*].

E. Under what circumstances?

F. In the case of [completing the vow and] cutting the hair in a state of cleanness.

G. But in the case of cutting the hair in a state of uncleanness, he would not cast it under the cauldron.

H. R. Meir says, "All cast hair under the cauldron except only for one who was unclean [and who cut off his hair outside the Temple] in the provinces."

M. 6:8

The pericope is in two parts, A-B, which conclude the line of thought begun at M. 6:7, and C-H. The point of A-B is clear as stated. C brings us to the disposition of the hair once it is cut off. It is burned in the fire in which the peace-offering is cooked. The readings of D are various, as indicated. The dispute, E-G *vs.* H, concerns the disposition of hair cut off on account of uncleanness. In Meir's view, the clean Nazir tosses the hair under the cauldron used for the peace-offering, and the unclean one, under the cauldron used for the guilt-offering. The unclean Nazir who cuts his hair outside of Jerusalem buries it. (T. 4:6B).

A. *All cast hair under the cauldron, except only for one who was unclean [and who cut his hair] in the provinces* [M. 6:8H],

B. because his hair is to be buried.

C. "He who was made unclean [and who cuts his hair] in the sanctuary casts his hair under the cauldron of the sin-offering or of the guilt-offering," the words of R. Meir.

D. R. Judah says, "The one who cuts his hair in a state of uncleanness here and there does not toss his hair under the cauldron.

E. "The one who cuts his hair in a state of cleanness here and there does cast his hair under the cauldron."

F. And sages say, "The one who cuts his hair by reason of uncleanness here and there, and the one who cuts his hair in a state of cleanness in the provinces do not cast their hair under the cauldron.

G. "You have only a Nazir who cut his hair in a state of cleanness and who does so at the door of the Tent of meeting who casts his hair under the cauldron, since it is said, *And the Nazir will cut his hair at the door of the tent of meeting*" (Num. 6:18) [M. 6:8F-G].

H. R. Simeon Shezuri says, "A man casts his hair under the cauldron, but a woman does not cast her hair under the cauldron,

I. "on account of the young priests."

J. How does one cast it under the cauldron?

K. One puts some broth on it and casts it under the cauldron of the peace-offering.

L. But if one cast it under the cauldron of the sin-offering or of the guilt-offering, he has fulfilled his obligation.

T. 4:6 L p. 138, ls. 24-32

A. Said Simeon the Righteous, "In my entire life I ate a guilt-offering of a Nazir only one time.

B. M'ŚH B: "A man came to me from the south, and I saw that he had beautiful eyes, a handsome face, and curly locks. I said to him, 'My son, on what account did you [become a Nazir and] destroy this lovely hair?'

C. "He said to me, 'I was a shepherd in my village, and I came to draw water from the river, and I looked at my reflection, and my bad impulse took hold of me and sought to drive me from the world.

D. " 'I said to him, 'Evil one! You should not have taken pride in something which does not belong to you, in something which is going to turn into dust, worms, and corruption. Lo, I take upon myself to shave you off for the sake of heaven.'

E. "I patted his head and kissed him said to him, 'My son, may people like you become many, people who do the will of the Omnipresent in Israel. Through you is fulfilled this Scripture, as it is said, *A man or a woman, when he will express a vow to be a Nazir, to abstain for the sake of the Lord*" [Num. 6:2].

T. 4:7 L pp. 138-139, ls. 32-40

T. 4:6 systematically goes over the materials of M. 6:8. A cites Meir's saying and glosses it at B. Then C-G go over the dispute of M. 6:8E-H. The positions of M.—in the Temple, in the provinces, in a state of uncleanness or of cleanness—are reworked in the several names of C, D, and F. Simeon Shezuri has yet another distinction on the subject. The unclarity of M.'s reading at D now falls into place.

6:9

A. He would cook the peace-offerings or seethe it.

B. The priest takes *the cooked shoulder of the ram and one unleavened cake out of the basket and one unleavened wafer and put them into the hand of the Nazir* (Num. 6:19).

C. And he waves them.

D. And afterward the Nazir was permitted to drink wine and to contract corpse-uncleanness.

E. R. Simeon says, "Once the blood of any one of the sacrifices has been tossed in his behalf, the Nazir was permitted to drink wine and to contract corpse-uncleanness."

M. 6:9

The description of the rite begun at M. 6:7A, M. 6:8C, continues at M. 6:9A-C. The dispute of D-E concerns the moment at which the vow is no longer binding. D defines it at the moment that the offering has been waved, in line with the sequence of Num. 6:19, 20. Simeon places it at the earlier point, at which one of the sacrifices has been slaughtered and its blood tossed on the altar. Simeon thus wants the shaving of the head to be done after the blood is tossed, with the notion that, at that point, the vow is null.

> A. A Nazir who was made unclean and again was made unclean and again was made unclean brings a single offering for the whole spell of uncleanness.
> B. "[If] he was made unclean on his seventh day and again was made unclean on his eighth day, he brings an offering for each one of the times he was made unclean," the words of R. Eliezer.
> C. R. Simeon says, "[He brings] single offering for all [the times he was unclean,] until he brings his guilt-offering.
> D. "[If] he brought his guilt-offering and was made unclean, brought his guilt-offering and again was made unclean, he is liable for an offering for each and every time he was made unclean."
> E. And sages say, "[He brings] a single offering for all such incidents until he brings his sin-offering.
> F. "[If] he brought his sin-offering and was made unclean, again brought his sin-offering and was made unclean, he is liable to bring an offering for each and every incident of uncleanness.
> G. "And he does not begin to count clean days until he brings his sin-offering.
> H. "If he brought his sin-offering but did not bring his guilt-offering, he nonetheless begins to count the days of his vow."
> I. R. Ishmael b. R. Yoḥanan b. Beroqah says, "Just as his sin-offering stands in his way, so his guilt-offering stands in his way."
>
> T. 4:8 L pp. 139-140, ls. 40-48

The relevance to M. is in defining the point at which one vow ends and another begins. The point of A is that several occasions of contracting uncleanness within a single spell produce the requirement of a single offering, such as is referred to at M. 6:6. What happens, however, if the man goes through a rite of purification, and, on the seventh day, is made unclean, and then keeps seven days, and on the eighth day after being sprinkled, he is made unclean? Now we have contamination *after* the beginning of the counting of days of cleanness—that is, after the beginning of a fresh spell. So, B, Eliezer maintains that he has to bring an offering for that new occasion. The disputing opinions raise the issue, not directly alluded to in Eliezer's opinion, of the point at which the new spell of counting begins. Simeon presents the familiar opinion that the end of the old vow and the beginning of the new one is at the point at which the Nazir brings the guilt-offering (for having been unclean at the time of his Nazirite-vow). Then he begins the count afresh. Sages put the end of the old and the beginning of the new vow on the occasion of the sin-offering, E-F. Then, G, sages apply their opinion to the opinion of Eliezer, B. At H they explicitly reject Simeon's view. Ishmael, I, takes up the position of Simeon. In all, the expansion of Eliezer's view by the disputants raises issues on which, on the face of it, Eliezer does not explicitly take up a position at all.

6:10

I   A. [If] he cut off his hair after a sacrifice and it turned out to be invalid, his cutting of the hair is invalid, and his sacrifices have not gone to his credit.

II   B. [If] he cut his hair after a sin-offering made not for its own name [under an incorrect designation], and afterward he brought his [other] offerings under their proper designation,

C. his cutting of the hair is invalid, and his sacrifices have not gone to his credit.

III   D. [If] he cut his hair after the burnt-offering or the peace-offering not properly designated and afterward he brought his [other] offerings under their proper designation,

his cutting of the hair is invalid, and his sacrifices have not gone to his credit.

E. R. Simeon says, "That particular sacrifice has not gone to his credit, but the other sacrifices have gone to his credit."

F. And if he cut his hair after all three of them and one of them turned out to be valid, his cutting of the hair is valid, and he brings the other sacrifices.

M. 6:10

We have the same point three times, A, which gives a general rule, then B-C, and finally, the dispute at D-E + F a unitary and nicely composed pericope. The main point is at A. If one makes an invalid sacrifice, then the hapless Nazir who, relying on that sacrifice, cuts his hair has to go through the whole process again. The hair-cutting is valid only in the aftermath of a valid sacrifice. Now B-C present the first exemplification. If the sin-offering is offered under an improper designation ("not for its own name") it is not valid, so M. Zeb. 1:1. It follows that if he cut his hair after such a sin-offering, but then brought the other offerings under a proper designation, his cutting of the hair is invalid. D makes the same point about cutting the hair after offering the burnt-offering or peace-offering under an improper designation. Here too the rule of A is invoked. The sole dispute is on whether the other sacrifices, which *have* been properly designated, go to his credit. Simeon's view is that since the burnt-offering or peace-offering which is not properly designated nonetheless is valid, we limit the invalidation of the hair-cutting and offering to the offering which is unacceptable. The others go to the man's credit. The final point is that if the man waited on cutting his hair until all three animals had been sacrificed, F, and one is not valid, the hair-cutting is valid since it follows some (other) valid sacrifice. The man has merely to bring a replacement for the invalid one.

J. R. Simeon concedes that if he cut his hair after offering a sin-offering under an improper designation, and afterward brought the [rest] of his offerings under their proper designation, [that] his cutting of the hair is invalid. And his sacrifices have not gone to his credit.

T. 4:8 (concluded) L pp. 139-140, ls. 48-50

Simeon explicitly concurs in M. 6:10B-C, which M. has not led us to doubt.

A. That which is appropriate to be brought at the age of one year which he brought at the age of two years,
B. at the age of two years which he brought at the age of one year,
C. or if one of the [animals which he brought] had committed bestiality with a human being, had suffered bestiality with a human being, had been set aside for idolatrous worship, had actually been worshipped, was the fee paid to a harlot or the price paid for a dog, or had one hip larger than the other, or had uncloven hoofs,
D. his cutting of the hair is invalid, and his sacrifices have not gone to his credit [M. 6:10A].
E. And as to the remainder of the peace-offering of a Nazir which he brought not in accord with its requirement, it is eaten for one day and the following night, and it does not require either a bread offering or the giving of the shoulder to the priest.

T. 4:9 L p. 140, ls. 50-53

T. augments M. 6:10A with examples of invalid offerings, A-D.

6:11

A. He in whose behalf one of the drops of blood has been properly tossed and who [then] was made unclean—
B. R. Eliezer says, "He loses the whole [set of offerings already offered up]."
C. And sages say, "Let him bring the rest of his offerings when he becomes clean."
D. They said to him, M'ŚH B: "In behalf of Miriam of Tadmor

[Palmyra] one of the drops of blood was properly tossed, and they came and told her that her daughter was dying, and she went and found her dead.

E. "And sages said, 'Let her bring the rest of her offerings when she will be clean.' "

M. 6:11

The Nazir has completed the vow and a drop of blood of one of the three offerings is tossed on the altar. Then he is made unclean. Eliezer holds that the offerings already made before the man was made unclean do not go to his credit. When he becomes clean, he has to bring a fresh set. One cannot offer the required sacrifices in parts. Sages say that when the man becomes unclean, he brings the remaining offerings. The precedent, D, produces a ruling at E in exactly the language of C.

F. *He in whose behalf one of the drops of blood was properly tossed and who was made unclean—*
G. R. Eliezer says, *"He loses all [the offerings he already has made]."*
H. And sages say, *"Let him bring the rest of his offering when he is clean* [M. 6:11A-C],
I. *"because the hair already has been sanctified by the blood."*

T. 4:9 L p. 140, ls. 50-55

A. MʿSH B: *One of the drops of blood had been properly tossed for Miriam of Tadmor, and then they came and told her that her daughter was dying.*
B. *She went and found her daughter dead,* and she was made unclean on her account.
C. Sages said, *"Let her bring the rest of her offering when she is clean,* because the hair already has been sanctified in the blood" [M. 6:11D-E].

T. 4:10 L p. 140, ls. 55-58

T. cites and at T. 4:9I and T. 4:10C lightly glosses M. The hair is sanctified once the blood is tossed, so the vow has been fulfilled.

A. He who took two vows of Naziriteship, counted out the first but did not bring his offerings, is prohibited from cutting his hair and from drinking wine and from contracting corpse-uncleanness.
B. [If] he was made unclean before he cut his hair,
C. R. Eleazar says, "He has to bring an offering on account of his having suffered uncleanness [while a Nazir]."
D. R. Yosé says, "He does not have to do so,
E. "because he has gone forth from the category of the first vow but has not yet entered into the category of the second vow."

T. 4:11 L p. 140, ls. 58-61

Before one drop of blood is properly tossed, all parties concur that the man remains a Nazir, A. The issue is joined at B. The man brings an offering on account of uncleanness, because the second vow now applies to him. Yosé says that the man is permitted to cut the hair, so clearly the second vow has not *yet* come into force (*TK* p. 555).

CHAPTER TWENTY

NAZIR CHAPTER SEVEN

This brief chapter is in two parts, M. 7:1, and M. 7:2-3 + 4. The former presents an exquisitely balanced dispute and debate on the responsibility of a high priest and a Nazir, both of them prohibited from contracting corpse-uncleanness, when together they come across a neglected corpse. Both must contract corpse-uncleanness in this circumstance, but which one does so? Eliezer assigns the work to the high priest, in the theory that he will not have to bring an offering to expiate his uncleanness, but the Nazir will. Sages have the Nazir do so, since he is consecrated for only a limited time, while a high priest is consecrated permanently. M. 7:2-3 + 4 then take up the more general question of the sorts of corpse-uncleanness which contaminate the Nazir and the modes of the transfer of corpse-uncleanness in this same regard. The construction is unitary but rather complex. The main point is that the Nazir is affected by diverse virulent forms of corpse-uncleanness, but is not forced to cut his hair because of being made unclean by reason of an attack of *sara'at* (Lev. 13-14) or *zob* (Lev. 15). In the former case the Nazir has to undergo a purification-rite and bring an offering. In the latter he simply immerses, awaits sunset, and then continues counting clean days. M. 7:4 contains two appendices for distinct elements in the foregoing construction.

7:1

A. A high priest and a Nazir do not contract corpse-uncleanness on account of [burying even] their close relatives.

B. But they do contract corpse-uncleanness on account of a neglected corpse.

C. [If] they were going along the way and found a neglected corpse—

D. R. Eliezer says, "Let a high priest contract corpse-uncleanness, but let a Nazir not contract corpse-uncleanness."

E. And sages say, "Let a Nazir contract corpse-uncleanness, but let a high priest not contract corpse-uncleanness."

F. Said to them R. Eliezer, "Let a priest contract corpse-uncleanness,

"for he does not have to bring an offering on account of his uncleanness.

"But let a Nazir not contract corpse-uncleanness,

"for he does have to bring an offering on account of his uncleanness."

G. They said to him, "Let a Nazir contract corpse-uncleanness,

"for his sanctification is not a permanent sanctification,

"but let a priest not contract corpse-uncleanness,
"for his sanctification is a permanent sanctification."

M. 7:1

This perfectly balanced dispute carries its own exegesis in the debate, F-G. Both parties must not contract corpse-uncleanness (A). When faced with a situation in which one of them must do so for overriding considerations (B = M. 6:5), Eliezer says the high priest become unclean in burying the corpse because of the reason at F, and sages have the Nazir do so, because of the reason at G. The sanctity of the Nazir is less than that of the high priest, which is permanent and transmitted to his children.

7:2-3

A. On account of what sorts of uncleanness does the Nazir cut his hair [and bring an offering for having become unclean]?

B. (1) On account of a corpse, and (2) on account of an olive's bulk of flesh from a corpse, and (3) on account of an olive's bulk of corpse-matter, and (4) on account of a ladleful of corpse-mould;

C. (5) on account of the backbone, and (5) on account of the skull, and (7) on account of a limb of a corpse, and (8) on account of a limb cut from a living human being on which is still proper flesh;

D. and (9) on account of a half-*qab* of bones, and (10) on account of a half-*log* of blood—

E. on account of touching them, and on account of carrying them, and on account of overshadowing them;

F. and on account of a bone, the bulk of a barley-seed—

G. on account of touching it and on account of carrying it.

H. On account of these the Nazir cuts his hair and is sprinkled on the third and seventh day [after contamination].

I. And he loses the prior days which he has observed.

J. And he begins to count [clean days] only after he is made clean and brings his offerings.

M. 7:2

A. But as to [uncleanness contracted by overshadowing] (1) interlaced foliage, (2) projecting stones, (3) a grave-area, (4) foreign land, (5) the sealing-stone and (6) the buttressing stone [of a grave],

B. a quarter-*log* of blood, and a Tent, and a quarter-*qab* of bones, and utensils which touch a corpse,

C. and because of the days of counting [after producing a symptom of ṣara'at (Lev. 14:8)] and the days during which he is certified [unclean with ṣara'at]—

D. on account of these, the Nazir does not cut his hair or sprinkle himself on the third and seventh days and he does not lose the prior days [observed in cleanness].

E. And he begins to count forthwith [after immersion and sunset].
F. And he is not subject to bringing an offering.
G. Truly did they rule: The days [of uncleanness] by reason of being a *Zab* or a Zabah [Lev. 15:2,25,28], and the days of being shut up as a *meṣoraʿ* [Lev. 13:4-5]—lo, these [nonetheless] go to his credit [in counting out his Nazir-days].

M. 7:3

The literary traits, specified in a moment, make it easy to state the substantive points made by the pericope. They are, first, that the sort of corpse-uncleanness which renders the Nazir unclean involves not only the corpse itself but various things deriving therefrom, and second, corpse-uncleanness then requires that a rite of purification-process be concluded. And on the contrary, if the Nazir is subjected to certain *others* kinds of uncleanness—e.g., a Tent which is not effective to impart uncleanness, or a source of uncleanness insufficient in volume to contaminate, or—especially—if he becomes unclean by reason of a separate and distinct sort of bodily excretion, whether *ṣaraʿat* or *zob*, he is not subjected to a process of purification. It follows that he continues his count, not losing the prior days observed in cleanness, and of course does not have to bring an offering. Truly does M. 7:3G state what is the principal message of the final hand of this complex and excellent piece of work. For the whole tale is in the contrast of M. 7:2H-J and M. 7:3D-F.

The basic structural lines of the pericope clearly are at M. 7:2A, H-J, M. 7:3D-F, the last two being in perfect balance. Then M. 7:3G supplements M. 7:3C and is certainly a secondary addition to the superstructure. The interesting question is, What are the principal components of the construction of M. 7:2? Here we have to turn to M. 7:3's counterpart, and it clearly is at B, so M. 7:2D appears to be basic to that component of the construction as well. M. 7:3A and M. 7:2B do not list parallel items, and the point made by M. 7:3A concerns the overshadowing alone. That is, M. 7:3A's items are not deemed virulently unclean as corpse-matter in such wise that one who overshadows them is made unclean. This same point comes out at M. 7:3B.

Now is the main issue of M. 7:2 really the matter of overshadowing? Hardly, since M. 7:2E is important only in its contrast to M. 7:2G, and the whole—M. 7:2E, F, and G—are clearly interpolated to introduce the issue of *how* the uncleanness is transmitted, specifically to make the point contained in F. That is, M. 7:2B, C, D are able to stand on their own without specification as to how the Nazir comes into contaminating contact with them, whether through touching, carrying, or overshadowing them. The upshot is that M. 7:2-3 as a whole hardly are constructed to make the point of contrast between overshadowing, on the one side, and touching, carrying, or having contact with a source of uncleanness, on the other. Their principal message is in the contrast between the volume of contaminating blood and bones of M. 7:2D and M. 7:3B, on the one side, and the inclusion of M. 7:3C, on the other. The issue of M. 7:2I-J, M. 7:3E-F + G surely confirms that the final hands wanted very much to contrast these two matters, and much else would then appear to be secondary. Overall, moreover, we see how many distinct issues have been drawn together in what is, in fact, a rather impressive piece of tradental work.

> A. All those concerning whom they have ruled, *He does begin to count [the days of his Nazirite-vow] only after he becomes clean* [M. 7:2J]—
> B. if he becomes unclean, he does not bring an offering on account of his uncleanness.
> C. All those concerning whom they have ruld, *He begins to count* and counts [his Nazirite-days] *forthwith* [M. 7:3E]—
> if he is made unclean, he does bring an offering on account of uncleanness.
> D. [If] a bit of corpse-uncleanness is located above the wall, even half on one side and half on the other,
> E. and so too: a living row of cattle, wild beasts, or fowl, which were walking one after the other, even if the head of one is between the hind-legs of the other—
> a Nazir does not cut his hair on account of their [having overshadowed both him and a bit of corpse-matter].
> F. And people [affected by their overshadowing] who enter the Temple or touch its Holy Things are not liable for contaminating the Temple and its Holy Things [M. 7:4A-C].
>
> T. 5:1 (continued) L p. 141, ls. 1-5

T.'s complement to M. 7:2-3 makes the point, A-C, that if a Nazir does not begin to count the days of his vow until he has completed the purification process, then, if he was made unclean before the conclusion of the purification process, he does not have to bring an offering. This new contamination is covered by the one to which he is subject anyhow. If, on the other hand, a Nazir is made unclean but does not have to undergo the purification process and bring a sacrifice, but merely immerses, waits for sunset, and then continues his counting of clean days without bringing an offering (= M. 7:3), if he is made unclean on that day by a source of uncleanness on account of which he does have to cut his hair and bring an uncleanness, then he has to bring such an offering. This is pretty obvious. The sole point is that if one does not have to bring an offering on one count but does on some other within the same time-span, then that latter count is effective.

C-F go over the ground of M. 7:3 in line with M. 7:4A-C. These are sources of uncleanness which do not effect uncleanness through forming a Tent, E, or through bringing to bear a sufficient volume of corpse-uncleanness to begin with, D. It follows that the Nazir is not affected, nor are people kept out of the Temple.

7:4

A. Said R. Eleazar in the name of R. Joshua, "For every form of corpse-uncleanness on account of which a Nazir cuts his hair are people liable on account of entering the sanctuary.

B. "And for every form of corpse-uncleanness on account of which a Nazir does not cut his hair, people are not liable on account of coming into the sanctuary."

C. Said R. Meir, "Let this matter not be less stringent [than when uncleanness is contracted] from a dead creeping thing."

D. Said R. ʿAqiba, "I reasoned before R. Eliezer as follows:

E. "Now if on account of a bone the bulk of a barley-kernel, which does not impart uncleanness to man in a Tent, a Nazir nonetheless cuts his hair for touching or carrying it [M. 7:2F-G],

F. "a quarter-*log* of blood, which does impart uncleanness to man in a Tent—

G. "is it not logical that a Nazir should cut off his hair for having touched or carried it [*vs.* M. 7:3B]?"

H. "He said to me, 'Now what's going on, ʿAqiba! In this area of law people don't adduce arguments *a fortiori* at all!'

I. "But when I came and laid matters out before R. Joshua, he said to me, 'You stated matters very well. But thus have they ruled that the law should be.'"

M. 7:4

This is a rather odd conglomeration, in that M. 7:4A-C and M. 7:4D-I are completely unrelated to one another. The attributive used at A and D signifies continuity with some antecedent unit of thought. In fact, both pericopae, A-C and D-I, constitute two distinct, secondary formations based on M. 7:2-3.

Eleazar's point, A-B, is that people made unclean by the forms of corpse-uncleanness listed at M. 7:2 are liable if they enter the Temple and violate its cleanness. People made unclean by the forms of corpse-uncleanness listed at M. 7:3 are not liable if they come into the Temple. Meir, commenting on the latter proposition, says that even those forms of corpse-uncleanness listed at M. 7:3 should prohibit a person from entering the Temple, by analogy with contact with the dead creeping thing, which prevents a person from going into the Temple.

ʿAqiba, D-I, wishes to reject the proposition of M. 7:3B that a quarter-*log* of blood, which has the capacity to impart uncleanness in a Tent, should be insufficient to contaminate a Nazir in such wise that he must cut his hair. His argument *a fortiori* is clear as stated at E. The framer of the pericope accepts that argument and claims that the sole reason ʿAqiba's position is not decided law is the arbitrary character of the law.

G. R. Eliezer says, "At the outset the elders were divided.

H. "Some of them say, 'A quarter-*log* of blood and a quarter-*qab* of bones,' and some of them say, 'A half *qab* of bones and a half-*log* of blood' [impart corpse-uncleanness in a Tent].

I. "The court which followed them ruled, 'A quarter-*log* of blood and a quarter-*qab* of bones [require burning] heave-offering and Holy Things [made unclean on their account].

J. " 'A half-*qab* of bones and a half-*log* of blood [are sufficient as regards rendering unclean] the Nazir and the sanctuary.' "

K. Said R. Leazar, "When I went to ʿArdasqim, I came upon R. Meir and R. Judah b. Betera, the Chief, who were in session and reasoning about matters of law.

L. "R. Judah b. Paterah said, 'On account of a quarter-*log* of blood a Nazir does not cut his hair and people are not liable who come into the sanctuary or touch its Holy Things.'

M. "Said to him R. Meir, '*Now why should this be less stringent than a dead creeping thing* [M. 7:4C]?

N. " 'Now if on account of a dead creeping thing, which is of lesser weight, a Nazir cuts his hair and they are liable for entering the sanctuary and touching its Holy Things, on account of a quarter-*log* of blood, which is more stringent, is it not logical that a Nazir should cut his hair and that people should be liable for entering the sanctuary and touching its Holy Things?'

O. "R. Judah b. Paterah remained silent before him.

P. "I said to him, 'Meir, don't disgrace him. He was an expert in your behalf in the matter of Joshua b. Mamal.'

Q. "He said to me, 'Indeed so, and he was a true master of laws.'

R. "I stated to him [a rule] in the following language: 'He said to me in the name of R. Joshua,

S. " '*For every form of corpse-uncleanness on account of which the Nazir cuts his hair are they liable for entering the sanctuary, and for any form of corpse-uncleanness on account of which a Nazir does not cut his hair, they are not liable on account of entering the sanctuary*' [M. 7:4A].

T. "And I recognize the correctness of his opinion."

T. 5:1 L pp. 141-142, ls. 5-18

T. gives its own picture of the matter of M. 7:4D-I. Then, K-T, we have an elaborate narrative version of the rule of M. 7:4A-C.

CHAPTER TWENTY-ONE

NAZIR CHAPTER EIGHT

This brief chapter takes up the final question on the Nazirite-vow, doubt as to whether or not a person is made unclean and how in this circumstance he carries out his required sacrifices. M. 8:1 has two Nazirs who are told that one is unclean. But the witness cannot say which one. The two then have to work matters out so that they bring one offering on account of cleanness, fulfilling the vow of the clean one, and one on account of uncleanness. They assign to the one (whichever it was) who was unclean this latter offering. The two then fulfill a second vow of thirty days and repeat the process. They thereby have covered both possibilities, and each has carried out his obligation. But what happens if one of the two dies before the process has worked itself out? Then Joshua has the survivor call upon an outsider to carry out the task of the other party and go through the same procedure. Ben Zoma points out that the survivor will not likely find a willing partner, and he provides for a different procedure.

M. 8:2 then goes on to yet another conundrum, this time a Nazir who may or may not have been unclean and who also may or may not have been certified as a *meṣoraʿ*. Such a person first of all has to complete the processes of purification of a *meṣoraʿ*, which involve two cuttings of the hair. Since he is a Nazir, these can take place only at a thirty-days' interval, instead of at the seven days specified for the purification of the *meṣoraʿ* in Lev. 14:9. At the end of sixty days he will have completed the purification for *ṣaraʿat*. Then he goes through two Nazirite vows, one for the uncleanness, the other for cleanness. After one hundred twenty days he has done all that is required of him. T. presents an immense essay on this same matter, which we shall examine only cursorily.

8:1

A. Two Nazirs, to whom someone said, "I saw one of you made unclean, but I don't know which one of you it was"—

B. they cut their hair and bring an offering, [owed by a Nazirite] because of uncleanness and an offering because of cleanness.

C. And each one of them says, "If it was I who was unclean, the offering because of uncleanness is mine, and the offering because of cleanness is yours. And if it was I who was the clean one, then the offering of cleanness it mine, and the offering of uncleanness if yours."

D. Then they count out thirty days and bring an offering because of cleanness.

E. And each of them says, "If it was I who was unclean, the offering because of uncleanness was mine and the offering of cleanness was yours, and this offering is now because of my being clean. But if it was I who was the clean one, the offering because of uncleanness was mine, and the offering because of cleanness was yours, and this offering now is because of your being clean."

F. If one of them died—

G. Said R. Joshua, "Let [the survivor] seek out someone from the market to take a vow as a Nazir as his counterpart, and let him say, 'If I was unclean, lo, you are a Nazir forthwith. And if I was clean, lo, you will be a Nazir after thirty days.' Then they count thirty days and bring an offering because of uncleanness and an offering because of cleanness.

H. "And he says, 'If I was the one who was unclean, the offering because of uncleanness is mine, and the offering because of cleanness is yours, and if I was the clean one, then the offering because of cleanness is mine, and the offering because of uncleanness is subject to doubt.'

I. "And they count out another thirty days and bring an offering because of cleanness.

J. "And he says, 'If I was the one who was unclean, then the offering because of uncleanness was mine, and the offering because of cleanness was yours, and this is the offering because of my being clean. And if I was the one who was clean, then the offering because of cleanness was mine, and the offering because of uncleanness is subject to doubt. And this is the offering because of your being clean.'"

K. Said to him Ben Zoma, "But who in the world would agree to take a vow as a Nazir to serve as his counterpart?

L. "But he [alone, the surviving Nazir] offers a sin-offering of fowl and a burnt-offering of cattle and says, 'Now if I was the unclean one, the sin-offering is offered in fulfillment of my obligation, and the burnt-offering is a freewill-offering. But if I was the clean one, then the burnt-offering is in fulfillment of my obligation, and the sin-offering is subject to doubt.'

M. "He counts out thirty days [more as a Nazir] and brings an offering because of cleanness and he says, 'If I was the unclean one, the first burnt-offering was a freewill-offering, and this one is in fulfillment of an obligation. But if I was the clean one, the first burnt-offering was in fulfillment of an obligation, and this one is a freewill-offering.

N. "And these are the rest of the offerings which I owe.'"

O. Said R. Joshua, "This one turns out to bring his offerings in bits and pieces."

P. But sages concurred with the opinion of Ben Zoma [M. 6:11].

M. 8:1

The pericope is a unity, but in two parts, M. 8:1A-E, which lay the groundwork, then M. 8:1F-J *vs.* K-N + O,P. It is E which provides the basis for all that follows. The point is that in a situation of doubt, we do have a means of resolving the doubt. What we do is go through a two-stage process of fulfilling the requirements of the first vow, through taking on yet a second vow. On the first go-around, B-C, both Nazirs bring an offering, one for uncleanness, the other for cleanness, and each one makes a conditional declaration concerning it, C. Now we do not know which of them was unclean, which clean. So in the second go-around, they trade-off, as at E. The issue, F, is whether this procedure can be followed sequentially. Joshua has the survivor find a mate for the offering, G, H, I-J. The mate has to keep two successive vows, just as at B-C, D-E. In the first, the survivor has the counterpart become a Nazir either at that time or after thirty days. They bring an offering and go through the procedure of C. Then they repeat the process of D-E. Ben Zoma's criticism, K, leads to a different procedure. The survivor goes through the rite, stating the operative condition, L, then repeats the matter thirty days later, M. The sin-offering of fowl is offered as the offering on account of the doubt about the Nazir's having become unclean, and the burnt-offering is offered as a sacrifice for the completion of the vow in a state of cleanness. If, then, the man had been unclean, this same beast may be designated to have been a freewill-offering. Then, at M, the man brings a complete set of offerings on account of fulfilling the vow in a state of cleanness. Joshua's criticism is that the man is bringing in bits and pieces the offerings for the completion of the vow in a state of cleanness. If he had been clean, the burnt-offering was in fulfillment of his obligation, and now—only now, long afterward—he produces the offerings serving as his sin-offering and peace-offerings. Joshua then concurs with Eliezer at M. 6:11 and Ben Zoma with sages.

A. *Two Nazirs, to whom someone said, "I saw one of you made unclean, but I do not know which one of you it was"* [M. 8:1A]—
B. they count out *thirty days and bring an offering for uncleanness and an offering for cleanness* [M. 8:1B].
C. *And they say, "If I was the unclean one, then the offering for uncleanness is mine and the offering for cleanness is yours, and if I am the clean one, then the offering for cleanness is mine, and the offering for uncleanness is yours"* [M. 8:1C].
D. *And they count out thirty days more and bring an offering for cleanness* [M. 8:1D].
E. *And one says, "If I am the unclean one, then the offering for uncleanness was mine and the offering for cleanness is yours, and this offering is now because of my being clean. But if I was the clean on then the offering for cleanness was mine, and the offering for uncleanness was yours, and this offering is because of your being clean"* [M. 8:1E].

T. 5:3 L p. 143, ls. 30-36

A. *If one of them died,*

B. *Said R. Joshua, "Let [the other] seek out someone from the market to take a vow as a Nazir as his counterpart, and let him say,*

C. *" 'If I was unclean, lo, you are a Nazir forthwith. And if I was clean, you will be a Nazir after thirty days.' Then they count thirty days and bring an offering because of uncleanness and an offering because of cleanness* [M. 8:1F-G].

D. *"And he says, 'If I was the one who was unclean, the offering because of uncleanness is mine, and the offering because of cleanness is yours. And if I was the clean one, then the offering because of cleanness was mine, and the offering because of uncleanness (of yours) is subject to doubt"* [M. 8:1H].

E. *"And they count out another thirty days and bring an offering because of cleanness.*

F. *"And he says, 'If I was the one who was unclean, then the offering because of uncleanness was mine, and the offering because of cleanness was yours, [and this is the offering because of my being clean]. If I was clean, the offering because of cleanness was mine, and the offering because of uncleanness was yours, and this is the offering because of your being clean' "* [M. 8:1I-J].

G. *"[During both] the first thirty days and the second thirty days he [the new Nazir] is prohibited from cutting his hair and from drinking wine and from contracting corpse-uncleanness.*

H. *"And if he cut his hair, drank wine, or contracted corpse-uncleanness, he incurs forty stripes.*

I. *"He himself [the survivor of the original pair] is liable for the first days, but exempt for the second days."*

T. 5:4 L pp. 143-144, ls. 36-45

The brief gloss of Joshua's advice, T. 5:4G-I, deals with the status of the original Nazir, that is, the survivor, and the man who has joined him in the matter. The latter is subject to G-H, the former, I, since the former has now completed his vow at the conclusion of the first thirty days.

8:2

A. A Nazir who was subject to doubt as to being made unclean [on the day he took the vow] and subject to doubt as to being a confirmed [victim of ṣara'at]

B. eats Holy Things after sixty days [= two Nazirite-periods].

C. And he drinks wine and contracts corpse-uncleanness after a hundred and twenty days [four Nazirite-periods].

D. For cutting of the hair in the case of a *nega'[ṣara'at]* overrides [the prohibition against] cutting the hair of the Nazir [only] when it [the ṣara'at] is certain.

E. But in a case when it is subject to doubt, it does not override [the other].

M. 8:2

We conclude this sequence of thought with a conundrum, surely the product of a single hand, since A-C form a single long declarative sentence, and D, E, explain the foregoing: Why does the man have to execute four hair-cuttings. At A we have a Nazir who, on the same day as he took his vow, turns out to be subject to two different matters of doubt. First, he may or may not have been in contact with a corpse. Second, on that same day, he may or may not have been certified as a meṣoraʿ. If he was made unclean, he must cut his hair at the end of his process of purification. If he was a meṣoraʿ, he cuts his hair (shaves his body) twice when he recovers, as I shall now explain.

Our pericope takes for granted a number of facts, which we had best specify at the outset (Maimonides, *Comm.*).

The first is that a meṣoraʿ is among those whose atonement is not yet complete and who cannot consume food in the status of Holy Things. Only when the atonement has been completed through the bringing of the necessary atonement-offering may such a person make use of food in that status. A Nazir, by contrast, is not in that status.

Second, the person afflicted with ṣaraʿat—the meṣoraʿ—cuts his hair two times, then brings his atonement-offering. The first hair-cutting (shaving) is done when the meṣoraʿ is purified from his ṣaraʿat, after he has immersed. The second is done seven days later. He then brings his offerings on the eighth day and may eat Holy Things, as specified in Leviticus Chapter Fourteen.

Third, we already know that the days on which the meṣoraʿ counts out seven days between one shaving and the other, and the days when he is certified unclean, do not diminish the days of the Nazirite-vow (M. 6:5).

Fourth, a single hair-cutting cannot go to a person's credit both in connection with ṣaraʿat and in connection with the Nazirite-vow. This is what generates the conundrum.

Fifth, when the Nazir suffers corpse-uncleanness, even on the last day of his vow, he loses all the days he has observed.

Sixth, the rule stated at D-E must be brought to mind.

With these principles in hand, we may understand the statements of B and C.

After the Nazir has completed his process of purification from the corpse-uncleanness, he cuts off his hair for the first time, with reference to the possibility that he suffers from ṣaraʿat. This he does at the end of thirty days. Why so long? Because he cannot cut off his hair forthwith. He might be a clean Nazir. A matter of doubt concerning his suffering from ṣaraʿat does not override the prohibition against his cutting his hair on account of being a Nazir (D-E). So it is only at the end of thirty days that he cuts off his hair in fulfillment of the requirement of both hair-cuttings—that of the

Nazir, that of the *meṣoraʿ*. He counts seven days, as a *meṣoraʿ* must (Lev. 14:9). But he does not execute the second cutting of hair until thirty days have passed from the first. Why not? Because—again—he may be a clean Nazir. The second hair cutting takes place, therefore, at the end of sixty days. Now he brings the offering of a *meṣoraʿ* and is clean in that regard. He therefore is permitted to eat food which is in the status of Holy Things (B).

But he still is prohibited to drink wine and to contract corpse-uncleanness. Why? Because he may have been a confirmed *meṣoraʿ*, and the cutting of the hair on account of his being a *meṣoraʿ* does not fulfill the requirement for the cutting of the hair after the conclusion of his Nazirite-vow (4). He therefore has to effect two more hair cuttings, each at the end of thirty days: one at the end of ninety days, in fulfillment of the doubt that he may have been an unclean Nazir, and one at the end of the one hundred twenty days, to complete the fulfillment of his Nazirite-vow in a state of cleanness.

Then, as I said, D-E explain the whole procedure. That is we know (M. 6:5) that a Nazir who is a confirmed *meṣoraʿ* cuts his hair for his *ṣaraʿat* in the first hair-cutting forthwith; after seven days he does the second; then he counts out his Nazirite-days. But in a case of doubt, as I said, we do not permit this procedure.

    A. They said to R. Simeon b. Yoḥai, "Lo, if one was a Nazir and a *meṣoraʿ*—

    B. "What is the law as to [the Nazir's] cutting his hair one time and receiving credit on that account both for his Nazirite-vow and for his *ṣaraʿat* purification-rites, [both of which require it]?"

    C. He said to them, "He does not cut his hair [one time for both purposes the purification]."

    D. They said to him, "Why not?"

    E. He said to them, "Now if this one were cutting his hair merely to remove the hair, and that one were cutting his hair merely to remove the hair, you would have ruled quite well.

    F. "But the Nazir cuts his hair to remove the hair, and the *meṣoraʿ* cuts his hair in order thereafter to grow [more] hair."

    G. They said to him, "But we too stated the rule only so that it should not count for him for the days of the certification of his uncleanness. But let it count for him toward the days of his counting."

    H. He said to them, "If this one cut his hair after entering water and that one cut his hair after entering water, you should have ruled quite well.

    I. "But a Nazir cuts his hair after entering water, while a *meṣoraʿ* cuts his hair *before* entering water."

J. They said to him, "But we too started the rule not so that the hair-cutting should go to his credit in a state of cleanness, but let it go to his credit if he brings his offerings on account of uncleanness."

K. He said to them, "If this one cut his hair after the tossing of blood, and that one cut his hair after the tossing of blood, you should have ruled quite well.

L. "But a Nazir cuts his hair after the tossing of blood [of sacrifices] while a *meṣoraʿ* cuts his hair before the tossing of blood."

M. They said to him, "The correct view of the matter: Let it not go to his credit in the days of the completion of his certification for uncleanness, but let it go to his credit for the days of counting.

N. "Let it not go to his credit in a case of cleanness, but let it go to his credit in a case of uncleanness, thus:

O. "A Nazir who was afflicted by *ṣaraʿat* and a *meṣoraʿ* who took a vow as a Nazir will then cut the hair at one time for both requirements."

T. 5:2 L pp. 142-143, ls. 19-30

The point of relevance to M. 8:2 is to explain why a single cutting of hair does not serve two purposes, just as we said in M. (4). The point of E-F is that the *meṣoraʿ* shaves his hair in preparation for a second hair-cutting, before he brings his offerings. The reply, then, is at G: The *meṣoraʿ* of whom we speak already has counted out seven days. He now cuts his hair for the second time—solely to remove the hair, just like a Nazir in a state of cleanness. That sets the stage for the next phase, H-J. At H-J, B. Naz. 60B reads, "If both were required to cut the hair before sprinkling of the blood, your ruling would be valid. But here the *meṣoraʿ* cuts the hair before sprinkling of the blood [Lev. 6:16-18], while the Nazir does so after sprinkling the blood [Num. 6:16-18]." It follows that B. corrects the erroneous text at H-J by dropping that phase of the argument, since the clean Nazir does *not* have to immerse. The conclusion, M-O, is that the single hair-cutting will not go to the credit of a clean Nazir who is a *meṣoraʿ*, for the latter has to grow hair. But it does go to the credit of both purposes in the case in which both cut the hair only for the sake of finally removing it. It further should not go to the credit of a clean Nazir, but it should go to the credit of an unclean Nazir.

A. [If] it is a matter of doubt whether a Nazir was unclean or clean, but it is certain that he was a Nazir,

B. [if] it is a matter of doubt whether a *meṣoraʿ* was unclean or clean, but it is certain that he was a *meṣoraʿ* [= M. 8:2A],

C. *he eats Holy Things after sixty days.*

D. *He drinks wine and contracts corpse-uncleanness after one hundred and twenty days* [M. 8:2A-C].

E. *How so?*

F. [If] they said to him, "You are an unclean Nazir, and an unclean Nazir cuts his hair only after seven days, so go and count out seven days," and he was sprinkled and the sprinkling-process was repeated, and he cut his hair and brought an offering—

G. [and] he counted out seven days and sought to cut his hair, and they said to him, "You are a clean Nazir, and a clean Nazir cuts his hair only after thirty days, go and count out twenty-three more days to complete the required thirty days,"

H. he cut his hair and brought his offering.

I. He counted out thirty days and sought to cut his hair, and they said to him, "You are a clean Nazir, and a clean Nazir cuts his hair only after the blood has been tossed"—

J. what should he then do?

K. He brings a burnt-offering in the form of a beast and makes the following condition concerning it, saying,

L. "Now if I am clean, lo, this is brought in fulfillment of by obligation, and if not, lo, this is a freewill-offering."

M. How should it be done for him to impose the more stringent ruling upon him [as *possibly* a confirmed *meṣoraʿ*]?

N. He brings a new clay jug and puts into it a quarter-*log* of spring water and brings two wild birds and slaughters one of them over the earthenware utensil into the spring water.

O. He digs a hole and buries it in his presence, and it is prohibited for the benefit of anybody.

P. Then he brings a sin-offering in the form of a bird and makes the following condition concerning it, saying,

R. "Now if I am unclean, the sin-offering is in fulfillment of my obligation, and the burnt-offering is a freewill-offering.

S. "But if I am clean, then the burnt-offering is in fulfillment of my obligation and the sin-offering is subject to doubt."

T. And he cuts the hair on his head, beard, and eyebrows, just as *meṣoraʿs* cut their hair, and he brings the burnt-offering of a beast and makes the following condition concerning it, saying,

U. "Now if I was unclean, the first burnt-offering was a freewill-offering and this one is in fulfillment of my obligation. And the sin-offering in the form of fowl is on account of his obligation.

V. "But if I am clean, then the first burnt-offering is in fulfillment of my obligation, and this one is a freewill-offering. And the sin-offering in the form of a bird is subject to doubt."

W. And he cuts off the hair of his head, beard, and eyebrows, just as the *meṣoraʿs* cut off their hair.

X. R. Simeon says, "On the morrow he brings his guilt-offering and its *log* of oil with it and sets them up at the Nicanor gate and makes the following condition concerning them, saying:

Y. " 'If I am a *meṣoraʿ*, lo, this is his [my] guilt-offering, and if not, lo, this is a peace-offering given as a freewill-offering.'

Z. "This guilt-offering then is slaughtered on the north side of the altar. And its blood has to be placed on the thumbs and big toes of the man, and it requires laying on of hands, and drink-offerings, and the waving of the breast and thigh, and it is eaten by the male priests."

AA. But sages did not concur with R. Simeon,

BB. for the man thus brings Holy Things to the house invalidly.

CC. [How so?] To offer a sin-offering of a beast is something he cannot do,

DD. because a sin-offering in the form of a beast is not offered in a case of doubt.

EE. To offer a sin-offering in the form of a bird is something he cannot do.

FF. *For a rich man who brought the offering of a poor man has not fulfilled his obligation* [M. Neg. 14:12].

GG. So what should he do?

HH. Let him write over his property to someone else and then bring the offering of a poor man.

II. It turns out that the poor man brings a sin-offering in the form of a bird, and makes the following condition concerning it, saying.

JJ. "If I was a *meṣoraʿ*, lo, this is in fulfillment of my obligation. And if not, lo, this is given because of the doubt concerning me."

KK. And he is permitted to eat Holy Things forthwith.

LL. But as to drinking wine and contracting corpse-uncleanness, these are things he cannot do.

MM. For the days of his Nazirite-vow are not credited on account of the days in which he is subject to *saraʿat*.

NN. How should he do things in accord with the opinion of Ben Zoma [M.8:1]?

OO. Let him count out thirty days and bring a burnt-offering in the form of a beast and cut his hair, and bring a sin-offering in the form of a bird and make the following condition concerning it, saying,

PP. "If I was unclean, this sin-offering is in fulfillment of my obligation, and the burnt-offering is a freewill-offering. If I am clean, the burnt-offering is in fulfillment of my obligation, and the sin-offering is subject to doubt."

QQ. Then he counts out thirty days and brings the whole of his offering.

RR. And he brings a burnt-offering in the form of a beast and makes the following condition concerning it, saying,

SS. "If I was unclean, the first burnt-offering was in fulfillment of my obligation, and this one is a freewill-offering.

TT. "And the sin-offering in the form of a bird is on account of his obligation.

UU. "If I was clean, the first burnt-offering was a freewill-offering, and this one is brought in fulfillment of my obligation. And the sin-offering in the form of a bird is on account of the doubt which concerns me."

VV. Then he drinks wine and contracts corpse-uncleanness forthwith.

WW. Under what circumstances?

XX. When he took the vow of a Nazir for thirty days.

YY. But if he took the vow as a Nazir for twelve months, he eats Holy Things only after two years have passed.

ZZ. And he drinks wine and contracts corpse-uncleanness after four years have passed.

AAA. If one was in doubt as to being unclean but certainly shut up as a *meṣoraʿ*, he eats Holy Things after eight days.

BBB. He drinks wine and contracts corpse-uncleanness after sixty-seven days.

CCC. If he was certainly unclean but subject to doubt as to whether he was a *meṣoraʿ*,

DDD. he eats Holy Things after thirty-seven days,

EEE. he drinks wine and contracts corpse-uncleanness after seventy-four days.

FFF. If he was unclean of a certainly and determined to be a *meṣoraʿ* of a certainty,

GGG. he eats Holy Things after eight days.

HHH. And he drinks wine and contracts corpse-uncleanness after forty-four days.

T. 6:1 L pp. 144-147, ls. 1-39

A-D go over the ground of M. Then T. spells out the story of the Nazir who may or may not have been unclean, F-G. Then at M we introduce the possibility that he also is a confirmed *meṣoraʿ*. So he has to go through the purification-rite of the *meṣoraʿ* which is described from M through KK. CC then goes back and explains how the *meṣoraʿ* offers his sacrifices after the cutting of the hair at the conclusion of the days of counting, between the first hair-cut and the second. NN points out that our authority does not require a guilt-offering. He now has taken care of the issue of *ṣaraʿat* by having a sin-offering of fowl brought.

We then turn to the concern for the man's Nazirite-vow. If, after all, he was a *meṣoraʿ*, everything done up to now has had nothing to do with his Nazirite-vow. He may be a clean Nazirite, or he may be an unclean one. We turn then to that problem once more. XX-ZZ repeat M.'s proportions, now with a long Nazirite-vow, lasting for a year.

AAA now turns to one who was confirmed as a *meṣoraʿ*. He completes his purification-rite in a week, that is, beginning on the day following the decision that he is clean. At BBB, we calculate the eight days in which the man was confirmed as a *meṣoraʿ*, plus thirty days, and an additional thirty days in which the man was subject to doubt as to whether or not he was a clean Nazir. If, CCC, he was an unclean Nazir but may or may not have been a *meṣoraʿ*, he keeps thirty days to fulfill a Nazirite-vow in cleanness and owes yet seven days to work out the condition of *ṣaraʿat*, hence thirty-seven days, DDD. The point of EEE is that he may have had *ṣaraʿat*, in which case the days he counted do not go to his credit for his Nazirite-vow. He counts out seven days as an unclean Nazir—he was surely that—and then undergoes purification. He counts thirty days for his Nazirite-vow as a clean Nazir, thus thirty-seven, and in addition he has already counted out thirty-seven days, hence seventy-four. At FFF-HHH, the man was certainly unclean as a Nazir and certainly a *meṣoraʿ*, a case M. has left out. He works out the *ṣaraʿat* as expected, GGG, and counts seven days for the *ṣaraʾat* to which he was certainly subjected, seven for the uncleanness which he certainly had suffered, then thirty days for his Naziriteship in a state of cleanness, forty-four in all (HHH). Further discussion is at Lieberman, pp. 144-147, *TK,* pp. 562-569.

CHAPTER TWENTY-TWO

NAZIR CHAPTER NINE

The power and successful effect of Mishnah's principal mode of redactional organization, by theme and its necessary and logical unfolding, become clear when we see a failed experiment in another such mode, by a *general principle* and its application to diverse themes. The present, unsuccessful chapter consists of three units, a miscellany, concluding discussion of the Nazir, an extended essay on the principle that, when there are grounds for making a decision in a case of doubt, one makes such a decision on the basis of those grounds—hence carrying forward Chapter Eight's general thematic interest in matters of doubt and their resolution—and a concluding homily of no impressive weight. So at the center of the chapter is the essay into organizing materials around a given principle, whether or not it is spelled out, applied to diverse and unrelated themes. Indeed, the miscellany at the outset may be seen in that same context.

We start with a brief, rather tightly woven pericope on the applicability of Nazirite-vows to women and slaves; gentiles are excluded. The rules applying to the one are compared with those applying to the other: the husband annuls the Nazirite-vows of the former, not of the latter. If a slave takes a Nazirite-vow, he keeps it after he goes free. If he escaped from his master we have a dispute. Meir says the slave may not drink wine, and Yosé says that he may. Now there are diverse ways to read the matter. One is to impose the notion that Meir confirms the status quo. Since the slave left the master alive, he should suppose he still is alive until he knows that he has died. The slave therefore continues to be exempt from keeping his vow, since by no stretch of the imagination can he be regarded as free.

If this view of what is at issue is correct, then the redactor's plan in placing M. 9:2-4 where they are is to be rather simply understood. For the next set of essays brings us further instances in which we make a decision on the basis of the status quo, "for there are grounds for such a decision" (at M. 9:2M, M. 9:3H, and M. 9:4F, J). In the first instance in a situation of doubt we confirm the unclean person in the presumption of being unclean, and the clean person is confirmed as clean. M. 9:3 is M. Oh. 16:3, an essay on estasblishing a graveyard on the basis of finding a few corpses near one another. Obviously, its principal locus is at Ohalot. M.

9:4A-B cite M. Neg. 5:4, M. 9:4C-F are the same as M. Zab. 2:2, and M. 9:4G-J belong at M. San. 9:1.

The concluding unit, M. 9:5, is an Ushan dispute on whether or not Samuel was a Nazir. Following Maimonides, we may suppose that the practical consequence will be the effect of saying, "Lo, may I be like Samuel!" It is, in any event, an unusually weak conclusion to a sustained and important tractate.

9:1

A. Gentiles are not subject to the Nazirite-vow.
B. Women and slaves are subject to the Nazirite-vow.
C. A more strict rule applies to women than to slaves.
D. For a master forces his slave [to be subject to a Nazirite-vow], but a husband does not force his wife [to be subject to a Nazirite-vow].
E. A more strict rule applies to slaves than to women.
F. For the husband has the right to annul the vows of his wife, but he does not [permanently] annul the vows of his slaves.
G. [If] he annuled [the vow] of his wife, it is annuled for all time.
H. [If] he annulled the vow of his slave,
I. [if] the slave went forth to freedom,
J. he has to complete his Nazirite-vow.
K. [If] he escaped from his master—
L. R. Meir says, "He may not drink wine."
M. And R. Yosé says, "He may drink wine."

M. 9:1

A may or may not be essential to what follows. Since it does stand in contrast with B, it would appear to me that the entire construction, A, B + C-D, E-F, is unitary. G-J form a useful, secondary accretion to A-F. At the same time, K-M are integral to H-J. So the whole is rather deftly woven together. The points are clear as given. The contrast of G to H-I is noteworthy. If the master annuls the Nazirite-vow of his slave, it is only for the time that the slave belongs to the master. That is an important qualification of F—or F and H-J disagree with one another. If the slave escapes, he then does not know whether or not the master is alive. Meir has the slave assume the master is alive; we confirm matters in the last known condition. Yosé says the slave may assume the master has died, so that the slave is now subject to his Nazirite-vow. Alternatively for H-J: If the master annuls the slave's vow, the slave is free and must keep it; then H-J and F surely concur (compare B. Naz. 62b, Albeck, pp. 379-380, Maimonides, *Comm.*, *vs.* Rabad, followed here).

A. A more strict rule applies to a man's wife and his daughter which does not apply to his boy-servant or his girl-servant,

B. [and a strict rule applies] to his boy-servant and girl-servant which does not apply to his wife and his daughter.
C. For as to his wife and his daughter, he annuls their vows.
D. And he cannot force them to drink wine or to contract corpse-uncleanness.
E. But as to his boy-servant or his girl-servant, he does not annul their vows.
F. But he does force them to drink wine or to contract corpse-uncleanness [M. 9:1C-F].
G. And they drink wine only when in his presence and they contract corpse-uncleanness only in his presence.

T. 6:4 L p. 148, ls. 52-56

A. R. Yosé says, "A slave whose master said to him, 'Drink wine for two years,' or 'Contract corpse-uncleanness for two years,' drinks wine in his presence and not in his presence, and contracts corpse-uncleanness in his presence and not in his presence" [cf. M. 9:1K, M].

T. 6:5 L pp. 148-149, ls. 56-58

A. Why does his master force him in the case of a Nazir but not in the case of vows or oaths?
B. A slave who took a Nazirite-vow and [completed it and] cut his hair and then went forth to freedom has fulfilled the terms of his Nazirite-vow.
C. [If] he took a Nazirite-vow and did not cut his hair and went forth to freedom, he has not fulfilled the terms of his Nazirite-vow.
D. [If] he was made unclean and then went forth to freedom, he counts the days of his Nazirite-vow from the time at which he become unclean.

T. 6:6 L p. 149, ls. 58-60

T. 6:4 rephrases M. 9:1C-F in obvious ways. T. 6:4G, 6:5 go over the ground of M. 9:1K-M: whether or not the slave who escapes is bound by his Nazirite-vow. G's view is that of Meir, and T. 6:5 restates Yosé's position. T. 6:6A has no answer. At B the slave takes the vow and completes it while he was a slave. It no longer is binding after he goes forth to freedom. He is credited with keeping the vow, and his sacrifices are valid. But if he took the vow and did not complete it, then he has to complete it when he goes forth, just as at M. 9:1H-J. He has to bring the sacrifices. If he was in process of observing the vow and was made unclean and then is freed, he is deemed to be in the midst of the vow, D, in line with the thinking of B.

9:2-4

A. A Nazir who cut his hair and then [before he brought his offerings] learned that he had been unclean—
  B. if it was a known uncleanness
  C. he loses [all the days he has counted in cleanness].

D. But if it was an uncleanness located in the nethermost deep, he does not lose the days he already has counted out.

E. If before he had cut his hair he learned that he had been made unclean, one way or the other, he loses the days he already has observed.

F. How so?

G. [If] he went down to immerse in a cave and a bit of corpse-matter turned out to be floating at the mouth of the cave,

H. he is unclean.

I. [If] it was located imbedded in the floor of the cave—

J. [if] he had gone down only to cool himself in the water, he is deemed still clean.

K. [If he had gone down] to clean himself from corpse-uncleanness, he is yet unclean.

L. For the unclean person is confirmed in the presumption of being unclean, and the clean one is confirmed in the presumption of being clean,

I M. for there are grounds for such a decision [in either case].

M. 9:2

A. He who finds a corpse in the first instance lying in usual fashion removes it and the earth affected by it.

B. [If] he found two, he removes them and the earth surrounding them.

C. [If] he found three,

D. if there are between one and the other from four to eight *amahs*,

E. lo, this is deemed a graveyard.

F. He examines the dirt twenty *amahs* from it.

G. [If] he found a corpse at the end of the twenty *amahs*, he examines the dirt another twenty *amahs* from that corpse.

II H. For there are grounds for such a decision.

I. But if he had found it at the outset, he would have removed it and the dirt affected by it [= M. Oh. 16:3].

M. 9:3

A. Any matter of doubt concerning *nega‛s* at the outset is ruled as clean before a decision has been made in favor of uncleanness.

B. [But if] a decision has been made in favor of uncleanness, a matter of doubt in its regard is deemed unclean [M. Neg. 5:4].

C. In seven ways do they examine the *Zab* before he has been confirmed to be subject to *Zibah*: In regard to food, drink, carrying things, jumping up and down, sickness, something he had seen, and something in his fantasy.

D. Once he has been confirmed as to *Zibah*, they do not examine him.

E. Any flux he produces through inadvertence, or which is subject to doubt, or his semen is unclean.

III F. For there are grounds for such a decision [= M. Zab. 2:2].

G. He who hits his friend and the reckoned that he would die and the friend got better than he was, but then he got worse and died—

H. he [the one who hit him] is liable.

I. R. Neḥemiah says, "He is exempt.

IV J. "For there are grounds for such a decision" [M. San. 9:1].

M. 9:4

M. 9:2, which makes the point that we confirm a possibility in line with prevailing assumptions, is given four appendices, M. 9:3 and M. 9:4 A-B, C-F, and G-J, taken from other contexts. We need not be detained with their exposition. M. 9:2A-E are a complete unit. G-M go over the same ground. The point of the former is that if the Nazir was in the midst of his purification-rite, cut his hair, but then learned that he had been made unclean, he loses the days already observed if the uncleanness was confirmed and known. But if it was one located deep in the ground, then he does not lose the days he has counted. E makes the point that this latter leniency applies only in the present circumstances. F links the former to what follows, but the case of F-M is quite distinct. Now we have a Nazir immerse in a cave, which thus forms a Tent over the corpse-matter. He is unclean on account of the corpse-matter. But if the corpse-matter turned out to be imbedded in the floor of the cave, and if the man was clean and went only to cool himself, he is confirmed as clean. If he was unclean and went to immerse himself for purposes of purification, he is confirmed in that status. I see no reason to read A into G-M. L-M explain why in each case, and, as I said, the next two units say the same thing in other contexts.

A. For all offerings of the community and the individual, the priestly frontlet effects expiation for uncleanness of the blood and for uncleanness of the body [of the owner],

B. except for the case of the Nazir and the one who prepares the Passover.

C. For in these cases the priestly frontlet effects expiation for uncleanness of the blood, but it does not effect expiation for uncleanness of the body.

D. But if he is made unclean by reason of uncleanness of the nethermost depths, lo, it does effect expiation uncleanness in his behalf.

E. How so?

F. [If] he was going along to slaughter his Passover or to circumcise his son, and they said to him, "There was a corpse with you in that house which you entered," or "...under the stone on which you were sitting,"

G. and if he was informed of this fact, whether he had already prepared his Passover or whether he had not already prepared his Passover,

H. he has to prepare a second Passover.

I. But [if] they said to him, "There was a grave in the nethermost depths with you in that house into which you entered," or "...under that stone on which you were sitting,"

J. if he was so informed of that fact before he had prepared his Passover, then he has to prepare a second Passover [in a state of cleanness].

K. But if he was so informed after he had prepared his Passover, he does not have to prepare a second Passover.

T. 6:2 L pp. 147-148, ls. 40-47

A. And so is the rule in the case of a Nazir who went to offer his offerings, and they said to him, "There was a corpse with you in that house which you entered," or "...under the stone on which you were sitting,"

B. and he was so informed, whether this was before or after he brought his offerings,

C. he has to bring an offering on account of uncleanness.

D. But if they told him, "There was a grave in the nethermost depths with you in that house which you entered," or "...under that stone on which you were sitting,"

E. and he was so informed before he had brought his offerings,

F. he has to bring an offering on account of uncleanness.

G. But if this was told to him after he had brought his offerings, he does not have to bring an offering on account of uncleanness.

T. 6:3 L p. 148, ls. 47-52

T. 6:3 goes over the ground of M. 9:2A-E.

9:5

A. "Samuel was a Nazir," according to the words of R. Nehorai,

B. "since it is said, *And no razor [morah] shall come upon his head* (I Sam. 1:11).

C. "Since in regard to Samson it is said, *[And no] razor [shall come upon his head]* (Judges 13:5), and concerning Samuel it is said, *And no razor...*,

D. "just as the reference to *razor* in the case of Samson means that he was a Nazir, so the reference to a *razor* in the case of Samuel means that he was a Nazir."

E. Said R. Yosé, "But is not the word *morah* said only with regard to fear (*morah*) of a human being?"

F. Said to him R. Nehorai, "But has it not already been said, *And Samuel said, How can I go? If Saul hears it, he will kill me* (I Sam. 16:2).

G. "For he *was* subject to the *morah* of flesh and blood."

M. 9:5

Yosé's claim is that *morah* at I Sam. 1:11 refers to fear. Samuel then was not a Nazir, but was not subject to fear of mortal man, E. F-G then show that that is not possible, leaving A-D to stand.

INDEX TO BIBLICAL AND TALMUDIC REFERENCES

BIBLE

Deuteronomy
  22:24 87
  24:19 95

Exodus
  24:8 36

Ezekiel
  32:23-25 36

Genesis
  17:1 35-36

Jeremiah
  9:26 35
  33:25 35-36

Judges
  13:5 197
  14:3 36

Leviticus
  5:8 167
  13-14 175
  13:4-5 177
  14:8 167, 176
  14:9 165, 181, 186
  14:9-10 187
  15 175
  15:2 177
  15:25 177
  15:28 177
  19:9 95
  19:17 74
  19:18 74

  25:36 74
  27:32 26

Numbers
  6:2 126, 169
  6:9 135
  6:9-12 107
  6:10 115
  6:11 17
  6:12 135, 137
  6:13-20 107
  6:14 115, 167
  6:16-18 187
  6:18 116, 125, 168
  6:19 116, 170
  6:20 170
  10:14 81
  30:1-16 7
  30:2 22, 64-65, 94
  30:3 24
  30:6-15 92
  30:9 99-100
  30:10 92
  30:13 92-93, 95
  30:14 86, 89

I Samuel
  1:11 197
  16:2 197
  17:36 35

II Samuel
  1:20 35
  1:24 80

MISHNAH

ʿArakhin
  8:6 26

Bekhorot
  9:8 155

Ḥagigah
  2:5 26

Ketubot
  5:2 86
  5:4 96

Menaḥot
  12:3 127
  13:10 127

Nazir
  1:1 105, 108, 114-16, 123, 141, 155
  1:1-2 114
  1:1-7 108
  1:1-4:3 108
  1:2 114-18
  1:3 108, 114, 117-18, 120, 163

INDEX TO BIBLICAL AND TALMUDIC REFERENCES 199

1:3-7   114
1:4   108, 114, 118-19
1:5   119-20
1:5-7   108, 114, 119-20
1:6   119-20
1:7   120
2:1   115, 121-23, 155
2:1-2   108, 121-23, 126-27
2:1-4   126
2:1-8   121
2:2   122
2:3   108, 123, 126
2:3-4   121-22
2:4   108, 121, 124-27
2:5   121, 125-27
2:5-6   108, 121-22, 125-27
2:6   125-27
2:7   121-127-28
2:7-8   108, 121-22, 127-29
2:8   127-29, 153, 158
2:9   121, 129
2:9-10   108, 121-22, 129-31
2:10   121, 129-30, 163
3:1   109, 133-35, 138
3:1-2   132
3:1-7   109
3:2   109, 134-36
3:3   135-36, 156
3:3-4   109, 132, 135-36
3:4   135-36
3:5   109, 132-136-38
3:5-6   132
3:6   109, 132, 138
3:7   109, 132-33, 139
4:1   140-43
4:1-2   109, 141-45, 164
4:1-3   109, 140-41, 147
4:2   140-42, 144
4:3   109, 140, 145-46
4:4   109-10, 140-41, 146-50
4:4-7   105
4:4-5:4   109
4:4-5:7   109
4:5   110, 140-41, 149-50
4:6   110, 140-41, 150-51
4:7   110, 140-41, 151-52
5:1   154-55
5:1-3   110, 153-56, 158
5:2   154-55
5:3   153, 155-56
5:4   110, 153, 156-59
5:5   157-59
5:5-7   110, 153, 157-59

5:6   157-58
5:7   110, 153, 158-59
6:1   110, 160-62, 164
6:1-2   160
6:1-4   110
6:1-8:2   110
6:2   111, 162
6:3   111, 160, 162-63
6:4   111, 160, 163-64
6:4-5   160
6:5   111, 160-61, 164-66, 176, 185-86
6:6   111, 160, 166-67, 170
6:6-11   111, 160
6:7   111, 160, 167-68, 170
6:8   111, 160, 167-70
6:9   111, 137-38, 160, 169-71
6:10   111, 161, 171-72
6:11   111, 161, 172-74, 182-83
7:1   111, 165, 175-76
7:1-4   111
7:2   137-38, 176-79
7:2-3   111, 175-79
7:3   177-80
7:4   111, 175, 178-80
8:1   111, 181-84, 189
8:2   112, 181, 184-91
9:1   110, 112, 193-94
9:1-5   110
9:2   110, 112, 192, 195-97
9:2-4   192, 194-97
9:3   110, 192, 195-96
9:3-4   110, 112
9:3-5   111
9:4   192-94, 196
9:5   110, 112, 193, 197

Nedarim
1:1   8, 15-17, 19, 114
1:1-2   15-18
1:1-2:5   8
1:1-3:11   8
1:2   8, 15-17
1:3   8, 18-20
1:3-4   15, 18-20
1:4   8, 15, 19, 24-25
2:1   8, 21-24, 26-27
2:1-2   21-25
2:1-3   21
2:2   8, 21-25
2:3   8-9, 21, 25, 117
2:4   8-9, 21, 25-28
2:4-5   9, 34
2:5   9, 21, 27-28

3:1   29-32, 66, 153
3:1-3   9, 29-31
3:1-4:5   9
3:2   30-31, 75
3:3   30-31
3:4   9, 29, 31-32, 73, 123
3:5   9, 29, 32-33
3:6   33-34
3:6-10   9, 29, 33-34, 36
3:6-11   9, 29
3:7   34
3:8   34
3:9   34
3:10   29, 34, 36
3:11   9, 29, 34-36
4:1   9-10, 37-39, 41-42, 62
4:1-4   41
4:1-5:6   10
4:1-8:6   10
4:2   37-39, 41
4:2-3   10, 27-40, 99
4:3   39, 41
4:4   10, 37, 40-41
4:5   10, 37, 41-42
4:6   10, 37, 42-43
4:7   37, 43
4:7-8   10, 37, 39, 43-44
4:8   43-44, 49
5:1   46, 48
5:1-2   10, 45-46
5:2   46
5:3   10, 45-47
5:4   47-48
5:4-5   10, 45, 47-49
5:5   10, 48
5:6   45, 49
6:1   51-54
6:1-3   11, 50-52
6:1-7:2   11
6:2   51, 53
6:2-3   52
6:3   51-52
6:4   11, 52, 54
6:5   11, 50, 52-53
6:6   11, 50, 52-55
6:6-7   55
6:7   51, 54-55
6:7-9   11, 50, 54-56
6:8   51, 54-56
6:8-9   51
6:9   51, 55, 58
6:10   11, 50-51, 56-58
7:1   11, 59-60, 62, 95

7:1-5   59
7:2   11, 59-60, 62
7:3   11, 56, 59, 61-62
7:3-5   11
7:4   62-63
7:4-5   11, 59, 62-63
7:5   63
7:6   63-64
7:6-7   11, 59, 63-64
7:6-9   59
7:6-8:6   11
7:7   63-64
7:8   64
7:8-9   11, 59, 64-65
8:1   67
8:1-3   11, 66-67
8:2   67, 69
8:3   67
8:4   68-69
8:4-5   68
8:4-6   11, 66-69
8:5   68-69
8:6   68-69
8:6-11:12   12
8:7   66, 69-71
9:1   71-75
9:1-2   12, 73-74
9:2   72-74, 80, 153, 157
9:2-3   73
9:3   74, 80
9:3-4   12, 72, 74-75
9:4   72, 74-76
9:5   12, 72, 75-76
9:5-10   72
9:6   72, 76-78
9:6-8   12, 76-79
9:7   73, 76-78, 123, 142
9:8   73, 77-78
9:9   12, 72-74, 79-80
9:10   12, 73, 80-81
10:1   82-83
10.1-2   82
10:1-3   12, 81-82, 85, 87
10:1-4   12
10:2   81-85
10:3   81-85, 99-100
10:4   13, 81, 85
10:5   85-87
10:5-7   13, 81, 85-90
10:5-8   13
10:6   81, 86-88
10:7   81, 86, 88-90
10:8   13, 81-82, 90-91, 98, 100

INDEX TO BIBLICAL AND TALMUDIC REFERENCES 201

11:1   92-95
11:1-2   14, 92-93, 102
11:1-4   93
11:1-8   13
11:2   93-95
11:3   92, 95-96
11:4   13, 92, 94, 96, 102
11:5   13, 96-97, 99
11:5-8   92
11:6   13, 97-99
11:7   13, 98-99
11:8   13, 92, 99
11:9   13, 92, 99-101
11:9-10   13
11:10   14, 92, 100-101
11:11   14, 92, 101-102
11:12   14, 93, 102

Nazir
 1:1   115
 1:2   118
 1:3   120
 1:4   119
 1:5   116-17
 1:6   117
 1:7   117
 2:1   123
 2:2   125
 2:3   125
 2:4   126-27
 2:5   126-27
 2:6   126-27
 2:7   126-27
 2:8   128
 2:9   128
 2:10   130, 133
 2:11   134
 2:12   136
 2:13   136
 2:14   137
 2:15   142
 3:1   139
 3:2   142, 144
 3:3   143-44
 3:4   143
 3:5   143-44
 3:6   143-44
 3:7   143
 3:8   143-44
 3:9   144
 3:10   144

Negaʿim
 5:4   193, 195
 14:12   189
ʾOhalot
 9:4   192
 16:3   192, 195
Sanhedrin
 9:1   193, 195
Yebamot
 16:6   115
Zabim
 2:2   193, 195
Zebaḥim
 1:1   147, 171
 5:6-7   147

TOSEFTA

 3:11   144
 3:12   145
 3:13   145
 3:14   146, 150
 3:15   146
 3:16   148
 3:17   151
 3:18   152
 3:19   156, 159
 4:1   162, 164
 4:2   164
 4:3   163
 4:4   165
 4:5   166
 4:6   168-69
 4:7   169
 4:8   170, 172
 4:9   172-73
 4:10   173
 4:11   173
 5:1   178, 180
 5:2   183
 5:4   184
 6:1   190
 6:2   196
 6:3   197
 6:4   197
 6:5   194
 6:6   194

Nedarim
 1:1   17
 1:2   18-19

1:3	20	4:6	65
1:4	24	4:7	69
1:5	21, 23-24	4:8	71
1:6	27	4:9	71
2:1	31	5:1	76, 78
2:2	32	5:2	78
2:3	33	5:3	79
2:4	36	5:4	79
2:5	36	5:5	79
2:6	36	5:6	80
2:7	36, 41	6:1	91
2:8	42	6:2	83-84
2:9	44, 46, 48	6:3	83-84
2:10	49	6:4	84-85
3:1	53-54	6:5	89
3:2	53-54	6:6	89-90
3:3	56	6:7	90
3:4	56	7:1	94, 99
3:5	54	7:1-3	92
3:6	58	7:2	94-95
3:7	58	7:2-3	95
4:1	61-62	7:3	95
4:2	61-62	7:4	96-98
4:3	62	7:5	98
4:4	62	7:6	100
4:5	65	7:7	102
		7:8	102

BABYLONIAN TALMUD

Nazir
2-b	115
9a	122
16a-b	124
34a	159
45a	168
60b	187
62b	193

11a	124
13b	19
38b	40
41b	40
42b	42
62b	69
75b	90
81a	95
89a	100

Nedarim
9a	122

MAIMONIDES

Naziriteship
4:3-5	130

Trespass
4:11	33

GENERAL INDEX

Abba Saul, binding effects of vows, 52; food, vows not to eat, 52
Absolution of vows, 12-14, 69-102
Albeck, Ḥanokh, language of vows, 33; Nazirite, restrictions on, 193
ᶜAqiba, absolution of vows, 12, 72-73, 75-78, 81, 85-89, 96, 100; binding effect of vows, 60; corpse-uncleanness, Nazirite, 179-80; daughter, annulment of vows of, 81; food, vows not to eat, 60; grapes, Nazirite restrictions, 161-62; hair cutting, 111, 166; husband, power to annul vows of wife, 96, 100; language of vows, 16; Nazirite: offerings, 149; restrictions on, 111, 161-62, 166, 179-80; vows on becoming, 146; wife, annulment of vows of, 13, 85-89, 96

Ben Zoma, Nazirite, restrictions on, 112, 181-83
Benefits, vows not to derive, 10, 32-49
Binding effect of vows, 10-11, 32-69

Corpse-uncleanness, Nazirite, 111, 175-80

Daughter, annulment of vows of, 12, 81-85

Eleazar, corpse-uncleanness, Nazirite, 111, 179; grapes, Nazirite restrictions, 162-164; hair cutting, 111, 167, 173; Nazirite: offerings, 152; restrictions on, 111, 162, 164, 167, 173, 179
Eleazar b. ᶜArakh, absolution of vows, 88-89; grapes, Nazirite restrictions, 162, 164; language of vows, 35; Nazirite, restrictions on, 162; wife, annulment of vows of, 88
Eleazar b. R. Ṣadoq, language of vows, 27
Eleazar b. R. Simeon, absolution of vows, 91
Eliezer, absolution of vows, 12, 72-74, 81, 85-89; benefits, vows not deriving, 39; corpse-uncleanness, Nazirite, 175-76, 179-80; daughter, annulment of vows, 81; grapes, Nazirite restrictions, 161, 164; hair cutting, 170-73; Nazirite: offerings, 157; restrictions on, 161, 164, 170-73, 175-76, 179-80; vow on becoming, 109, 132, 135-37; wife, annulment of vows of, 13, 85-88
Eliezer b. Jacob, benefits, vows not to derive, 45-46; language of vows, 29-31

Food, vows not to eat, 11, 50-60

Gamaliel, absolution of vows, 94-95, 99
Grapes, Nazirite restrictions, 110-11, 160-64

Hair cutting, 111, 164-74
Hillel, absolution of vows, 83-85; daughter, annulment of vows of, 83-84; language of vows, 30-32; Nazirite: offerings, 110, 151, 153-59; vows on becoming, 108-109, 115, 117, 121-23, 133, 138-39
Husband, power to annul vows of wife, 13-14, 93-102

Ishmael, absolution of vows, 80, 100; grapes, Nazirite restrictions, 163; hair cutting, 171; husband, power to annul vows of wife, 100; language of vows, 35; Nazirite, restrictions on, 163, 171
Ishmael b. R. Yoḥanan b. Beroqah, hair cutting, 170; Nazirite, vow on becoming, 139
Ishmael b. R. Yosé, absolution of vows, 75

Jacob, language of vows, 20
Joshua, absolution of vows, 85-89; corpse-uncleanness, Nazirite, 111, 179-80; Nazirite, restrictions on, 111-12, 179-84; wife, annulment of vows of, 13, 85-89
Joshua b. Qorḥa, language of vows, 35
Joshua b. Mamal, corpse-uncleanness, Nazirite, 180
Judah, absolution of vows, 71, 101; benefits, vows not to derive, 40-41, 48; binding effect of vows, 40-41, 48, 52-55, 57-58, 61-62, 68; food, vows not to eat, 52-55, 57; grapes, Nazirite restrictions, 162; hair cutting, 111, 167-68; husband, power to annul vows of wife, 101; language of vows, 17-19, 21, 26-27-36; Nazirite: offerings, 152, 159; restrictions

on, 111, 162, 168; vows on becoming, 116, 120-23, 127-28, 136, 138, 145-46; objects, vows not to use, 61-62; temporal limitations on vows, 68

Judah b. Betera, absolutions of vows, 76, 80; binding effect of vows, 51-55; corpse-uncleanness, Nazirite, 180; food, vows not to eat, 51, 54-55; Nazirite, restrictions on, 180

Judah b. Peterah, corpse-uncleanness, Nazirite, 180

Language of vows, 8-9, 15-36, 108-109

Leazar, Nazirite, restrictions on, 180

Lieberman, Saul, absolution of vows, 78-79, 84; daughter, annulment of vows, 84; hair cutting, 174; Nazirite; restrictions on, 174, 191; vow on becoming, 145

Maimonides, language of vows, 33; Nazirite: restrictions on, 185, 193; vow on becoming, 130

Meir, absolution of vows, 12, 70, 72, 74, 76-77, 80, 96, 98-99; benefits, vows not to derive, 44; binding effect of vows, 44, 59-60, 62-63, 67-69; corpse-uncleanness, Nazirite, 111, 179-80; food, vows not to eat, 59-60; hair cutting, 168-69; husband, power to annul vows of wife, 96, 98-99; language of vows, 19, 21, 26-28, 34; Nazirite: offerings, 152; restrictions on, 111, 168-69, 179-80, 192-93; vow on becoming, 115, 121-22, 125-27, 145; objects, vows not to use, 11, 62-63; temporal limitations in vows, 67-69; wife, annulment of vows of, 96, 98-99

Nahum the Mede, Nazirite, offerings, 156

Nathan, absolution of vows, 77-78, 83-85, 102; daughter, annulment of vows of, 83-85; husband, power to annul vows of wife, 102

Nazirite: offerings, 109-10, 146-59; restrictions on, 110-12, 160-97; vow on becoming, 108-109, 114-46

Neḥemiah, language of vows, 35; Nazirite, restrictions on, 195

Nehorai, Nazirite, restrictions on, 197

Objects, vows not to use, 11, 61-63

Pappyas, Nazirite, vow on becoming, 134

Ṣadoq, absolution of vows, 73

Shammai, absolution of vows, 85; language of vows, 30-32; Nazirite: offerings, 110, 151, 153-59; vow on becoming, 108-109, 115-16, 121-23, 126, 133, 138-39

Simeon, benefits, vows not to derive, 40, 44; binding effect of vows, 40, 44, 56; food, vows not to eat, 56; grapes, Nazirite restrictions, 163; hair cutting, 169-72; Nazirite: offerings, 152, 157-59; restrictions on, 163, 169-72, 188-89; vow on becoming, 116-17, 121-22, 124-28, 137, 144-45

Simeon b. Eleazar, binding effects of vows, 54-56; food, vows not to eat, 54-56; Nazirite, vow on becoming, 133

Simeon b. Gamaliel, binding effect of vows, 53-54, 61, 68; hair cutting, 167; language of vows, 17-18; Nazirite: restrictions on, 111, 167; vow on becoming, 118; objects, vows not to use, 61; temporal limitations in vows, 68

Simeon b. Judah, grapes, Nazirite restrictions, 163

Simeon the Righteous, hair cutting, 169; Nazirite, restrictions on, 169

Simeon Sheruzi, hair cutting, 168-69

Simeon b. Yoḥai, Nazirite, restrictions on, 186

Ṭarfon, binding effects of vows, 53; hair cutting, 111, 166-67; Nazirite: offerings, 153, 157-59; restrictions on, 111, 166-67

Temporal limitations in vows, 11, 63-69

Wife, annulment of vows of, 13, 85-99

Yoḥanan b. Nuri, absolution of vows, 96; wife, annulment of vows of, 13, 96

Yosé, absolution of vows, 75, 93-95; benefits, vows not to derive, 43-44; binding effects of vows, 43-44, 52, 57-58, 67-69; food, vows not to eat, 52, 57-58; grapes, Nazirite restrictions, 162; hair cutting, 173-74; husband, power to annul vows of wife, 92-95; language of vows, 27, 35-36; Nazirite: offerings, 151-52, 159; restrictions on, 162, 173-74, 192-94, 197; vow on becoming, 145; temporal limitations in vows, 67-69; wife, annulment of vows of, 13, 92-94

Yosé b. R. Judah, absolution of vows, 91

www.ingramcontent.com/pod-product-compliance
Lightning Source LLC
Chambersburg PA
CBHW070315230426
43663CB00011B/2143